THE INFORMATION HIGHWAY

Other Books in the Current Controversies Series:

THE INFORMATION HIGHWAY

David L. Bender, *Publisher*
Bruno Leone, *Executive Editor*

Scott Barbour, *Managing Editor*
Brenda Stalcup, *Senior Editor*

Charles P. Cozic, *Book Editor*

CURRENT CONTROVERSIES

Cover Photo: © Charly Franklin/FPG International

Library of Congress Cataloging-in-Publication Data

The information highway / Charles P. Cozic, book editor.
    p. cm. — (Current controversies)
    Includes bibliographical references and index.
    ISBN 1-56510-374-2 (pbk. : alk. paper) — ISBN 1-56510-375-0
(lib. bdg. : alk. paper)
    1. Information superhighway—United States. 2. Telecommunication
policy—United States. 3. Telecommunication—United States.
I. Cozic, Charles P., 1957–   . II. Series.
HE7572.U6I537 1996
384.3—dc20   95-35486
                                                                CIP

Contents

Chapter 3: Will the Information Highway Benefit Society?

Yes: The Information Highway Can Benefit Society

No: The Information Highway May Not Benefit Society

Chapter 4: Should Computer Content Be Regulated?

Yes: Computer Content Should Be Regulated

No: Computer Content Should Not Be Regulated

Foreword

By definition, controversies are "discussions of questions in which opposing opinions clash" (Webster's Twentieth Century Dictionary Unabridged). Few would deny that controversies are a pervasive part of the human condition and exist on virtually every level of human enterprise. Controversies transpire between individuals and among groups, within nations and between nations. Controversies supply the grist necessary for progress by providing challenges and challengers to the status quo. They also create atmospheres where strife and warfare can flourish. A world without controversies would be a peaceful world; but it also would be, by and large, static and prosaic.

The Series' Purpose

The purpose of the Current Controversies series is to explore many of the social, political, and economic controversies dominating the national and international scenes today. Titles selected for inclusion in the series are highly focused and specific. For example, from the larger category of criminal justice, Current Controversies deals with specific topics such as police brutality, gun control, white collar crime, and others. The debates in Current Controversies also are presented in a useful, timeless fashion. Articles and book excerpts included in each title are selected if they contribute valuable, long-range ideas to the overall debate. And wherever possible, current information is enhanced with historical documents and other relevant materials. Thus, while individual titles are current in focus, every effort is made to ensure that they will not become quickly outdated. Books in the Current Controversies series will remain important resources for librarians, teachers, and students for many years.

In addition to keeping the titles focused and specific, great care is taken in the editorial format of each book in the series. Book introductions and chapter prefaces are offered to provide background material for readers. Chapters are organized around several key questions that are answered with diverse opinions representing all points on the political spectrum. Materials in each chapter include opinions in which authors clearly disagree as well as alternative opinions in which authors may agree on a broader issue but disagree on the possible solutions. In this way, the content of each volume in Current Controversies mirrors the mosaic of opinions encountered in society. Readers will quickly realize that there are many viable answers to these complex issues. By questioning each author's conclusions, students and casual readers can begin to develop the critical thinking skills so important to evaluating opinionated material.

Current Controversies is also ideal for controlled research. Each anthology in the series is composed of primary sources taken from a wide gamut of informational categories including periodicals, newspapers, books, United States and foreign government documents, and the publications of private and public organizations. Readers will find factual support for reports, debates, and research papers covering all areas of important issues. In addition, an annotated table of contents, an index, a book and periodical bibliography, and a list of organizations to contact are included in each book to expedite further research.

Perhaps more than ever before in history, people are confronted with diverse and contradictory information. During the Persian Gulf War, for example, the public was not only treated to minute-to-minute coverage of the war, it was also inundated with critiques of the coverage and countless analyses of the factors motivating U.S. involvement. Being able to sort through the plethora of opinions accompanying today's major issues, and to draw one's own conclusions, can be a complicated and frustrating struggle. It is the editors' hope that Current Controversies will help readers with this struggle.

"Like print, video, and other media that preceded them, computer networks such as the Internet . . . have become a medium for sexually explicit words and images."

Introduction

In June 1995, *Los Angeles Times* writer Kim Murphy described separate incidents involving a fifteen-year-old boy in Washington and a thirteen-year-old girl in Kentucky who ran away from their homes, apparently after corresponding with strangers via electronic mail (e-mail) on their personal computers. After spending several weeks in California, both teens were located and returned to their homes. According to Murphy, these stories reveal that there is a "very real possibility that children could be lured into illicit sex, prostitution or worse by contacts gleaned from their home computers." Child welfare groups report that cases of adults having had unlawful sex with minors they have met through e-mail are becoming more common.

In a related development, in 1995, Robert and Carleen Thomas, who lived near San Francisco and operated a computer bulletin-board system (BBS) called Amateur Action, were convicted by a Memphis, Tennessee, jury of transmitting pornographic images to that state, thereby violating local obscenity standards. The couple, sentenced to three years in federal prison, had been charged after a state postal inspector signed on to the BBS and downloaded several sexually explicit images.

Like print, video, and other media that preceded them, computer networks such as the Internet—a patchwork network used by the runaway teens and more than thirty million other computer users worldwide—have become a medium for sexually explicit words and images. On portions of the Internet, users can view or produce risqué stories and computer-scanned nude photographs or join "chat" groups discussing sex.

According to *Time* and other newsmagazines, such electronic material is both popular and easily available. In the words of *Time* writer Philip Elmer-DeWitt, "There's an awful lot of porn online" and "it is immensely popular." After estimates of the precise amount became a controversy itself among computer users and journalists in 1995, Wyoming newspaper editor Charles Levendosky challenged Elmer-DeWitt's perception: "A realistic estimate puts sex-related information at less than one-tenth of 1 percent of the sites on the Internet and other interactive computer services."

In response to the availability of on-line porn and the risk of its exposure to minors, U.S. legislators have begun targeting computer networks. In 1995, Nebraska senator James Exon proposed the Communications Decency Act, legislation that would make transmission of sexually explicit material via computers a federal crime. Exon had become alarmed about some of the more explicit on-line images. "I knew it was bad," Exon said. "But then when I got on [the computer], it made *Playboy* and *Hustler* look like Sunday-school stuff."

The senator aimed to fill a void in the law regulating such material. Although an existing federal law bans any transmission of child pornography, no federal statute prohibits computer users from transmitting other forms of pornography or sexually explicit content. In Exon's view, his amendment (specifying a maximum fine of $100,000 and a maximum jail sentence of two years for violators) places a justifiable restriction on free speech in order to protect children's well-being. Exon argues that the increase in both the number of minors using computers and the amount of on-line sexual material creates the need for such a law and that government's failure to act accordingly would be "an open invitation to some of the hardcore pornography getting into our homes." As of October 1995, Congress was considering Exon's amendment as part of its telecommunications reform bill.

But many civil liberties advocates, parents, and others argue that proposals such as Exon's are ill-advised for several reasons. Most importantly, they contend, laws targeting computers would violate Americans' First Amendment right of freedom of speech, not only producing a chilling effect on computer users' speech but criminalizing some of it as well. In the words of *Los Angeles Times* columnist Lawrence J. Magid: "I worry that some overzealous prosecutor, anywhere in the country, might use this law to go after a discussion of reproductive rights, birth control, [or] gay rights."

Free-speech advocates fear that government—with a license to regulate computer content and images—would become a censor of what has been a virtually uninhibited and democratic form of communication. Charles Levendosky asserts that with such a mandate, government would "inevitably stick [its] nose in business you thought was your family's private affair."

Some observers contend that Exon's amendment threatens to undermine the Supreme Court's 1973 *Miller v. California* decision, which stipulated that local standards should determine what constitutes obscenity. They argue that the legislation would, in effect, impose a national obscenity standard, thereby impinging on the right of local communities to establish and enforce standards consistent with their own values. For example, critics of the Thomases' conviction argue that images produced in one community (San Francisco) should not be forced to meet the standards of a community that holds a markedly different ideology or philosophy (Memphis).

Despite their differences, Exon and many of his opponents do agree on the attractiveness of one approach: "lock-out" mechanisms that allow parents to block children from accessing computer network areas containing material they consider indecent. Several software companies and on-line service providers have introduced this option to parents, giving them greater control over what children can view.

Introduction

As the information highway expands into more areas of society and people's daily lives, debate about what types of images and words are suitable for viewing promises to continue. Whether broader restrictions are necessary to prohibit any computer transmission of sexually explicit material is one of the issues examined in *The Information Highway: Current Controversies*. Other viewpoints assess what constitutes the information highway, whether it benefits society, and how the information highway should be developed.

Chapter 1

What Is the Information Highway?

CURRENT CONTROVERSIES

The Information Highway: An Overview

by Philip Elmer-DeWitt

About the author: *Philip Elmer-DeWitt is a writer for* Time *magazine.*

It started, as the big ideas in technology often do, with a science-fiction writer. William Gibson, a young expatriate American living in Canada, was wandering past the video arcades on Vancouver's Granville Street in the early 1980s when something about the way the players were hunched over their glowing screens struck him as odd. "I could see in the physical intensity of their postures how *rapt* the kids were," he says. "It was like a feedback loop, with photons coming off the screens into the kids' eyes, neurons moving through their bodies and electrons moving through the video game. These kids clearly *believed* in the space the games projected."

That image haunted Gibson. He didn't know much about video games or computers—he wrote his breakthrough novel *Neuromancer* (1984) on an ancient manual typewriter—but he knew people who did. And as near as he could tell, everybody who worked much with the machines eventually came to accept, almost as an article of faith, the reality of that imaginary realm. "They develop a belief that there's some kind of *actual space* behind the screen," he says. "Some place that you can't see but you know is there."

Gibson called that place "cyberspace," and used it as the setting for his early novels and short stories. In his fiction, cyberspace is a computer-generated landscape that characters enter by "jacking in"—sometimes by plugging electrodes directly into sockets implanted in the brain. What they see when they get there is a three-dimensional representation of all the information stored in "every computer in the human system"—great warehouses and skyscrapers of data. He describes it in a key passage in *Neuromancer* as a place of "unthinkable complexity," with "lines of light ranged in the nonspace of the mind, clusters and constellations of data. Like city lights, receding . . ."

In the years since, there have been other names given to that shadowy space where our computer data reside: the Net, the Web, the Cloud, the Matrix, the

Metaverse, the Datasphere, the Electronic Frontier, the information superhighway. But Gibson's coinage may prove the most enduring. By 1989 it had been borrowed by the online community to describe not some science-fiction fantasy but today's increasingly interconnected computer systems—especially the millions of computers jacked into the Internet.

Now hardly a day goes by without some newspaper article, some political speech, some corporate press release invoking Gibson's imaginary world. Suddenly, it seems, everybody has an E-mail address, from Hollywood moguls to the Holy See. Billy Graham has preached on America Online; Vice President Al Gore has held forth on CompuServe; thousands chose to celebrate New Year's this year with an online get-together called First Night in Cyberspace.

In Washington cyberspace has become a political hot button of some potency, first pressed during the 1992 presidential campaign by Al Gore and Bill Clinton, who rode to the White House in part on the promise that they would build the so-called information superhighway and route it through every voter's district—if not to his home. But the Clinton Administration lost the high ground of cyberspace, having, among other transgressions, come out on the wrong side of the privacy debate when it endorsed the Clipper Chip security device favored by its intelligence services. The Republicans were quick to grab the initiative. No sooner had incoming House Speaker Newt Gingrich taken office than he made his bid, staging a big press conference to unveil a new House computer system. At a Washington confab called "Democracy in Virtual America," attended by his old friends, futurists Alvin and Heidi Toffler, the Speaker talked expansively about wiring the world. "Cyberspace is the land of knowledge," proclaimed an information age Magna Carta issued in his name. "And the exploration of that land can be a civilization's truest, highest calling."

Corporations, smelling a land rush of another sort, are scrambling to stake out their own claims in cyberspace. Every computer company, nearly every publisher, most communications firms, banks, insurance companies and hundreds of mail-order and retail firms are registering their Internet domains and setting up sites on the World Wide Web. They sense that cyberspace will be one of the driving forces—if not the primary one—for economic growth in the 21st century.

> *"Suddenly, it seems, everybody has an E-mail address, from Hollywood moguls to the Holy See."*

All this is being breathlessly reported in the press, which has seized on cyberspace as an all-purpose buzz word that can add sparkle to the most humdrum development or assignment. For working reporters, many of whom have just discovered the pleasures of going online, cyber has become the prefix of the day, and they are spawning neologisms as fast as they can type: cyberphilia, cyberphobia, cyberwonk, cybersex, cyberslut. A Nexis search of newspapers, magazines and television transcripts turned up 1,205 mentions of cyber in the month of January, up from 464 the previous January and 167 in January 1993.

One result of this drum roll is a growing public appetite for a place most people haven't been to and are often hard-pressed to define. In a TIME/CNN poll of

> *"The rush to get online, to avoid being 'left behind' in the information revolution, is intense."*

800 Americans conducted in January by Yankelovich Partners, 57% didn't know what cyberspace meant, yet 85% were certain that information technology had made their life better. They may not know where it is, but they want desperately to get there. The rush to get online, to avoid being "left behind" in the information revolution, is intense. Those who find fulfillment in cyberspace often have the religious fervor of the recently converted.

These sentiments have been captured brilliantly in an IBM ad on TV showing a phalanx of Czech nuns discussing—of all things—the latest operating system from Microsoft. As they walk briskly through a convent, a young novice mentions IBM's competing system, called Warp. "I just read about it in *Wired*," she gushes. "You get true multitasking . . . easy access to the Internet." An older sister glances up with obvious interest; the camera cuts to the mother superior, who wistfully confesses, "I'm dying to surf the Net." Fade as the pager tucked under her habit starts to beep.

Cybernuns.

What is cyberspace? According to John Perry Barlow, a rock-'n'-roll lyricist turned computer activist, it can be defined most succinctly as "that place you are in when you are talking on the telephone." That's as good a place to start as any. The telephone system, after all, is really a vast, global computer network with a distinctive, audible presence (crackling static against an almost inaudible background hum). By Barlow's definition, just about everybody has already been to cyberspace. It's marked by the feeling that the person you're talking to is "in the same room." Most people take the spatial dimension of a phone conversation for granted—until they get a really bad connection or a glitchy overseas call. Then they start raising their voice, as if by sheer volume they could propel it to the outer reaches of cyberspace.

Cyberspace, of course, is bigger than a telephone call. It encompasses the millions of personal computers connected by modems—via the telephone system—to commercial online services, as well as the millions more with high-speed links to local area networks, office E-mail systems and the Internet. It includes the rapidly expanding wireless services: microwave towers that carry great quantities of cellular phone and data traffic; communications satellites strung like beads in geosynchronous orbit; low-flying satellites that will soon crisscross the globe like angry bees, connecting folks too far-flung or too much on the go to be tethered by wires. Someday even our television sets may be part of cyberspace, transformed into interactive "teleputers" by so-called full-service networks like the ones several cable-TV companies (including Time Warner) are building along the old cable lines, using fiber optics and high-speed switches.

But these wires and cables and microwaves are not really cyberspace. They are the means of conveyance, not the destination: the information superhighway, not the bright city lights at the end of the road. Cyberspace, in the sense of being "in the same room," is an experience, not a wiring system. It is about people using the new technology to do what they are genetically programmed to do: communicate with one another. It can be found in electronic mail exchanged by lovers who have never met. It emerges from the endless debates on mailing lists and message boards. It's that bond that knits together regulars in electronic chat rooms and newsgroups. It is, like Plato's plane of ideal forms, a metaphorical space, a virtual reality.

But it is no less real for being so. We live in the age of information, as Nicholas Negroponte, director of M.I.T.'s Media Lab, is fond of pointing out, in which the fundamental particle is not the atom but the bit—the binary digit, a unit of data usually represented as a 0 or 1. Information may still be delivered in magazines and newspapers (atoms), but the real value is in the contents (bits). We pay for our goods and services with cash (atoms), but the ebb and flow of capital around the world is carried out—to the tune of several trillion dollars a day—in electronic funds transfers (bits).

Bits are different from atoms and obey different laws. They are weightless. They are easily (and flawlessly) reproduced. There is an infinite supply. And they can be shipped at nearly the speed of light. When you are in the business of moving bits around, barriers of time and space disappear. For information providers—publishers, for example—cyberspace offers a medium in which distribution costs shrink to zero. Buyers and sellers can find each other in cyberspace without the benefit (or the expense) of a marketing campaign. No wonder so many businessmen are convinced it will become a powerful engine of economic growth.

At this point, however, cyberspace is less about commerce than about community. The technology has unleashed a great rush of direct, person-to-person communications, organized not in the top-down, one-to-many structure of traditional media but in a many-to-many model that may—just may—be a vehicle for revolutionary change. In a world already too divided against itself—rich against poor, producer against consumer—cyberspace offers the nearest thing to a level playing field.

> *"Cyberspace, in the sense of being 'in the same room,' is an experience, not a wiring system."*

Take, for example, the Internet. Until something better comes along to replace it, the Internet *is* cyberspace. It may not reach every computer in the human system, as Gibson imagined, but it comes very close. And as anyone who has spent much time there can attest, it is in many ways even stranger than fiction.

Begun more than 20 years ago as a Defense Department experiment, the Internet escaped from the Pentagon in 1984 and spread like kudzu during the personal-computer boom, nearly doubling every year from the mid-1980s on. Today 30 million to 40 million people in more than 160 countries have at least E-mail access to the Internet; in Japan, New Zealand and parts of Europe the number of Net users has grown more than 1,000% during the past three years.

One factor fueling the Internet's remarkable growth is its resolutely grass-roots structure. Most conventional computer systems are hierarchical and proprietary; they run on copyright software in a pyramid structure that gives dictatorial powers to the system operators who sit on top. The Internet, by contrast, is open (non-proprietary) and rabidly democratic. No one owns it. No single organization controls it. It is run like a commune with 4.8 million fiercely independent members (called hosts). It crosses national boundaries and answers to no sovereign. It is literally lawless.

> *"Today 30 million to 40 million people in more than 160 countries have at least E-mail access to the Internet."*

Although graphics, photos and even videos have started to show up, cyberspace, as it exists on the Internet, is still primarily a text medium. People communicate by and large through words, typed and displayed on a screen. Yet cyberspace assumes an astonishing array of forms, from the utilitarian mailing list (a sort of junk E-mail list to which anyone can contribute) to the rococo MUDs, or Multi-User Dungeons (elaborate fictional gathering places that users create one "room" at a time). All these "spaces" have one thing in common: they are egalitarian to a fault. Anybody can play (provided he or she has the requisite equipment and access), and everybody is afforded the same level of respect (which is to say, little or none). Stripped of the external trappings of wealth, power, beauty and social status, people tend to be judged in the cyberspace of the Internet only by their ideas and their ability to get them across in terse, vigorous prose. On the Internet, as the famous *New Yorker* cartoon put it, nobody knows you're a dog.

Nowhere is this leveling effect more apparent than on Usenet—a giant set of more than 10,000 discussion groups (called newsgroups) distributed in large part over the Internet and devoted to every conceivable subject, from Rush Limbaugh to particle physics to the nocturnal habits of ring-tailed lemurs. The newsgroups develop their own peculiar dynamic as participants lurch from topic to topic— quick to take and give offense, slow to come to any kind of resolution.

But Usenet regulars are fiercely proud of what they have constructed. They view it as a new vehicle for wielding political power (through mass mailings and petitions) and an alternative system for gathering and disseminating raw, uncensored news. If they are sometimes disdainful of bumbling "newbies" who go online without learning the rules of the road, they are unforgiving to those who violate them deliberately. Many are convinced that the unflattering press accounts (those perennial stories about Internet hackers and pedophiles, for example) are part of a conspiracy among the mainstream media to suppress what they perceive as a threat to their hegemony.

The Usenet newsgroups are, in their way, the perfect antidote to modern mass media. Rather than catering to the lowest common denominator with programming packaged by a few people in New York, Atlanta and Hollywood and broadcast to the masses in the heartland, the newsgroups allow news, commentary and humor to bubble up from the grass roots. They represent narrowcasting in the extreme: content created by consumers for consumers. While cable-TV executives still dream of hundreds of channels, Usenet already has thousands. The network is so fragmented, in fact, that some fear it will ultimately serve to further divide a society already splintered by race, politics and sexual prejudice. That would be an ironic fate for a system designed to enhance communications.

The Internet is far from perfect. Largely unedited, its content is often tasteless, foolish, uninteresting or just plain wrong. It can be dangerously habit-forming and, truth be told, an enormous waste of time. Even with the arrival of new point-and-click software such as Netscape and Mosaic, it is still too hard to navigate. And because it requires access to both a computer and a high-speed telecommunications link, it is out of reach for millions of people too poor or too far from a major communications hub to participate.

But it is remarkable nonetheless, especially considering that it began as a cold war postapocalypse military command grid. "When I look at the Internet," says Bruce Sterling, another science-fiction writer and a great champion of cyberspace, "I see something astounding and delightful. It's as if some grim fallout shelter had burst open and a full-scale Mardi Gras parade had come out. I take such enormous pleasure in this that it's hard to remain properly skeptical."

> *"While cable-TV executives still dream of hundreds of channels, Usenet already has thousands."*

There is no guarantee, however, that cyberspace will always look like this. The Internet is changing rapidly. Lately a lot of the development efforts—and most of the press attention—have shifted from the rough-and-tumble Usenet newsgroups to the more passive and consumer-oriented "home pages" of the World Wide Web—a system of links that simplifies the task of navigating among the myriad offerings on the Internet. The Net, many old-timers complain, is turning into a shopping mall. But unless it proves to be a total bust for business, that trend is likely to continue.

The more fundamental changes are those taking place underneath our sidewalks and streets, where great wooden wheels of fiber-optic cable are being rolled out one block at a time. Over the next decade, the telecommunications systems of the world will be rebuilt from the ground up as copper wires are ripped up and replaced by hair-thin fiber-optic strands.

The reason, in a word, is bandwidth, the information-carrying capacity of a medium (usually measured in bits per second). In terms of bandwidth, a copper telephone wire is like a thin straw, too narrow to carry the traffic it is being asked to bear. By contrast, fiber-optic strands, although hair-thin, are like great fat pipes, with an intrinsic capacity to carry tens of thousands of times as many bits as copper wire.

> *"Over the next decade, the telecommunications systems of the world will be rebuilt from the ground up."*

It's not just the Internet surfers who are crying for more bandwidth. Hollywood needs it to deliver movies and television shows on demand. Video game makers want it to send kids the latest adventures of Donkey Kong and Sonic the Hedgehog. The phone companies have their eyes on what some believe will be the next must-have appliance: the videophone.

There is a broad consensus in government and industry that the National Information Infrastructure, as the Clinton Administration prefers to call the info highway, will be a broadband, switched network that could, in theory, deliver all these things. But how it will be structured and how it will be deployed are not so clear. For example, if cable-TV and telephone companies are allowed to roll out the new services in only the richest neighborhoods—a practice known as "cream skimming"—that could exacerbate the already growing disparity between those who have access to the latest information and the best intelligence and those who must be content with what they see on TV.

An even trickier question has to do with the so-called upstream capacity of the network. Everybody wants to build a fat pipeline going into the home; that's the conduit by which the new information goods and services will be delivered. But how much bandwidth needs to be set aside for the signal going from the home back into the network? In some designs that upstream pathway is quite narrow—allowing just enough bits to change the channel or order a zirconium ring. Some network activists argue that consumers will someday need as much bandwidth going out of the home as they have coming in. . . .

How these design issues are decided in the months ahead could change the shape of cyberspace. Will it be bottom up, like the Internet, or top down, like broadcast television? In the best case, says Mitch Kapor, cofounder (with John Perry Barlow) of the Electronic Frontier Foundation, we could collectively invent a new entertainment medium, one that taps the creative energies of a nation of midnight scribblers and camcorder video artists. "In the worst case," he says, "we could wind up with networks that have the principal effect of fostering addiction to a new generation of electronic narcotics."

The Myths of the Information Highway

by Laurent Belsie

About the author: *Laurent Belsie is a staff writer and columnist for the* Christian Science Monitor *newspaper.*

When Juan Ponce de Leon arrived in the New World, he found what is now the Bahamas and Florida. But he was disappointed; he was searching for the Fountain of Youth.

In the 1540s, Francisco Coronado established Spain's claim to a stretch of land from California to Kansas. But it was almost an afterthought. He wanted El Dorado: The Seven Cities of Gold.

That's the problem with conquistador-explorers. They often chase the wrong things. When today's corporate chieftains describe cyberspace, history seems to be repeating itself.

In mid-1994, Bell Atlantic and Nynex announced their desire to combine cellular telephone operations, creating a $13 billion behemoth. Columbia Broadcasting System (CBS) and home-shopping channel QVC Network were said to be close to a merger. The strategy? To be big enough and diversified enough to take over the so-called information highway. But the notion that bigness ensures survival is nearly as far-fetched as the Fountain of Youth.

Small Entrepreneurs

The history of technology is rife with examples of how small entrepreneurs have wrested away new markets from larger competitors. In the computer industry, for example, Microsoft successfully challenged IBM in software; hundreds of companies sprang up to build personal computers while mainframe manufacturers stood idly by.

The same may hold true in the new world of communications known as cyberspace.

"Some traditional forms of enterprise will survive," says Daniel Spulber, professor of management strategy at Northwestern University in Evanston, Illinois.

But the big winners may be entrepreneurs no one's heard of yet, he adds.

Telephone, television, and computer companies are excited about cyberspace because it borders each of their domains.

If two people one thousand miles apart hold a telephone-carried, video-enabled conference, they're meeting in a space that is not physical. That's cyberspace.

These kinds of communications will become even easier and more pervasive as telephones, televisions, and computers begin to speak the same digital language.

There's huge business potential in sending text, voice, and video as easily as making a phone call. But because this cyberspace is unfinished, no one knows what it will look like. Only the myths are coming into focus.

Myths of the Information Highway

Myth No. One: The information highway.

"It perpetuates the myth that it is one thing," says Jeff Johnson, chairman of Computer Professionals for Social Responsibility, a national organization concerned with the social implications of computer technologies. "There is not just one highway in the United States. There is a highway 'system.' And highways are only one of many types of road, and roads are just one of many transportation routes, in our national transportation system."

Alan Blatecky, vice president of information technologies at MCNC, a research consortium in Research Triangle Park, North Carolina, says: "You may get on [the information highway but] you are not going to follow a path. You may go up."

Myth No. Two: Cyberspace means five hundred channels of television, mostly movies.

Cyberspace will not be television—not television as we know it. Yes, viewers will probably be able to sit in front of a set and select any movie they want. But that's not where the action will be, technology gurus predict. "Movies-on-demand will come but almost instantly become a commodity," says Paul Saffo, director of the Institute for the Future in Menlo Park, California. "The cable companies will find it's more difficult" than they thought, he adds. Video will become interactive. That means viewers will not only receive signals but send back messages, thanks to a small, computerized box that sits on top of the set. Even then, it's not clear how dynamic this market will be.

> *"Telephone, television, and computer companies are excited about cyberspace because it borders each of their domains."*

"The set-top box is probably the least important" innovation, adds Avram Miller, vice president of corporate business development at Intel Corporation in Santa Clara, California. "We are going from television where we watch when they want . . . to television where we watch when we want. But you're not going to pay your bills that way."

Myth No. Three: The all-in-one appliance.
While cyberspace will quite possibly create new information machines, these appliances will do separate things.

You wouldn't pay your bills through a television screen fifteen feet away.

In cyberspace, one size does not fit all. "Game machines," Mr. Miller says, "won't take over the world."

Placing a Value on the Internet

Myth No. Four: Cyberspace means the Internet.
This international web of communicating computers is an intriguing experiment, but probably too utopian to survive in its current form. "To some extent, the Internet is a myth," Miller says. "It's probably unsustainable in its current form. . . . People have to be allowed to make money or they won't invest."

> *"No one knows what it will take to make cyberspace as popular as, say, the car or the telephone."*

Myth No. Five: Cyber-Utopia.
According to this vision, everyone will be able to log on, download, and upload anything they want. The services will be free or nearly free. We'll all be members of a single electronic village.

"I think there's a great danger in these arguments," Mr. Johnson says. "It's a mistake to require universal access to the information superhighway." If it's not valuable, then government and industry will waste enormous sums of money.

Myth No. Six: Electronic commerce will drive the future.
The promises glitter: on-line shopping, electronic malls. Cyberspace has already begun to create such things. But it's doubtful these will dominate the traffic. "The overwhelming bulk [of traffic] will be people talking to each other," Johnson says.

How they will communicate is unclear. Miller thinks electronic mail will be the application that lures business people into cyberspace. Mr. Saffo of the Institute for the Future believes that "live" communication will become more important.

Myth No. Seven: The future is far off/The future is here.
Some people are already using on-line services to shop, carrying portable phones that enable anytime/anywhere communication, and sending electronic mail all over the world. But it's doubtful the current set of services are cheap enough and compelling enough to appeal to the mainstream. No one knows what it will take to make cyberspace as popular as, say, the car or the telephone.

Nearly one hundred years before Coronado searched for El Dorado, Johannes Gutenberg used movable type to produce his famous Bible. It wasn't until fifty years later that Aldus Manutius in Italy created inexpensive, pocket-sized editions that assured the printing industry's future, Saffo says. It may take entrepreneurs quite a while to figure out the real opportunities in cyberspace, he adds. "The . . . secret of the information revolution is that it takes almost as long today as in the 1400s."

A Critical Look at the Internet

by Chris O'Malley

About the author: *Chris O'Malley is a contributing editor for* Popular Science, *a monthly science and technology magazine.*

With one hand in a tub of M&Ms and the other gripping my mouse, I am electronically flipping through the pages of the Internet's World Wide Web. Two hours later, I'm sick to my stomach. I've done it again. I let those pretty colors and addictive little morsels get the best of me. And it has nothing to do with the M&Ms.

Set aside for a moment the hype about what the Internet represents ("the assembly line of the electronic era"), what it could become ("the bedrock of the information superhighway"), or what it might turn us into ("a global community of data-seeking homebodies"). Instead, let's take stock of what it *is*. This worldwide computer network you hear and read so much about is today little more than a high-tech candy dispenser for the eyes, ears, and mind. It is fuzzy satellite weather maps, canned audio clips from the President, unfettered access to obscure college journals, and, very likely, not one damn thing that will make a lasting difference in how you work, play, or live.

A Surreal World

But this much is equally true: The Internet's eccentricity is almost irresistible. AT&T's famed Bell Laboratories posts some of its important newsletters there, and a Purdue graduate student named Sho posts what he eats for lunch everyday (if you click on his lunch bag with your mouse). The Census Bureau lets you dig into its population data archives, and CBS lets you search through David Letterman's Top Ten list archives. Superminds and supermodels vie for your attention. In short, the Internet is one big digital Gumpism: You never know what you're gonna get.

Information superhighway? Alice in Wonderland is more like it. The Internet is a surreal world filled with words and pictures and sounds that manages to be fascinating while remaining largely impractical. You can see pictures of what it's like to stroll down the streets of Paris or London, but you can't stop and make plane or hotel reservations if the experience moves you. Its scope is incredibly broad—every conceivable interest is covered—yet it's remarkably shallow. There are countless spots devoted to music and movies, for example, but don't expect to get more than a tiny snippet of sound or video through your PC.

> *"The Internet is a surreal world filled with words and pictures and sounds that manages to be fascinating while remaining largely impractical."*

It's a world that invites and insults ordinary (nontechnical) people. All are welcome to join in the idle chatter of discussion groups, but know that you run the risk of receiving extraordinarily nasty messages known as flame mail if you irk the sensibilities of the Internet regulars. Simply not being a regular is frequently offense enough.

Paradoxically, the Internet is also the fast lane of the online world that somehow slows to a crawl by the time it reaches your PC. That's because it was constructed by the world's technocracy, who are connected to each other by incredibly fast computer networks and high-speed telephone wires—the equivalent of a five-lane highway. But the Internet's wide load barely squeaks through the narrow neighborhood streets where we, the PC proletariat, are linked by modems and regular phone lines.

Cool and Hip

And, oh yes, the Internet is one more thing: It's the trendiest nonplace in the universe. You want to be hip? Or at least be able to hold up your end of a conversation over the latter half of the nineties? Better know about the Net. You better know that something called the World Wide Web is where all of the Net's really cool "sites" are at. You better know that an electronic mail address on the Net (you@hiway.com) is way cooler than a phone number. And you certainly better know that, according to the Internet Society, the number of cool people on the Net is projected to equal the human population of the planet by 2001. Universally cool.

Cool? Hip? Are we still talking about computers? Strange, but true. Revenge of the nerds? Quite the opposite. It's more like the invasion of the masses (or at least their first platoon) into a medium that until 1992 was the exclusive domain of colleges, government agencies, defense contractors, and assorted technical types. Apparently, we want what they got—information, and lots of it.

The land rush for a stake in this cyberspace has been recorded eagerly and encyclopedically by the media. In the 12 months prior to this viewpoint being written, a search (online, of course) through the annals of mainly U.S. newspapers, magazines, and wire services reveals no fewer than 43,475 other stories about the Internet.

The media frenzy may be self-induced and self-important—many of these publications are themselves flocking to establish a "presence" on the Net—but no doubt this digital delirium is fueling the foggy feeling that the Internet is the place to be.

But the real gas in this engine is formulated from more potent stuff. The whole online phenomenon, and the Internet in particular, is the first substantially new communications medium since television. Technically, it's a medium assembled out of old parts: computers, software, modems, and phone lines. And it's not as if we haven't been exposed to words, photographic images, moving pictures, and recorded sound before. But the use of these elements to create, in effect, a parallel universe for ourselves marks one of the most profound social changes of our time. Whether it's for better or worse remains to be seen.

For now, the worse part has a firm grip on this netherworld. Like opening Al Capone's secret vault in Chicago, it is preceded with great fanfare and expectations yet must be attempted methodically and cautiously. Once inside, you may find it fascinating to be there, but find little of value to take home.

There's an entrance fee too. The Internet is not a free ride. First, you pay at the door. The door, in this case, is the online service or "provider" that extends its own digital pathway into the Internet to your PC. That'll cost you $10 or more per month, and from there the meter is running. After a few hours, generally, you'll pay $2 to $10 per hour to peruse the Net.

The place is tailor-made for loitering. The Internet is not organized with the idea of getting you back to the real world quickly—many parts aren't organized at all. And as superficial as it can be, there's always something that looks intriguing. Snicker, if you will, at the concept of an online pub in which you can't see the patrons and you can't imbibe. But just try to keep from stepping inside to see exactly what is going on.

Should you be along for the wild ride? For the serious-minded pursuit of information and services that can directly and immediately enhance the quality of your life, the answer is clearly "no." The Internet is far too much sports car, albeit a sputtering one, and far too little delivery vehicle for such pragmatic aims. But if the notion of an electronic joyride through a curious new world—a medium that will someday be much more than a curiosity—is intriguing enough to get you beyond this paragraph, then the answer is "why not?"

"The whole online phenomenon . . . is the first substantially new communications medium since television."

The Internet is a digital funhouse, though, and the confusion begins almost as soon as you decide to step inside. Aside from a PC and a modem pumping at least 9,600 bits per second, you'll need special software to move around. Sometimes, the online service connecting you to the Internet provides all the software; sometimes it doesn't. Computing hasn't been this confounding since the days of building PCs from kits.

Recently, the commercial online services have taken it upon themselves to make things a little easier. Prodigy, America Online, Genie, CompuServe, and Delphi each offer access to the Internet to some degree, and they supply both the service and the software needed to get there. In January 1995, Prodigy became the first of these to include access to Internet's most popular area, the World Wide Web, as part of its basic monthly service. The others each offered the same deal in 1995.

> *"The World Wide Web is the only part of the Internet that's really fit for public consumption."*

The World Wide Web

The World Wide Web is becoming synonymous with the Internet, but it's actually only one part—and a recent one at that—of this loose confederation of computers strung together by phone wires. The Internet has become the world's clearinghouse for electronic mail, easily its most vital role in cyberspace, if a mundane one. The Net also hosts countless discussion groups and file archives, and lets you remotely control other computers, such as the Library of Congress' card catalog system, from your PC. Each of these requires a different type of software and varying levels of expertise and interest.

But the World Wide Web is the only part of the Internet that's really fit for public consumption. The arcane procedures and heavy technical flavor of the Net's older avenues make them unappealing destinations for normal folks. Moreover, much of what they offer can be accessed through the Web.

What's the Web? The World Wide Web is a collection of colorful onscreen documents (or pages) that can contain words, pictures, data files, audio snippets, and video clips. These pages also have highlighted words, known as hypertext links, that let you jump to related pages on Web computers anywhere in the world by simply clicking your mouse on one of these words. All of this happens with the aid of "browsing" software such as Mosaic, Netscape Navigator, and their many variations.

A Web document called the NASA Homepage, for example, presents a U.S. map with the locations of its 13 centers marked. Clicking on the Kennedy Space Center button transports you to computers at the Cape Canaveral, Florida, facility. From there, you have many choices. You can learn more about the Center, thumb through its (nonclassified) historical archives, see photos of recent launches, and even, if your timing is right, receive information, images, and audio clips from an ongoing space shuttle mission. It also offers links to numerous other space-related sites.

Your curiosity will be exhausted long before the Web's pages will be. There are about 18,000 "host" computers around the globe serving up an estimated 3.5 million documents on the World Wide Web, according to Carnegie-Mellon's Center for Machine Translation. Roughly 6,000 more documents are being added daily.

A Navigation Problem

Here's the catch: There's no table of contents. Instead, you're left to meander through this vast electronic encyclopedia, jumping from page to page and stopping as fate or fancy decides. And since there's no person or group with the authority to organize or set rules for the Internet, there likely won't be a definitive table of contents—or in computer lingo, main menu—anytime soon.

There are people and companies trying to fill the void, however. Several companies have posted "navigator" pages that attempt to organize the Web's contents by subject. The Whole Internet Catalog is perhaps the best navigator; it offers an ample but not overwhelming overview of the Web, and it provides brief but insightful summaries of the places it lists—so you have a clue to what lies at the end of a teasing title. The Catalog reports that there's "not much beyond lists" in a Web page called Bookwire, for example. Instead, perhaps, you should venture into the Children's Literature Web Guide, which the Catalog calls "a must-visit site for parents, teachers, and young people."

The trouble is, these navigating pages generally—and understandably—cover only a small fraction of the places on the Web. Consequently, you never feel confident that you're seeing the most complete or most appropriate lists of Web documents for your interests.

Web-searching services, such as Carnegie-Mellon's Lycos page, do a far better job of spanning the Web. But these services are essentially indexes, not subject listings. You have to know what key words to search for, and the results aren't always as accurate or descriptive as you'd like. Fully half of all the entries from a search for pages containing the word "rocket," for example, had nothing whatever to do with space or aviation. Two interesting misfires: a software company (Rocket Science Games Inc.) and musician Elton John ("Rocket Man").

> *"Navigating pages generally— and understandably—cover only a small fraction of the places on the Web."*

Even if you know exactly what you want and know it exists on the Web, getting to it can be unduly difficult. To go somewhere directly (as opposed to jumping there from a hypertext link), you have to obtain and type in its electronic address, known as a Universal Resource Locator, or URL. And that can be a fingerful. Want to check out that NASA "home page"? You'll need to tap out the following precisely: http://www.gsfc.nasa.gov/NASA_ homepage.html.

Happily, most browsing software at least lets you save the location of your favorite pages in a "hotlist"—or personalized menu—so you can get there quickly the next time around.

Did I say quickly? Here's the other catch: The Web is s-l-o-w. Often excruciatingly slow. That's because the Web is transporting graphics-laden documents, not just plain text, and there's not much room in the phone company's copper wires for visuals. The more pictures in the document, the longer it takes to appear on your PC screen. Even with a fast modem, waiting ten to 20 seconds for a single page to appear is typical. Waiting a minute or more is not unusual. Downloading a separate picture or data file to your PC usually takes several minutes.

> *"The majority of Web sites are dedicated to what might be broadly termed special interests."*

Receiving a digitized audio or video clip can require the patience of Job. Short clips can take 15 minutes; longer ones can take a half hour or more. Even then, the quality of the pictures and sounds is considerably inferior to your TV and CD player. This "bandwidth" problem, as the computer and communications people like to call it, is the online world's dirty little secret. The vision of the Internet as a multimedia servant that offers you a host of audio and video delights is not merely fantasy, it's fraud. It will be years before the Internet can begin to compete with MTV or HBO.

Racy hardware can help, but not a lot. My Pentium system with a 28,800bps [bits per second] modem worked better than a slower 486 machine with a 14,400 bps modem, but the difference was not dramatic. The same held true with a Power Macintosh and an older Mac sibling. That's because the problem is mainly in the limits of the phone lines, not your PC. Some companies are using or experimenting with faster lanes to the Internet, including digital and fiber-optic phone lines and cable TV wires, which have ten to 500 times the capacity of regular phone lines. But for the foreseeable future, we'll have to plod along the plain old telephone "highway."

Web Traffic

Traffic is a problem too. Popular Web sites are frequently overwhelmed by the growing number of people vying for access to them. You may be refused entry—the online equivalent of a busy signal—or cut off in the process of exploring a Web page. More than once, the computers at AT&T have suggested I reach out and touch somebody else for the time being.

Once you've endured the potholes, speed bumps, and congestion, you're ready to . . . well, cruise the Net. And a fascinating drive it is. All of the hype about the Internet has produced at least one very tangible benefit: Seemingly, every organization in the real universe is represented in this ethereal one. Many government agencies, research centers, universities, corporations, and media outlets are there now, and the rest are on the way.

The cyber-merchants are enroute too. Right now, shopping on the Internet is a good way to keep money in your pocket. There are online flower shops offering the equivalent of FTD services, a disproportionately high number of lingerie catalogs, and hundreds of miscellaneous cyberstores selling odds and ends. Some fill the growing number of online "malls." But don't expect to find Sears or J.C. Penney there. Nor will an electronic edition of the full L.L. Bean catalog be dropping in your e-mail box soon.

The fat-cat capitalists aren't simply being cautious—they're being realistic. Though some merchants bravely accept credit card orders online, the security of such transactions is still dubious at best. A moderately wily computer hacker could swipe your credit card number online in seconds. Various companies and committees are now attempting to hammer out standards and safeguards for "electronic commerce." In the meantime, the Internet is mainly window shopping.

Special Interests

But the majority of Web sites are dedicated to what might be broadly termed special interests. These run the gamut from the serious to the sublime: AIDS information and Alaska vacations, biotechnology news and Barbie worship, cognitive psychology and Cajun cooking, and so on through the alphabet. The Countdown Page calculates that, as of this writing, there are only 155,627,247 seconds left until the dawn of the second millennium. This has me worried enough about the passage of time that I've begun regularly checking the Endurance Training Journal page ("the journal of the monomaniacal athlete") hoping for tips to live well into the next century. But if things begin to look grim, I'm logging onto the DeathNet page to investigate "end-of-life issues."

It seems no imaginable pursuit goes unpursued.

That includes some "adult" interests you may want to avoid—or at least have your kids avoid. There is as yet no censorship on the Internet, and predictably, the envelope of good taste gets pushed hard. It's easy to stumble upon too. A Web site called Our House, for example, is an innocuous visual tour of an attractive home until you get to the bedroom, where you're offered a menu of saltier sites. And among the discussion groups on the Usenet section of the Internet, "alt.sewing" is listed just above "alt.sex" and its many variations. Talk about seamy.

> *"Most of the words and pictures on the Internet are lifted from the pages of newspapers, journals, and magazines."*

Some in Congress have already seen enough. At this writing [June 1995], a bill to curb the erotic excesses of the Internet is working its way through the House. However, whether even the FBI could enforce such a measure on the freewheeling Net is questionable.

Ultimately, though, it's the lack of genuine interactivity, not the hyperactivity, that may sour you on the Web. In the big dreamscape, interactivity means doing, changing, requesting, buying, and otherwise seizing control of your electronic destiny. On the Internet, interactivity is defined by typing messages and clicking buttons. Net surfing is a spectator sport.

Electronic voting? Sorry, not on the agenda. But sit back and take a virtual tour of the White House with its fuzzy stills of the Oval Office and Blue Room. Music or concert tickets by wire? Well, no, but you can order a T-shirt on the U2 and the Rolling Stones pages. TV on your PC? Not over the Internet, but try a 30-second sound bite from the Melrose Place Home Page. Grocery shopping online? Not yet, but you can order brownies and flowers. Tickets to "The Late Show"? Sorry, the home office says you'll need to send a postcard.

Drawn from Elsewhere

If the dead ends don't deter you, a pervasive sense of déjà vu might. Most of the words and pictures on the Internet are lifted from the pages of newspapers, journals, and magazines. The audio and video clips are usually cribbed from compact discs and TV shows. All of which may lead you to the inescapable conclusion that the Internet—for all its alleged grandeur—is little more than a low-fidelity version of real life.

The Internet, in other words, is far more eccentric than it is essential. So too, in many respects, is television. That doesn't make cyberspace a bad medium, but it doesn't make it a compelling one, either. The Internet may eventually find its versions of CNN, "Monday Night Football," "E.R.," "Sesame Street," and the other things that do make TV an integral part of our lives. Until then, it's high-tech sitcoms for everyone.

A Revolution in Multimedia Communications

by John S. Mayo

About the author: *John S. Mayo served as president of American Telephone & Telegraph's (AT&T) Bell Laboratories from 1991 until his retirement in 1995.*

It's clear that the key underlying information technologies are the prime drivers and the key enablers behind the emerging multimedia communications revolution and the evolution of information superhighways—as well as a host of other advances that together are changing the way we live, work, play, travel and communicate. Because these key information technologies are changing the work and home environments, these same technologies are helping to address customer needs. The more they can do, the more new products and services the customer wants. It has been an upward spiral that has lasted over three decades, and will surely last at least one or two decades more.

What are these key underlying information technologies? They are silicon chips, computing, photonics or lightwaves, and software. And we've seen technology capabilities doubling every year in a number of such domains—for example, in computing and photonics—and doubling every eighteen months in silicon chips. Even software—once a "bottleneck" technology because of quality and programmer-productivity problems—is beginning to advance rapidly in major areas like telecommunications, thanks to advanced programming languages and reuse of previously developed software modules.

Powerful Silicon Chips

To cite perhaps the most widely known example, we've witnessed explosive growth in the power of silicon chips—one measure of which is the number of transistors we can cram onto a chip the size of a fingernail. And this number, now in the millions, is moving steadily toward known physical limits. In the

From "Information Technology for Development," a videotaped speech by John S. Mayo, delivered at the NRC/World Bank Symposium "Marshalling Technology for Development," Irvine, Calif., November 28, 1994. Reprinted with permission.

early part of the twenty-first century, today's familiar solid state devices may mature with transistors measuring about four hundred atoms by four hundred atoms each—the smallest such transistors likely to operate reliably at room temperature. The new frontier then will not be in making the devices smaller, but in creatively and economically using the vast increase in complexity and power made possible by this remarkable technology.

> *"Today's familiar solid state devices may mature with transistors measuring about four hundred atoms by four hundred atoms each."*

The amazing progress of silicon chips forms a microcosm of the broad thrust of information technology and all the associated forces that are leading to the multimedia communications revolution and the evolution of information superhighways. Let's look at the progress and impacts of these related driving forces.

After the invention of the integrated circuit, every time the number of transistors on a silicon chip increased by a factor of a thousand, something had to be reengineered—that is, something had to be radically changed or improved, because it was a new ball game. So the first reengineering that we did—as we headed toward that first thousand-fold increase—was to change all of our design processes, which had been based on discrete components.

When we reached a thousand transistors per chip, we used the new digital circuitry to reengineer our products from analog to digital, as did many other industries. Let me stress that this early progress toward digital products, enabled by silicon chips and software, brought about the digitalization of most systems and services—domestically and, more and more, globally. This digitalization created a powerful force that is driving us toward multimedia communications and information superhighways.

The Beginning of Multimedia Communications

Then, around 1984, we reached toward a million transistors per chip—and powerful microcomputers became possible, along with all the periphery related to microcomputers and the needed software systems. All this led to an explosion of advanced communications services that forced the judicial process that led to the reengineering of our company: from a company that provided largely voice and data-on-voice telecommunications services to a company focused on universal information services. The theme of universal information services is voice, data and images anywhere, anytime with convenience and economy. Providing advanced services on an increasingly intelligent global network was the beginning of multimedia communications, now emerging as the revolution of the 1990s and beyond.

We are currently in the era of yet another thousand-fold increase in transistors per chip. And reengineering has now extended beyond our company and is leading to the merging of communications, computers, consumer electronics and entertainment. The bringing together of these four industries has started out in obvious ways—that is, through joint projects, joint ventures, mergers, acquisitions and some new start-up companies. This reengineering of our industry appears to be the next-to-the-last step of the information revolution brought on by the invention of the transistor.

The last step, and one that may go on forever, is the reengineering of society—of how we live, work, play, travel and communicate. It will create a whole new way of life. For example, it will change education through distance learning and school at home; it will change work life through virtual offices and work at home; and it will diminish the need to transport our bodies for work or routine tasks such as visiting and shopping. Let me quickly add, however, that it will take social change as well as technology to make many of these changes happen.

Common Standards

Another driving force toward multimedia communications and information superhighway evolution is the worldwide push toward common standards and open, user-friendly interfaces that will encourage global networking, and maximum interoperability and connectivity. Photonic or lightwave transmission facilities, for example, will be based on the evolving international standard called SDH—for Synchronous Digital Hierarchy. Because SDH defines standard network interfaces, service providers and customers will be able to use equipment from many different vendors without worry about compatibility. This will facilitate the upgrading of existing networks and the construction of new networks on a worldwide basis. SDH will also provide efficient transport of broadband services and will simplify networks. Similar standards in domestic networks will enable digital communications to the workplace and home, and will make possible high data-rate services.

But let me be clear on this point: although we have a lot of good work on standards, universal connectivity and interoperability will remain a big challenge as the communications and computing industries merge.

Of considerable help will be the Broadband Integrated Services Digital Network, or B-ISDN standard. B-ISDN is a new digital format as well as an international standard that supports multiple services such as voice, data and new video services over lightwave transmission facilities. And it could introduce an exciting new era in global communications networking as equipment vendors and service providers adopt compatible standards to provide sophisticated high-bandwidth, or high-information-capacity, services. B-ISDN is currently defined at so-called interface rates of 155 million bits per second and 622 million bits per second.

"We are currently in the era of yet another thousand-fold increase in transistors per chip."

The Multimedia Revolution

Now, the pacing force behind the multimedia and information superhighway revolution is not so much the technology as it is marketplace demands. For the greater part of this century, the user willingly accepted whatever technological capabilities we were able to achieve. Thus, the telecommunications industry was supplier-driven, and the suppliers managed the evolution of the industry and the information highways. But, as you may know, the technology became so rich that it made many more capabilities possible than the user could accept. To put it differently, we could design a lot more products and services than the customer was willing to pay for. That marked the transition from a supplier-driven industry to today's customer-driven industry—from supplier push to marketplace pull.

> *"Emerging competition is another force driving the evolution of both multimedia communications and information superhighways."*

And, importantly, the global transfer and assimilation of information technology are combining with political and regulatory forces such as the move to privatization of telecommunications around the world—in both developed and developing countries. The result is the growth of ever-stronger global competition in the provision of communications products and services. Such emerging competition is another force driving the evolution of both multimedia communications and information superhighways. And there is an on-going challenge to public policy—not just in the United States, but globally—to provide a framework for that evolution to occur, a framework that ensures full and fair competition for all players.

These, then, are some of the important forces driving us into the multimedia communications revolution and the associated evolution of information superhighways.

Let's look a bit further into these subjects and start with the multimedia revolution. After all, the pursuit of multimedia is creating social pressures on the evolution of information superhighways—both here and around the world. So what is "multimedia"? A reasonable working definition is that the term "multimedia" refers to information that combines more than one medium, where the media can include speech, music, text, data, graphics, fax, image, video and animation. And we at AT&T tend to focus on multimedia products and services that are networked; that is, connected over a communications and information network.

Examples of such networked multimedia communications range from videotelephony and videoconferencing; to real-time video on demand, interactive video and multimedia messaging; to remote collaborative work, interactive information services such as electronic shopping, and multimedia education and training.

Eventually, we will have advanced virtual reality services, which will enable people to indirectly and remotely experience a place or an event in all dimensions.

Now, we are excited about multimedia because public-switched networks—or information highways, if you will—can presently accommodate a wide array of networked multimedia communications, and the evolutionary directions of those networks will enable them to handle an increasingly vast range of such communications. Moreover, there is also a potentially vast market for multimedia hardware and supporting software. Although actual projections differ widely, the most commonly quoted projection for the total worldwide market for multimedia products and services is roughly $100 billion by the year 2000.

We at AT&T are playing a major role in facilitating the emerging multimedia revolution—as a service provider, as a provider of network products to local service providers, and as a provider of products to end users. These are familiar roles for AT&T, so let me briefly describe another, perhaps less familiar, major role we are studying in relation to the multimedia revolution. That is the role of what we call "the missing industry"—and that role is a "host" for a wide variety of digital content and multimedia applications developed by others. Hosting is a function that connects end users to the content they seek. Customers will gain easy, timely and convenient access to personal communications, transactions, information services and entertainment via wired and wireless connections to telephones, handheld devices, computers and eventually television sets. Independent sources for this digital content eventually will range from publishers to large movie studios to small cottage-industry software houses.

This role is also of interest here because of the key information superhighway challenge it illustrates—specifically, because openness of critical interfaces and global standards are vital to this complex hosting function. The entertainment industry, for example, must have software systems that are compatible with those of the hosting industry, and these software systems must, in turn, be compatible with those of the communications and information-networking industry, which then must be compatible with the customer-premises equipment industry.

> *"Tremendous growth in available information and databases will stimulate the need for personal intelligent agents."*

"Smart Agents"

In addition, the tremendous growth in available information and databases will stimulate the need for personal intelligent agents. These "smart agents" are software programs that are activated by electronic messages in the network, and that find, access, process and deliver desired information to the customer. They can perform many of the time-consuming tasks that have discouraged a number of users from taking advantage of on-line services and the emerging electronic marketplace. "Smart agents" are one feature of AT&T's enhanced network service called AT&T PersonaLink[SM] Services.

Let me say I'm looking forward to these "smart agents"—software that can take the hassle out of life. Shopping for the best mortgage, or finding the best new car deal, or finding out which store has the item I want is a hassle, and has people at the interface who add negative value. Just last week I needed a replacement part. I called the store twice and got no satisfactory response to my calls. So I went to the store, waited in line, and then the salesperson queried the database and said, "We don't have it in stock." My "smart agent" could have queried their database and saved them and me a big investment in a zero-revenue operation. There was never a problem with the database; the problem was that people were inadvertently in the way of my ability to access it—adding negative value, but diligently trying to do their jobs. A "smart agent" could simply have done it better.

> *"The pursuit of multimedia communications is driving social issues relating to the evolution of the information superhighway."*

Now, it's important to note that in the age of multimedia communications, people who are geographically separated from each other will not, for example, just play games together over networks—they will visit and find what is emotionally nourishing, and build their relationships. . . .

Remote Collaboration

I must stress that networked multimedia communications will dramatically change the nature of work and will therefore have a broad impact on business—first in developed nations and eventually in developing nations. Videoconferencing, for example, is first coming into businesses to enhance productivity, save time, and reduce travel. And current developments in multimedia telephony are making the possibility of remote collaborative work more and more realistic. In a few years, for example, a person could be working with colleagues or suppliers in branch offices in New York, Irvine, Hong Kong, Paris, and Sydney. Working in real time, they could accomplish the combined task of producing printed materials, presentation slides, and a videotape introducing a new product line.

As I noted, the pursuit of multimedia communications is driving social issues relating to the evolution of the information superhighway. Now, what is AT&T's vision of the information superhighway?

Our vision is to bring people together, giving them easy access to each other and to the information and services they want and need—anytime, anywhere. In our view, the information superhighway is a seamless web of communications and information networks—together with other elements of our national information infrastructure, such as computers, databases, and consumer electronics—which will put vast amounts of information at the fingertips of a variety of users.

A Revolution in Television

by Shelly Schwab

About the author: *Shelly Schwab is the president of MCATV, a television program-*
ming and distribution division of MCA Universal in Universal City, California.

With dozens of cable channels now available to the average home, and hundreds more on the way, how many do we actually watch?

What is signal compression? Multiplexing? Video on demand? Interactivity?
What are the underlying questions and challenges posed by the coming electronic
or information "superhighway"? Beyond entertainment, what bearing will it have
on our lifestyles? Television in the nineties: revolution or confusion?

It's still really a medium in its infancy. Yet, even in just four short decades, it's
remarkable how many moments have touched, molded, and reshaped our lives.

However, even with its rich and colorful history, in terms of real practical potential television hasn't even scratched the surface.

The Early Days

Once upon a time it was a medium of limited options on limited channels. For
the three networks—ABC, CBS, and NBC—the underlying strategy was not so
much to "entice the viewer" as to schedule the "least objectionable programming."
But the day of targeting the passive viewer is over; no longer is a family of four
sitting down to watch *Bewitched* considered making optimum use of the medium.

We're entering an age of audience fragmentation where programmers will
find that their success depends on the aggressive pursuit of an individual viewer
with almost limitless options—500, 600, even 1,000 channels.

When I was growing up, I thought I had a big choice—seven channels to
choose from! But it was television, and it was new, and it was exciting. But today's viewers aren't as easily wooed. For broadcasters, the coming electronic
age is the technological equivalent of Columbus setting sail for the New World:
It's uncharted territory, but where there's great danger, there's also great opportunity—opportunity best realized by understanding the dynamics that brought
us to this point.

Excerpted from "Television in the Nineties," a speech by Shelly Schwab, delivered at the Stern School
of Business, New York University, March 1, 1994.

Let's look back for a few moments at the growth of television by decade. I can remember in the fifties when television watching was considered an "event." Milton Berle [a comedian nicknamed "Mr. Television"] was the talk of the country, but for my family to watch [him] we had to go to a neighbor's house—we didn't own a TV. And we weren't alone: the same was true all over the country. But in just a five-year span, television penetration in terms of households went from almost nothing to two-thirds of the country.

> *"The coming electronic age is the technological equivalent of Columbus setting sail for the New World: It's uncharted territory."*

In the sixties, the television terrain became more colorful, literally, with network schedules being converted to all-color lineups, and many of us getting our first color sets. The sixties were also the decade of the "demographic"—as ratings analysis turned from being strictly quantitative to qualitative as well. Advertisers began looking past raw numbers of households to find just who were their viewers—by age, sex, income.

A New Era

By the seventies, the networks were aggressively programming for young, urban viewers. Gone were such longtime favorites as Jackie Gleason, Ed Sullivan, Red Skelton, even Lassie, and the silly rural sitcoms of the sixties such as *Green Acres* and *The Beverly Hillbillies*. Instead, they were replaced by such landmark series as *All in the Family, M*A*S*H, Mary Tyler Moore Show,* starting a new era in television comedy featuring story lines more sophisticated and relevant than anything that preceded it.

The question as we entered the eighties was: Where are the audiences going? The terrain of television began shifting. Instead of having the three major networks, with all other options almost an afterthought, the television landscape began taking on the look it has today . . . with the networks being just one of the viewers' alternatives.

First, there was the phenomenal growth of the independent stations (stations not affiliated with any of the big three networks). In 1975, there were only 102 of these so-called "indies" throughout the country. By 1985, there were 300, and there are now more than 430. This not only provided a major new alternative for viewers but, in effect, created a gold rush among program producers. Fulfilling the need of these independent stations is what transformed syndication into what it is today . . . now a major competition to the networks. Today many of the most popular and watched series are not on the networks but in syndication, i.e., *Oprah, Donahue, Star Trek, A Current Affair, Wheel of Fortune, Jeopardy,* and *Baywatch*. As a result, the amount of advertising expenditures for non-network or syndicated programs has gone from $25 million annually in 1980 to $1.5 billion today.

Chapter 1

Cable TV and New Networks

A second new programming front was cable. In 1980 cable penetration stood at just 18 percent of all households. CNN and MTV were launched and are now staples of daily life, and by 1985 cable penetration had jumped to 43 percent. It now stands at over 60 percent.

But, in addition to these changes from without, the eighties also brought the networks change from within: All three networks were sold—ABC to Capital Cities, NBC to General Electric, and CBS to Laurence A. Tisch of the Loews Corporation. And television's founding fathers, William Paley, David Sarnoff, Leonard Goldenson, visionaries who shaped each network's philosophy, were replaced by corporate entities run by bottom-line investors.

Meanwhile, another visionary and entrepreneur on a global scale, Rupert Murdoch, was buying both 20th Century Fox and the Metromedia stations and forming the Fox Broadcasting Company (later to become the fourth network). Ted Turner was adding to his Turner broadcasting empire by starting up additional cable channels and, more recently, acquiring Hollywood production companies.

Another critical change facing television, and Madison Avenue in particular, was the skyrocketing number of "VCRs." Viewers were increasingly zapping through commercials when playing back tapes. With 55 percent of all homes having remotes by 1988, "grazing" or "channel hopping" during commercials became the advertisers' other big nightmare. (And a woman's nightmare as well, as men more than women are usually the zapping "culprits.")

This brings us to the nineties: With so many new entertainment alternatives coming into the field, what are the ramifications for the networks, the program suppliers, the advertisers, the viewers?

For the three major networks, their diminishing share of the audience pie is down to 60 percent and on any given night as low as 50 percent. In 1984 it was 80 percent.

> *"For the three major networks, their diminishing share of the audience pie is down to 60 percent and on any given night as low as 50 percent."*

Fox, for example, as the upstart network, has already siphoned off a significant number of the big three networks' most demographically desirable viewers—the 18- to 34-year-olds—by aggressively programming for them with such series as *In Living Color, Beverly Hills 90210,* and *The Simpsons.*

In addition, more competition is on the way from Paramount and Warners, who are now engaged in a race to sign up as many affiliates as possible for their proposed fifth and sixth networks. It prompted one network insider to wonder, "If networks are a dying business, how come everyone is in such a rush to start one?"

The answer is, of course, that the networks may not necessarily be dying, but to survive they may have to reconfigure significantly. Based on new FCC regulations, there is now a strong possibility that one or two of the networks could be bought by film studios, or vice versa. Networks that were until recently pure buyers of programs will increasingly become suppliers, producing not only their own programming but, in select instances, that of their competition. For example, Fox, which has its own network, is now producing the Emmy Award–winning series *Picket Fences* for CBS. The old definition of mixed emotions was "watching your

> *"Do you know what the fastest-growing form of programming on television is? Infomercials."*

mother-in-law drive off a cliff in your new Cadillac." The new equivalent may be producing the number one series in prime time—for your competition.

Other changes facing the networks? The news and sports divisions may not survive on all three. Networks will continue to buy stakes in more and more advertiser-supported cable channels such as ESPN, Lifetime, and A&E: Again, under the theory that as long as someone has to be in competition with me, why not let it be me?

What are the programming trends of the nineties? Or to be more pragmatic, I suppose, in which directions are the economic realities of the business forcing network programmers to turn?

Sitcoms and dramas will continue to be staples of the networks' lineup. On the other hand, "action-hours" series such as the *A-Team* and *Magnum P.I.* that once accounted for 21 percent of the networks' lineups will continue to be conspicuous by their absence. With only the occasional exception, they just don't make 'em like they used to. Why? Strictly economics—the dollars involved don't make any sense. Exploding buildings and crashing car scenes are just too expensive to produce.

Action-hours cost between $1.3 to $2 million per episode to produce versus $1 million for dramas and $700,000 for reality programming. Incidentally, if big-budget action series are endangered, conversely, do you know what the fastest-growing form of programming on television is? Infomercials! As a start-up business, it's gone from grossing nothing to $1 billion a year, virtually overnight (and growing).

Now and in the Future

So where do we stand in 1994 and beyond? There are now 94 million TV homes, reaching 98 percent of the country (1950: 4 million TV homes/10 percent of the country). Sixty-five percent of TV homes have two or more sets. Sixty-one percent of TV homes have cable. The average home receives 35 channels (1950s = 2.9).

Of those 35 channels, does anyone know how many the typical adult viewer watches in any given week? 7.5. How many will you watch when there are 500 channels?

The average household views over 7 hours a day/51 hours a week. VCR penetration is 83 percent. That's a lot of taping. But only half of all home-recorded tapes are ever played back. Thirty percent of all households have "PCs." Advertising is still the lifeblood of television: In 1950, $171 million was spent on total TV advertising. Now it's at $33 billion!

But beyond over-the-air broadcasting and cable, what are the alternate technologies being developed as means of delivering television?

There's "DBS," direct broadcasting satellite. This system will beam a package of channels directly to homes that have small dish antennae. This service was launched nationally in 1994. Another new competing delivery system is microwave technology. This simultaneously transmits dozens of channels for television, telephone, and data. Homes are reached by bouncing the signal off buildings or other objects until it reaches its destination.

But everything we've been discussing so far—the evolution of television, the new technologies—while dramatic and exciting, pales in comparison to the changes at hand.

A radically changed medium lies just around the corner, and the key to it is the coming electronic or information superhighway, which will use fiberoptic wires to compress and deliver 500, 600, or even 1,000 channels! But will this lead to revolution—or total confusion?

Enormous Potential and Cost

Here's where the real opportunities lie. John Sculley, the former chief executive of Apple Computer, estimated that the formation of a single interactive information industry could generate revenue of $3.5 trillion by the year 2001.

The potential is enormous, but so is the massive outlay of capital required to finance this superhighway: over $400 billion (that's more than the gross national product of Canada). That's also why cable companies that until now have enjoyed virtual monopolies in their service areas are suddenly rushing into a series of mergers and partnerships with the one industry they most feared as future competition: the telephone companies. The Baby Bells [regional telephone companies] are cash cows and they have the capital and resources to build and deliver the infrastructure to the information superhighway. Of course, a great deal of the direction and growth in this area is tied to government regulations. One of the greatest fears caused by all the recent megamergers is access, the ability of everyone—companies, consumers, institutions—to tap into the superhighway. Will a small number of "gatekeepers" be able to cause a "bottleneck"? How do Congress and the courts plan to enforce access?

"What shape will the superhighway take? One senior cable executive offered this example: one of a 600-channel universe."

There will be a lot of new words in our vocabulary—"multiplexing," "CD-ROM," "access"—that's the new language of the superhighway. Other buzzwords include fiber optics, infrastructure, signal compression, high definition, servers, interactive programming, multimedia, video dial tones, network time shifting, video on demand, bulletin board services, and virtual reality, with more and more coming on-line every day. But none of this is speculation. It isn't Buck Rogers fantasizing. It's what we are now capable of achieving.

Future Television Channels

What shape will the superhighway take? One senior cable executive offered this example: one of a 600-channel universe.

First, a 100-channel "grazing zone" that would be similar to current traditional cable television. Next, there would be a 200-channel "quality zone" providing two additional channels for each channel in the "grazing zone" on which their best programming would be repeated. Beyond that, a 50-channel "event TV zone" for live pay-per-view events such as boxing. And finally, a 250-channel "video store" that would be reserved for movies, and these movies won't all necessarily be previously released theatricals; they may be big-budget spectaculars running concurrently with or prior to their theatrical runs.

What about programming on the superhighway? As a viewer, what would I find in the proposed grazing zone? Programming not meant as a mass viewing experience but designed for the individual: What I or you want, when we want it. For instance, movies that can now be ordered at several specific times during the day will be available at any time at all—virtually "on demand."

Incidentally, another example of "video on demand" is a system developed by

"We're going to be replaced by a new generation of viewers raised on interacting with their sets."

a company called U.S.A. Video, which will digitize and compress full libraries of movie studios. Those compressed signals will be sent over telephone lines and stored in a box attached to a user's set, where they can keep the movie or event for up to 24 hours with the ability to rewind, fast forward, or pause it—just like a rented video.

But as a programmer, competing with hundreds of other channels, how will I effectively reach as many viewers as possible?

One of the strategies prominently mentioned by the broadcast networks and their cable counterparts is "multiplexing"—expanding their lineup to more than one channel at a time. For instance, it's Monday at 8 p.m. and HBO-One will be running a movie, while HBO-Two has a concert, and HBO-Three carries the series *Dream-On*.

What about the enormous potential of pay-per-view? Theatrical premieres and special events notwithstanding, the greatest example of a built-in pay-per-view audience is in sports. Thus far, only boxing, wrestling, and [talk-show host] Howard Stern have managed to take full advantage of this technology; but the day of the pay-per-view "season ticket" will soon be at hand. It's speculated that the NFL could soon be offering a weekly tray of "pay-per-view" games if you want to watch a game other than the one carried in your market. And there will be special plans offered, if you wish to follow one particular out-of-town team for an entire season.

Interactive Television

What about "interactive programming"? Forget the image of the couch potato who sits before his set going from channel to channel in a semivegetative state, the way my generation watches television. We're going to be replaced by a new generation of viewers raised on interacting with their sets. I can just hear an incredulous child saying to a parent, "You mean you used to watch movies without being able to decide what happens next?" Imagine reaching the last scene in *Casablanca* and then getting to choose who Ingrid Bergman goes off with at the end? Humphrey Bogart or Paul Heinreid? Heinreid wouldn't stand a chance!

But is this really what viewers want? To pick the end of their favorite television shows or films? Or does that somehow diminish the viewing experience? As a novelty, it might work, but on a regular basis?

At the 1993 superhighway summit at UCLA, opinion was split—Jeffrey Katzenberg, [then] chairman of the Walt Disney Studios, said that as a viewer he wouldn't want to sit home and determine the outcome of films. On the other hand, Lucie Salhany, the Fox Broadcasting Corporation chairman, says that this is something they are interested in and want to explore. Two major studios with opposite views. Again, revolution or total confusion?

"Virtual reality," the sexiest of the new buzzwords, is another form of interactivity. The user is able to interact in what is usually a computer-driven environment. For example, batting against a major league pitcher while sitting in your living room. This experience is enhanced with video, audio, and graphics and gives the senses a full three-dimensional effect.

> *"The quality of the images you'll be seeing on-screen, in the high-definition universe, will be taking a quantum leap."*

But "interactive programming" goes far beyond just playing simulated games or having your kids interact with *Beavis and Butthead*. By the way, that thought alone is enough to make me want to rethink the entire technology. But it's about interacting with other people. Interactive television will revolutionize education, politics, lifestyles.

Vice President Al Gore, the Clinton Administration's point man on the information superhighway, told CEOs at the UCLA summit that providing every school, library, and hospital with access to the superhighway's educational and informational tools was the highest priority and targeted the end of the nineties for them to meet that challenge, which the CEOs in turn pledged to do.

Without Leaving Your Home

Interactive television will change politics, careers, communication. Interest groups, scattered by geography, will be able to "link up," becoming much more effective, much more demanding. For those looking for a different quality of life, it will be much easier to run a business in a remote area, without leaving your home.

And you won't have to go out to do your marketing either. Instead of a trip to the supermarket, you'll be able to call up a market's entire inventory—by price, by brand, by size—and place your order by touching your screen. From foods, to fashion, to furnishing your home, to any aspect of your life —you'll soon be able to satisfy your shopping needs via video malls. In fact, *Joan Rivers Shopping Show* aside, the whole concept of home shopping has an enormous upside that has barely been scratched.

Also, let me mention briefly "high definition" television. It's important to realize that the quality of the images you'll be seeing on-screen, in the high-definition universe, will be taking a quantum leap. Not only will we have greater options regarding what to watch, but it will be provided in a wide-screen format with unprecedented clarity. The audio will also be beyond anything previously available, and you'll be able to hang it all on your wall. Today's sets will seem as primitive and outmoded as the black-and-white sets of the fifties.

Yet, even with all the terms used to describe the future of the superhighway— enormous, gargantuan, unlimited—the bottom line is that no one agrees regarding what form it will finally take. With companies investing hundreds of millions, even billions of dollars, there's still no consensus on how it will pay off. Mistakes will be made. There won't be a magic switch that you turn on and it will suddenly be there.

Again, returning to my earlier analogy about Columbus setting sail for the New World: Where there are great opportunities, there are also great dangers.

Chapter 2

How Should the Information Highway Be Developed?

CURRENT CONTROVERSIES

Development of the Information Highway: An Overview

by Amy Bruckman et al., interviewed by Herb Brody

About the authors: *Herb Brody is a senior editor for* Technology Review. *Amy Bruckman is a Massachusetts Institute of Technology doctoral student. Michael Dertouzos directs MIT's Laboratory for Computer Science. Robert Domnitz is a telecommunications industry expert in the Massachusetts Executive Office of Economic Affairs. Nathan Felde is executive director of video information service development at the NYNEX Science and Technology Center in Cambridge. Mitchell Kapor is chairman and cofounder of the Electronic Frontier Foundation advocacy group and founder of Lotus Development Corporation. Martyn Roetter is a vice president and market researcher at Decision Resources in Waltham, Massachusetts. Michael Schrage is a* Los Angeles Times *columnist and a research associate at MIT's Sloan School of Management.*

Brody: Two different visions of an information highway seem to be emerging. There's Vice-President Al Gore's view, where we all have access to libraries and vast databases through our personal computers. Meanwhile, the cable TV and telephone companies are moving forward with entertainment-oriented systems that offer things like video on demand, home shopping, and games. Which information highway are we going to get?

Envisioning the Information Infrastructure

Domnitz: It's almost inevitable that the private sector is going to be doing the heavy lifting on the development of infrastructure. Since the private sector is going to respond only to economic incentives, the services offered initially will be entertainment. But to put in the infrastructure necessary for such profit-making activities, the private sector needs access to public assets. Cable TV operators and telephone companies need rights of way. Broadcasters need spectrum space. And the government, representing the public interest, will probably decide that certain benefits should be provided to the public in return. So educational and public-service kinds of uses will come into the picture.

Felde: That sounds a little too neat, and unlikely. We'll get the information infrastructure that we pay for, and it won't be all things to all people. If it is driven opportunistically by one or two big revenue sources, like movies on demand, then it will be a different network than if it is deployed more to allow people to attend college classes remotely.

Dertouzos: The information infrastructure will reflect our society the way we function today—a certain amount of private-sector activity, a certain amount of political and educational and public-service work. TV-based recreation, with movies and home shopping and so on, is where it will start. After all, there are 80-million-plus TV sets in the United States. The cable TV companies are going to come in with a system that offers very little interaction. Information like movies or the L.L. Bean catalogue will mostly flow one-way—from a central source to you. But the information market that I envision is a medium where every person and every organization would be able to buy, sell, and exchange freely information and information services.

> *"Eighty percent of our $6 trillion GNP [gross national product] is information-related."*

Kapor: Michael, why do you emphasize buying and selling as the archetypal service? Noneconomic uses, like coordination of activities for political or educational purposes, are as important, if not more important, and none of them will be possible on a one-way system designed to deliver lowest-common-denominator, mass-market entertainment.

Dertouzos: The reason I say buy and sell is because 80 percent of our $6 trillion GNP [gross national product] is information-related. I also say "exchange freely."

Kapor: But if people don't understand that this is about more than business, and about more than the private sector making a lot of money as industry boundaries dissolve and realign, then we're going to miss an enormous opportunity to revitalize democratic values in society. It is all too easy to substitute an economically or technically focused discussion for what ought to be first a political and cultural discussion.

Dertouzos: Actually, the political and cultural effects will transcend buying and selling. To me, the primary feature of a true information infrastructure is the shrinking of geographical distance and the elimination of political boundaries. Think about what this means for the notion of national identity. I'm Greek. There are 9 million of us in Greece, 2 million on the East Coast of the United States, 1 million in Australia, a couple of million elsewhere in the world. Maybe it's not the Greek nation anymore. Maybe it's the Greek network.

This assaults head-on the national boundaries that shaped so much of our history and that led to so many wars. People talk about an NII—a national information infrastructure. I think we should drop the "N." It's very parochial to be thinking only of a U.S. infrastructure.

Universal Access

Brody: But whether the goal is an NII or a global information highway, we don't want to end up with a system that divides society into information haves and information have-nots. How can we ensure universal access?

Domnitz: We have to distinguish between two concepts here. Access to the conduit for, say, a conversation between you and me is not necessarily the same as access to information itself—which might mean, essentially, a conversation between a database and me. We do want to make sure that information is available to all. But to allow unlimited conversation at essentially no cost—that may cost more than society can afford to pay.

Bruckman: Oh, I disagree. One of the really exciting things about what is going on is that we're moving away from the idea that truth is contained only in libraries and official databases. People are realizing that truth is created by communities of people. Here's a personal example. I keep tropical fish, and sometimes I need some information about their care and feeding. Yes, I could go to the library and pore through a book on tropical fish—but I'll probably never find the right answer to my question. Or, I can post a message on the Usenet newsgroup alt.aquaria, and someone will respond in three minutes with exactly the information that I need. The network is changing our basic notion of the nature of information. We can't think of information and community as separate concepts any more.

Felde: Sure, but just because information is posted on the Internet as an immediate answer to a question doesn't guarantee that it's true. You might be putting something toxic in the fish tank as a result of some prankster's advice. What you're talking about sounds to me more like consensus than truth. The major "truth" that I see is that the advance in telecommunications technology has led people to expect a lot more than they used to as basic service.

> *"To allow unlimited conversation at essentially no cost—that may cost more than society can afford to pay."*

My two-year-old daughter used to come by our laboratory and use our videoconferencing system to talk with my colleagues. We didn't have a television in our home at the time—when we finally bought one, my daughter expected it to be as responsive as the one she had been using. She has developed the expectation that television allows direct communication with people who respond directly to you.

Dertouzos: I firmly believe that without explicit, vigilant attention by society, the information infrastructure will tend to increase the gap between rich and poor. First, there will be a disparity with respect to nations—Bangladesh is not going to have as sophisticated an information highway as the United States, Japan, or Germany. And as much as we'd like to theorize about educational applications and so on, the people in the inner city will not necessarily be able to afford these services. Not only that, but many will lack the educational background that would enable them to use the network even if they could afford it.

> *"Cyberspace clearly needs an Andrew Carnegie."*

Kapor: Cyberspace clearly needs an Andrew Carnegie. The public library system that we have today is supported by taxes, but it didn't start out that way. Carnegie endowed 2,000 libraries and gave such a jump-start to the notion that every community should have its own library that in a fairly short period of time, people accepted the idea. But even if initially the support for these information services comes philanthropically, eventually it will be supported out of a tax base. And it's not just a matter of putting in wires—software is going to have to be built that enables whatever level of free access we as a society decide to provide. The analog to Carnegie's libraries today is not to create some sort of new physical repository where there are computer terminals that you could come to. Many libraries are doing that, and that's a good thing as a transition. But it suggests that there's some level of service that is basic and ought to be available free to all citizens.

Roetter: We should keep in mind that public financing doesn't ensure equal access. Libraries, for instance, are locally funded. There are some very good libraries in Massachusetts, but some of the less wealthy towns have practically closed their libraries altogether. There's also the question of what devices people have in their homes to hook up to this network. Only about 25 percent of households now have a personal computer.

Domnitz: Look at the current public telephone network. Most people feel that telephone service is affordable, but it's not free and therefore not "universal." How can public policy deal with that?

Kapor: Maybe it doesn't have to—at least, not in terms of cost alone. In California, most people who don't have phones have made that decision for noneconomic reasons—a lot of them are illegal aliens and they're afraid if they get a phone that immigration is going to come and deport them. Meanwhile, 98 percent of U.S. households have TVs (only 93 percent have telephones) and all those people in the 98 percent *paid* for their TVs—television is important enough that people go out and actually spend money on it. . . .

Developing a Vision

Brody: Despite the blizzard of media coverage about the information highway, don't we really lack a vision of what the system itself should be?

Kapor: We have a vision, but it's the wrong one. Any vision of the information superhighway that focuses on video-on-demand and home shopping rather than on providing cyberspace with its equivalent of Andrew Carnegie is too narrow. The first-order issue ought to be: What are we shooting for as a society? How are we conceiving of this great project that we are engaged in? My hope is that we reach a consensus for the system to be open, inclusive, egalitarian, and decentralized, and that it be based in the private sector so that investments can be matched with the possibility of reward. Common sense suggests that if you make something too much of an entitlement before you give businesspeople a chance to recoup an investment in what they do—let's cut right to the bottom line of what capitalism worries about here—it's going to be an unhappy situation.

Dertouzos: It's all well and good to discuss how to configure the information highway so that it provides the best social value. But at this stage of the game, we should be concentrating mainly on developing fundamental technologies. Then we will have the technical means to address many of the social and political problems that arise in the future. Historically, this is how it has usually worked. Radar, for example, was developed as a weapon of war, and then, through no intention of its inventors, became the cornerstone of modern air transportation.

Felde: Yes, and in fact the metaphoric model for the information highway— the nation's interstate highway system—was conceived originally for national defense purposes. President Dwight D. Eisenhower didn't want to have trouble moving tanks around in tight, crooked, unpaved streets like they had in Europe. But if the interstate highway system had been built in the 1850s instead of the 1950s, it would

> *"At this stage of the game, we should be concentrating mainly on developing fundamental technologies."*

have been eight lanes wide going west. Today we seem to be designing an information highway that has eight lanes back from out west— Hollywood—and leaves only a footpath from the home.

Bruckman: I strongly agree with Mitch [Kapor] that we need to develop a vision of where we want this technology to go. In that spirit, I'll tell you where we ought to start—in the schools. That's where we can develop a vision for what we as a society want.

Schrage: No! The last thing we need to do is turn innocent little children into guinea pigs for the grandiloquent ambitions of technocrats. Schools would be the single worst place to experiment with the information highway. Let's have the *Fortune* 1000 suffer the pains of trying to apply leading-edge technology before we let thousands of inner city schools fall victim to people whose hearts are in the right place but who can't pull any of these things off.

Bruckman: Oh, Michael, come on. Do you want to hear real stories about the things that kids are doing on networks?

Schrage: I know those wonderful anecdotes. But I think they reflect a principle that's already been proven in the workplace: if you pay more attention to people—any kind of attention—they perform better. So when people like you are in the schools, those kids do better, whether they're using computers or pen and paper.

Bruckman: I couldn't agree with you more. The real value is not in the technology, but in forging connections between people. All the things that are exciting right now in education involve using technology to forge connections between people.

> *"The real value is not in the technology, but in forging connections between people."*

Felde: The ability to connect with other people is especially important nowadays because of the dislocation of families. The information infrastructure must allow people to define, reconstitute, and create their own "family."

Dertouzos: We could have had a discussion like this 120 years ago about the telephone. . . .

Schrage: Yeah, some visionary would be saying something crazy like, "Let's put a phone on every desk."

Dertouzos: Some people would focus on education. Others would say, no, this technology is really best suited for use by doctors or in commerce. As we look at the telephone in retrospect, people talk through it about everything—about all the economic and personal things, tangible and intangible, that govern our lives. I believe that this is what is going to happen here. Education is going to pick up its societal share of somewhere between 5 and 8 percent of the uses. There's going to be commerce on this thing, there's going to be personal communication, business communication, x-rays from labs to the family doctor, orders from factories to suppliers, people buying consumer products. It will be all of what happens today in society, but a little bit faster and maybe, if we're lucky, a little easier. That's my vision—what I call the information market. . . .

In Historical Perspective

Kapor: One of the things that's gotten lost here is the notion of who we are as Americans. We're citizens. Our democratic tradition emphasizes the value of active participation in the shaping of one's society. If we have an information infrastructure that is highly open and decentralized and egalitarian and supports diversity, and that lets lots of people make lots of money, then it will create numerous opportunities for types of civic participation that do not exist today. So the point is to tip the balance back in favor of those who do not have lots of money and lots of power by giving them more of an opportunity to have their voices heard—by each other, by their elected officials, by people in their community who may not share their views.

Let's put this in historical perspective. In the first decade of the republic—

when the United States was a start-up—it was Alexander Hamilton versus Thomas Jefferson for the dominant vision of what kind of government we were to have. Hamilton won, and we wound up with a highly centralized society. To fuel the engine of economic growth and raise the standard of living, we had to have centralized corporations, like the railroads, U.S. Steel, and Standard Oil. But now there's an opportunity to have sort of a rematch, under very different conditions, between the principles of Jefferson and those of Hamilton. We have the ability, given the construction of a high-capacity information infrastructure, to do things in a decentralized fashion that does not require large institutions, either public or private.

Brody: What's the Jeffersonian "game plan," then?

Kapor: It is to make sure that the information infrastructure that we build is a two-way, interactive network. When we get down to detail, of course, there are very legitimate questions, like, does everybody need a multimegabit-per-second digital line going into their living room? We'll probably conclude that they could get by with less. But we can't make practical decisions like that until we share a vision for the information infrastructure and agree on its purpose. . . .

Different Priorities

Brody: What if, tomorrow, you were named information highway czar. In that position, you'd have to act on pending decisions and formulate policy. What would you do? What would your priorities be?

Kapor: Unfortunately, it's a lot easier to make good policy by preventing bad things than by enabling good things. So if you want pragmatic advice, I'd say: kill the Clipper chip. The Clipper embodies an attempt by the Clinton administration to force-feed a crippled encryption technology into the telephone network. Copies of the keys that are used to decode information are kept in escrow by the federal government, so law-enforcement agencies will still be able to tap phone calls when they get a court order. The chip uses a secret encryption algorithm developed by the National Security Agency, and there's no guarantee it doesn't have a trap door that makes it possible to listen in without the escrow keys. My second act would be to urge anybody who has a dream or vision for the global information infrastructure to get on the Internet and try to build part of it—*now*. Take some direct action. Because I'm becoming less and less optimistic that the private sector will, left to itself, build the kind of infrastructure that's best for the citizens of the country. So I'd say *carpe diem* [seize the day].

> *"The point is to tip the balance back in favor of those who do not have lots of money and lots of power."*

Schrage: I have three suggestions. First, eliminate software patents. Intellectual property issues are going to become more and more important, but the attempts to enforce software patents create more problems than they solve. Second, in the interests of promoting accessibility, the government should make sure that any telecommunications carrier that does not provide nondiscriminatory access is disadvantaged in the marketplace—maybe through a higher tax rate, maybe through denial of government contracts. Third, forbid the proliferation of computers in the public schools, which have failed to effectively assimilate and adopt them.

> *"If you want pragmatic advice, I'd say: kill the Clipper chip."*

If there is some sort of revolution in the schools that turns them inside out and upside down, then perhaps the role of technology in the schools could be reevaluated.

Bruckman: I believe that the network should be a place that people construct, not just access. Individuals with nothing more than a personal computer and a modem should be able to create their own communities and businesses. There need to be multiple economic models to choose from—for-profit and not-for-profit, advertising-permitted and advertising-not-permitted. Governments should facilitate the network's development—not by legislating entitlements but by structuring incentives and by funding basic research. I don't know what those incentives should look like, and I don't think anyone else does either. If I were czar of the information highway, I'd fund many small research projects that would stretch our conception of what the network might be.

Two-Way Interaction

Felde: There are powerful forces now promoting an information highway that would be essentially one-way. That's what "500 channel" cable TV is all about. We need to make sure that it doesn't happen, and that we build instead a switched network that allows two-way interaction between everyone who connects to it. For example, I'd redesign the FCC's [Federal Communications Commission] "video dial tone." As presently conceived, video dial tone is a way of regulating the distribution of movies from central sources. It should instead be a means of providing individuals with universal access to the public switched network with their existing camcorders, televisions, and stereos.

I would create a tariff structure that ensures that telecommunications services cost the same regardless of geographical distance. The same stamp now gets a letter across town or across country; e-mail, video, and other new services ought to be just as distance-insensitive. We also need to study how grassroots users—those without a lobby or an organization to represent their interests—might shape the design of the network. And to anyone who is willing to relinquish their driver's license, I would issue a telecommunications card that gives them a network address, access privileges, tax credits, equipment discounts, and low-interest home improvement loans: let people trade hydrocarbons for photons/electrons.

Roetter: First, I'd repeal any restrictions on foreign ownership of common carriers or broadcasting licenses. In fact, I would create incentives to make sure that foreign television and other programming get distributed widely in the United States. Second, with regard to the new wireless personal communications services that are going to make portable telephone service cheaper and more widely available, I would try to get a third wireless operator in every area as soon as possible. You may need two to tango but you need three for real competition. I would also look at the electronic information services that government agencies provide and try to introduce some of the best commercial practices so that we can much more effectively deal with government as citizens and as consumers.

Domnitz: As my first official act I would put half my staff on furlough. The government should get out of the way of the private sector, which has done a great job of developing innovative concepts and tools for telecommunications that are responsive to the marketplace. The best and perhaps only role for government may be to ensure universal, affordable access in situations where the market fails to provide it. I would therefore initially advocate use of government's powers only to ensure competition. If the marketplace doesn't provide everything that society needs, government can easily step in later. The federal government has been effective in deregulating and enforcing competition in the long-distance telephone industry. States that emulate the federal approach will reap substantial social and economic benefits.

> *"Governments should facilitate the network's development . . . by structuring incentives and by funding basic research."*

Dertouzos: The first thing I'd do is try to build some awareness as to what an information infrastructure—an information market—is. I would educate people that an information market requires a lot more than just shipping uninterpreted bytes. Then I'd catalyze the establishment of agreements on standards so that computers can understand each other, so they can interpret the bytes and relieve us of work. The third thing would be to ensure more open access. That means wherever there's a question, err in the direction of shrinking the radius of control, consistent with American traditions. Finally, I would set up the beginnings of a national endowment for the information have-nots.

Schrage: I'd have really been impressed if you had led off with that one.

Dertouzos: Sometimes the most important things are last.

The Federal Government Should Expedite the Information Highway

by Rick Boucher

About the author: *Rick Boucher, a Democrat from Virginia, has been elected to six terms in the House of Representatives and is the chairman of the House Subcommittee on Science of the Committee on Science, Space, and Technology.*

In politics as in sports, Americans are accustomed to a fair amount of exaggeration. Just as the "greatest game ever" seems to be played three or four times a season, leaders in government often speak boldly about ideas that hold the promise of a vastly improved society, a wealthier and better educated public, or a more competitive economy.

Occasionally, history conspires to prove our leaders right. This is precisely the case with the much-heralded information superhighway, a development in technology so remarkable in scope that it could equal the telephone or the steam engine in its ability to reorder our economy and improve our quality of life.

Effects on Society

Exaggeration? Maybe, but I don't think so. Consider for a moment what the information highway could mean to American society:

- Businesses large and small could transmit sales orders, contract specifications, or detailed plans and drawings instantly from one coast to another without the loss of time, money, and clarity that hinders so much business communication.
- Students in every corner of the nation could have equal electronic access to new courses, the best teachers, and the widest selection of information.
- The health-care system could use high performance computing and networking to speed the development of new drugs, facilitate diagnoses from

Rick Boucher, "The Information Superhighway: Turning the Vision into Reality." Reprinted from *National Forum: The Phi Kappa Phi Journal*, vol. 74, no. 2 (Spring 1994), © Rick Boucher, by permission of the publishers.

remote locations, and achieve enormous improvements in administrative efficiency.

- Americans from every background could "telecommute" to their offices, watch the latest movies and sporting events, and access the vast resources of the nation's libraries.

This is just a snapshot of what the future will look like when the National Information Infrastructure (NII) is developed fully. A centerpiece of the Clinton administration's technology policy, the NII can best be defined as a nationwide communications system that will enable users to access information and communicate with one another easily and in virtually any medium, including voice, data, image, video, or any combination thereof. The system will link an extensive web of public and private communications networks that use fiber-optic cables, wireless technologies, copper wire, and coaxial cable.

Virtually everyone in Washington—in the Executive Branch and in Congress—agrees that the information superhighway should be built and built soon. The tougher question is the appropriate federal role in building the system.

The Federal Government's Role

As a preliminary matter, it bears repeating that the federal government should not own, deploy, control, or manage the information infrastructure. The physical network, including the fiber-optic lines, high speed switches, and associated software, should be deployed, owned, and controlled by the private sector. The federal government's role should consist of the following.

First, the government should ensure that the network is fully interoperable for the digital transmission of video, voice, and data seamlessly throughout the nation. Both wired and wireless means of data delivery should be accommodated through a government-

"Virtually everyone in Washington . . . agrees that the information superhighway should be built and built soon."

initiated standard-setting process. Specifically, Congress should direct the Federal Communications Commission to facilitate the creation of common standards and protocols for network operation by establishing an external advisory committee composed of technical experts from both the private and the public sectors.

Provide Research and Development Funding

Second, the government should provide research and development funding for the creation and demonstration of new networking technologies. Our immediate goal is a twenty-fold increase in the speed of network performance from the current level of 45 million bits per second (commonly known as a T-3 link), currently the fastest available commercial connection, to one billion bits per second (commonly known as gigabit speed). That level of performance would enable the transmission of large volumes of material at high speed; a file equal in size to the *Encyclopaedia Britannica* could be transferred in about one second.

To achieve that increase in network speed, a new generation of switches and software will be required. The federal government should provide funding for that development. The government also should create a testbed network in which the new technologies, once developed, could be demonstrated. The demonstration network also could serve as a link between the users of high bandwidth, such as supercomputer centers, which require a level of network performance not available from the private sector.

> *"The most immediate uses of a high-performance network will be for the delivery of health care."*

The government also should provide research and development funding for certain near-term applications of the information infrastructure. The most immediate uses of a high-performance network will be for the delivery of health care, including distant diagnoses, the transmission of patient billing and records, and the remote monitoring of vital signs, leading to an increased degree of freedom for patients who today must be kept in more confined settings. It also will help the nation achieve quickly the administrative reforms that President Clinton has identified as being so critical to the reduction of health care costs.

Expanding electronic classrooms, digitizing libraries, and assembling in a readily retrievable form the vast stores of government information will be the other near-term applications for which federal research funding is appropriate.

I have authored legislation to carry out these R&D [research and development] functions. H.R. 1757, the National Information and Infrastructure Act of 1993, authorized $1 billion over five years to demonstrate the applications of the information highway for health care, education, digital libraries, and government services. It also authorized the National Science Foundation to assist educational institutions at all levels to interconnect with each other and to connect with the Internet. The House of Representatives approved H.R. 1757 in July 1993 by a wide margin; it [was rejected] in the Senate in 1994.

Remove Outdated Restrictions

The third role for the federal government is to remove outdated restrictions on communications companies that serve as major disincentives to private sector network investment. To give private industry sufficient economic incentive to deploy fiber-optic lines and other broad band technology providing network access to homes, businesses, schools, and research laboratories throughout the nation, Congress should eliminate the following restrictions.

First, the provision of the 1984 Cable Act that prohibits telephone companies from offering cable TV service within their telephone service area should be repealed. This cross-ownership restriction of the 1984 law is the current major impediment to the willingness of telephone and cable television companies alike to deploy a high-performance network in local communities throughout the nation.

The interstate highways of the information infrastructure are already in place. These are the fiber-optic lines maintained by the long-distance telephone carriers (AT&T, MCI, and Sprint, among others) that carry telephone traffic on an inter-exchange basis from one city to the next, connecting telephone company central offices. What are missing are the off-ramps and city streets of the information highway, that portion of the network that connects telephone company central offices directly with users, including homes, businesses, and schools. This "last mile" of the information highway employs the most outdated technology, and, because of its combined length, it is the most costly segment of the infrastructure to deploy. In fact, it is variously estimated that the aggregate deployment cost will range between $150 billion and $400 billion.

The nation can obtain the benefits of deployment over the "last mile" without spending any taxpayer dollars if telephone companies are given the right to offer TV service where they also offer telephone service, and vice-versa. The ability of telephone companies to offer cable service and cable companies to offer telephone service carries with it an enormous financial incentive to deploy a network capable of offering the combination of services. In the case of the telephone companies, the deployment would consist of fiber-optic lines replacing the twisted pairs of copper wires currently in use. In the case of the cable companies, the deployment would consist of advanced switches enabling what is today a one-way network of coaxial cable to operate interactively in the future.

Given the convergence that is already taking place between telephone companies and entertainment companies, the outdated nature of the cross-ownership restriction is readily apparent, and Congress should repeal it. It also should be mentioned that repeal of the restriction would create competition in the delivery of both cable television service and telephone service, giving consumers meaningful choices in two markets that operate as monopolies today.

Second, the seven regional Bell operating companies should be empowered to manufacture telecommunications equipment and to offer long-distance service. It makes little sense to exclude from the market for high-end telecommunications equipment seven of the most capable competitors in the nation at a time when a large share of our domestic market is dominated by foreign manufacturers including Thompson, Seimens, and Northern Telecom. That provision of the Modification of Final Judgment, a court order that divested the seven Bell operating companies from AT&T in 1984, should be overwritten by Congress to permit these companies to become full competitors in the market for new networking technologies. Much of the innovation

> *"What are missing are the off-ramps and city streets of the information highway."*

that occurs in those companies today does not find its way directly into the marketplace because of this outdated restriction. We could encourage a far more rapid development of much-needed technology if it is removed.

That same court decree prohibits the seven Bell operating companies from offering long-distance service. That prohibition will inhibit the efficient delivery of cable television service and other information services by Bell operating companies. For the nation to receive the full benefit of investing in new technology, that prohibition too must be changed. It can also be argued that once the market for local telephone service is made readily competitive, little reason exists to prohibit the Bell companies from offering a full range of long-distance services, including voice transmission.

> *"Much of the innovation that occurs in [regional Bell] companies today does not find its way directly into the marketplace."*

What Congress Should Do

As a means of fulfilling the federal government's role of encouraging the development of the world's most capable information network, Congress should take the following actions as soon as possible:

- Pass [legislation that] carries forward the government's role in standard-setting and research and development for new networking technologies.
- Enact [legislation that] achieves the competitive reforms—including an end to the telecable and telecommunication industries' cross-ownership prohibition—that are so important in promoting the information superhighway.

The financial incentives and innovation that will flow from these changes will fulfill the Clinton-Gore administration's vision of the communications policy that will carry the nation into the twenty-first century.

The Information Highway Should Serve Public Interests over Commerce

by Canadian Conference of Catholic Bishops

About the author: *The Canadian Conference of Catholic Bishops has its head-quarters in Ottawa, Quebec.*

> One thing is clear: Major change is rapidly approaching in the area of communications, information and entertainment. It will not be long before telephones, television, cable and computers merge into an interactive communications network that will revolutionize our lives.
>
> —Claude Marcil and Lise Ravary, *Presence*, June/July 1994

The revolution of interactive communications is already under way. One hears about it every day. It has various names, including the information highway, the information superhighway, the electronic highway, the global network and Internet. Marshall McLuhan's "global village" is being constructed through the integration of countless invisible networks that will soon crisscross the planet. Information, education, entertainment, social and health services, commercial and financial activities as well as cultural and countless other "products" and services will be available on call—and as a means of fostering dialogue among people, societies and nations.

Our country has traditionally been at the forefront of communications technology development. One can only hope that our government will ensure that this latest critical development is managed in a completely democratic fashion. In order to do so, it will mean providing universal access at reasonable prices as well as adequately safeguarding Canada's sovereignty and cultural identity.

The Catholic Church, including the church in Canada, welcomes the advent of the information highway as another important technological innovation that

Reprinted from the Canadian Conference of Catholic Bishops statement, "Reflections on the Information Highway," as it appeared in *Origins*, vol. 24, no. 39, (March 16, 1995).

will enhance every aspect of communication among people and societies. New communications technologies have indeed transformed the face of the earth. The information society is bringing about a promised era of social communication as "the increasing number of communications networks transforms the democratic environment," remarks Canadian writer Carolyn Sharp. Human experience itself has become an "experience of media," according to the Vatican.

> *"Authorities must take appropriate steps to ensure that communications technologies do not concentrate too much power . . . into the hands of an elite few."*

On the other hand, one is also obliged to take seriously the concerns of critics and researchers, and remain vigilant. There are warnings that the media, including the public sector media, risk becoming the greatest menace to democracy unless their constant tendency to commercialization is properly limited and the common good, in the best sense of the term, becomes their fundamental criterion for evaluation.

For these reasons, the episcopal commissions for social communications (English and French sectors) of the Canadian Conference of Catholic Bishops are interested in the information highway, just as they have been in all the media for some decades. We recognize that the "use of new media . . . has given birth to new possibilities for the mission of the church as well as to new pastoral problems," as the Vatican stated in 1992.

From the particular perspective of the church, it is not the details of implementing the information highway or the resulting competition that concern us the most, but rather the contents themselves and the conditions for access, especially as regards human and Christian values.

Dialogue Among People, Societies and Nations

The information highway is a network of interactive communications networks. For the first time, communications can truly be characterized as fully interactive and bi- or multidirectional (question and answer, supply and demand, interface, exchange, dialogue and so on). The term that best expresses the aspects of mutuality, community and userfriendliness involved is certainly *dialogue*. This term indicates the window of opportunity that is opening up on a host of exciting and enriching new possibilities—although there is also new potential for manipulating social communication, unless safeguards are considered.

It is often said that the media have made the world grow smaller. Because of the advent of the communications society and the era of the global village, interdependence among nations is growing. Public authorities must take appropriate steps to ensure that communications technologies do not concentrate too much power (the media often being regarded as a Fourth Estate) into the hands of an elite few for their own benefit or for the sake of a capitalistic ideology. It is unfortunately true sometimes that, according to the World Association for Catholic Communication, "rather than bringing people together, the mass media often isolate or divide them."

The information highway by its very nature is focused on the user. Thus it has the potential to nourish community spirit, foster worldwide cultural exchange, and promote respect and cooperation among people. It can also transform understanding and knowledge as well as organizations and society itself.

It is not too far-fetched in this respect to speak of the information highway as facilitating dialogue among people, societies and nations. Can there be a better guarantee for peace?

Right to Information and Freedom of Expression

The right to information and freedom of expression are closely related but quite distinct concepts. They must, however, coexist in a dynamic and harmonious relationship, each respecting its particular conditions and limits, if people and the societies they form are to develop and live in peace throughout the world.

The right to information is first and foremost the right to complete and objective information, and thus also the right to have access to information sources. In practical terms, the right to information cannot be exercised unless there is freedom to communicate or, in other words, freedom of expression.

Human beings are social by nature; they need and desire to learn more about "the other"—their counterparts—and to engage in dialogue. From this need and desire is born public opinion, which is certain to be healthier as more people are empowered to participate in the life of society through better means of communications and through an exchange of ideas.

Society can only meet its information needs by taking steps to ensure that its citizens are kept well informed, especially through constant and easy access to a variety of information sources. Pluralistic societies such as our own have recognized the need for legislation that guarantees the public's right to information that is complete, consistent and accurate as well as the right to freedom of expression and an independent media. They have also enacted safeguards to protect the reputations of people and institutions "within the limits set by justice and charity," as Pope John Paul II said in 1987.

> *"There must be particular attention to what is required by the right to information and freedom of expression."*

The possibilities of the information highway are almost limitless. For that very reason, there must be particular attention to what is required by the right to information and freedom of expression, especially if public opinion is to be informed, enlightened and analytical.

Chapter 2

Protection of Cultural Values

According to the Vatican, "at the dawn of a new era, a vast expansion of human communications is profoundly influencing culture everywhere. Revolutionary technological changes are only part of what is happening."

More than ever before, ours is a society focused on communication and a civilization centered on images. Philosophers have even said that ultimately society is communication.

Communications technologies have developed audiovisual languages and new forms of rhetoric. The very concept of an audiovisual culture is now commonly accepted.

At first, the media simply disseminated the masterpieces of traditional culture, but they soon became adept at producing their own invaluable forms of art. In addition, recent technological developments such as satellites, fiber optics and digital compression, "in a manner that is unique," said the Vatican in 1971, "bring artistic and cultural achievements within the orbit of a great part of the human race. And soon, perhaps, they will do the same for the whole of it. This is as authentic a mark of social progress as is the removal of economic and social inequality."

In this regard, it has been noted by Pope John Paul II that:

> The culture of our time particularly seems to be dominated and shaped by the newest and most powerful among the means of communication . . . so much so that at times they seem to assert themselves as ends and not as simple means. . . .

> Indeed, the mass media, whether they deal with news or concern themselves with precisely cultural topics, or whether they are used for the purpose of artistic expression and entertainment, always return to a particular concept of man; and it is precisely on the basis of the exactness and completeness of this concept that they will be judged.

It is on this very point that there is need for vigilance. It is so much taken for granted that the impact of the information highway will be generally positive. However, ongoing research and reflection are needed in order to foresee and counteract the negative results that the information highway may have on information "carriers" such as schools, libraries, newspapers and other forms of publishing.

"More than any other form of the media, the information highway can promote intercultural communication among people."

Cultures are dynamic and, increasingly, in contact with one another. More than any other form of the media, the information highway can promote intercultural communication among people, thereby encouraging the expression and protection of basic cultural values. Accordingly, there must be clear and specific measures to provide steady and easy access to a variety of social and cultural contacts. This is especially true in the case of Canadians, whose cultural diversity and aspirations are so varied and rich, but who live in a North American economic context that strongly encourages the importation of American "products."

Safeguarding Privacy

The right of each citizen to privacy should be constantly monitored by the federal and provincial governments. In the widest sense, the right to privacy is the right of everyone to "being left alone. It means protecting an individual's personal and private life from intrusion or exposure to the public view," noted the Canadian Broadcasting Corporation.

> *"The media must present the entire 'picture' of the human person."*

Generally speaking, the Canadian as well as the Quebec charters of rights and freedoms and the common law of the other provinces make provision for the right to privacy. There is also specific legislation concerning violations and protection of property as well as several sections of the criminal code dealing with such activities as electronic eavesdropping.

Specifically in regards to communications, some aspects of the right to privacy are governed by the Access to Information Act and the Privacy Act. Furthermore, there are the Radiocommunications Act and the 1986 Canadian Radio-Television and Telecommunications Commission radio regulations.

It is reassuring to note that in its October 11, 1994, referral to the CRTC, the government specified that the fourth principle guiding the development and implementation of a strategy for the information highway was to be the protection of privacy and network security. However, it should be added that such regulation needs to be clear and easily comprehensible .

In an earlier section above, titled "Right to Information and Freedom of Expression," it was noted that there are limits to the right to information. Particularly in the case of personal reputation, this is a matter of ethics as well as of exercising professional standards with prudence and discretion.

Religious Values

On several previous occasions, the two social communications commissions of the Canadian Conference of Catholic Bishops have presented their views and recommendations regarding the policies and regulations that the CRTC should adopt in the area of religious broadcasting.

As well, on March 13, 1992, the archbishops of Montreal and Quebec City requested the CRTC to ask broadcasters to give reasonable space in their programming to the religious dimension.

Essentially, the positions that have been put forward by the Canadian church in its various briefs to the CRTC remain relevant. If anything, the communications explosion evidenced by the implementation of the information highway makes our concerns even more pertinent.

The media must present the entire "picture" of the human person. Arising out of the innate human need for transcendence, the religious dimension, like the psychological, ethical and intellectual dimensions, is an integral part of being human. Legislators need to ensure that the religious dimension in the lives of their fellow citizens is accorded its proper place in the information highway.

What Pope John Paul II, quoted by the Vatican, said in 1988 about the media applies in 1995 to the communication technologies that together constitute the information highway: "It is imperative that the media respect and contribute to that integral development of the person which embraces 'the cultural, transcendent and religious dimensions of man and society.'"

Proper Role of Advertising

Advertising and commercial activities will undoubtedly be central to the functioning of the information highway. As the Vatican stated in 1971:

> The importance of advertising is steadily on the increase in modern society. It makes its presence felt everywhere; its influence is unavoidable. It offers real benefits to society. It tells buyers of the goods and services available. It thus encourages the widest distribution of products and, in doing this, it helps industry to develop and benefit the population. All this is to the good so long as there is respect for the buyer's liberty of choice, even though in trying to sell some particular objects appeal is made to a person's basic need. Advertising too must respect the truth, taking into account accepted advertising conventions.

The information highway will not only carry a large amount of advertising but probably also new forms of advertising. It is the needs of those using the network that should be given primary consideration when creating new services, and not market forces alone. Precisely because of this, new forms of advertising should be evaluated and fine-tuned, according to the responsibilities of the various parties involved—including the state as well as broadcasters and those who are at the same time information consumers and producers.

"Media first and foremost are people, rather than technology."

In short, what may be regarded as excessive in media advertising is the emphasis on delivering audiences over to commercial interests, seeing human beings strictly as consumers and forgetting that they are first and foremost persons and citizens.

User Education

"Media first and foremost are people, rather than technology," said Cardinal Roger Etchegaray in 1979. This single phrase sums up the need for having competent professional communicators as well as the necessity for education to help people make optimum use of the media.

It is no secret that the media have their own language, syntax and rhetoric; they have indeed developed an audiovisual culture. They have marked contemporary humanity to its very core. Today, just as one learns to read, one must also learn to decode media images and sequences of images.

> *"Because the information highway is interactive, the consumer is also a producer."*

"The media are a parallel school. It is both necessary and urgent to become more aware of the growing interrelationship between the media and the democratic and social quality of life," noted the Institut Canadien d'Education des Adultes.

The challenge is significant. Our society stands on the brink of the 200- or 500-channel universe and poised to embark on the information highway. In the near future, radio and television programs, films, computer software, video games and so on will be developed and handled as "products" to be "sold" on the "consumer market." The longer the list of products, the larger the clout of consumer reaction on "supply." It will become more difficult to choose, and people may even become alienated if they feel unable to make free, informed and voluntary choices. . . .

It is to be hoped that public authorities, for their part, will recognize that democracy in Canada is best served by a discerning public that will support current efforts as well as new initiatives to develop media programs in schools and through continuing education.

"Today, only those who have been educated, who have learned to delay their reflexes by means of reflection, will be capable of learning the new forms of communication," according to Etchegaray.

To this, it should be added that because the information highway is interactive, the consumer is also a producer. Accordingly, users need to be aware of their responsibilities as to what they "send"—in other words, this is an ethical concern.

Six Objectives

In order for the information highway to be able to respond fully to the expectations being raised, it is vital:

1. That the objective of universal access at reasonable prices be central to its development, and that this be expressed in a way that is explicit, detailed, clear and simple.
2. That universal access be commonplace—that is, that everyone who wants can be appropriately and easily trained to contribute to the information highway and to profit from the services that should benefit all.
3. That it indeed facilitate dialogue among people, societies and nations.

4. That there be adequate protection to the right to information, freedom of expression, the protection of cultural values and the expression of religious values.

5. That advertising, which will play a most prominent role, be developed and regulated as a service, not a disservice, to people.

6. That in Canada the information highway never be allowed to contribute to a two-tiered society divided between the privileged haves with access to information and the have-nots, who lack access to information.

In closing, let us recall those significant lines at the beginning of the 1963 decree of the Second Vatican Council in which the church expressed its openness to and acceptance of the means of social communication:

> By divine favor, especially in modern times, human genius has produced from natural materials astonishing inventions in the field of technology. Some of these have extraordinary bearing on the human spirit, since they open up new and highly effective means of communication for all kinds of information, ideas and directives. . . .
>
> [T]he church welcomes and watches such inventions with special concern. Chief among them are those which by their very nature can reach and influence not only individual people, but the masses themselves, even the whole of society.

The Private Sector Alone Should Build the Information Highway

by William F. Jasper

About the author: *William F. Jasper is a senior editor for the* New American, *a biweekly conservative magazine.*

The White House folks who want to bring you socialized medicine under the rubric of "managed competition in health care" are pushing hard to socialize cyberspace under the guise of "managing the transition" to the new "information age." In his campaign manifesto, *Putting People First,* Bill Clinton called for: "A national information network to link every home, business, lab, classroom and library by the year 2015. To expand access to information, we will put public records, databases, libraries and educational materials on line for public use."

Vice President Al Gore has been given the role of pitch man for this effort and has taken to it with the same gusto that Hillary Clinton has shown for promoting her brand of fascist medicine. Assisting Gore in this undertaking is Commerce Secretary Ron Brown, chairman of the Information Infrastructure Task Force, and Laura D'Andrea Tyson, chairman of Mr. Clinton's Council of Economic Advisers. That is certainly a trio to inspire confidence in a national effort to harness and promote dynamic new technologies: a vice president who authored one of the most embarrassing, technophobic, Luddite [antitechnological] diatribes ever written (*Earth in the Balance*); a commerce secretary who has hopped from one corruption scandal to another involving charges of influence peddling and bribery; and a socialist economist from the People's Republic of Berkeley.

Hypemeister in Action

Al Gore was the logical choice to lead the fedgov charge into the electronic frontier. While still a senator, he authored the High Performance Computing and Communications Act, a five-year, $3 billion boondoggle signed into law in

William F. Jasper, "Electronic Fascism," *New American*, July 25, 1994. Reprinted with permission.

1991, ostensibly for the purpose of advancing our nation's high-tech research and development. He has been nearly as passionate about the need for federal intervention into, and management of, the exploding technological revolution as he has been for UN regulation of the global environment.

In a speech at the National Press Club in Washington, DC, on December 22, 1993, Gore stated:

> Today more than ever, businesses run on information. A fast, flexible information network is as essential to manufacturing as steel and plastic. If we do not move decisively to ensure that America has the information infrastructure we need, every business and consumer in America will suffer.
>
> To understand what new systems we must create though, we must first understand how the information marketplace of the future will operate.

And the "marketplace," you can be sure, always takes on interesting new meaning when discussed by anyone from Clinton, Gore & Co. The vice president continued: "Some highways will be made of fiber optics, others of coaxial cable, others will be wireless. But this is the key point: They must and will be two-way highways so that each person will be able to send information in video form as well as just words, as well as receiving information."

No, here is the key point: For all its disingenuous bows to the "market" and "private sector initiative," the Clinton Administration is determined to dictate the development of the exciting new frontier of interactive, multi-media communications. It doesn't trust consumers and producers (and state and local governments) to work out solutions to the challenges presented by the new technologies. It cannot countenance the idea of this huge and lucrative new arena of human activity being outside of its control. Why *must* the new highway be two-way, i.e., interactive? Is there any proof that consumers even *want* such services? If so, at what cost? Private companies are already racing feverishly and

> *"The Clinton Administration is determined to dictate the development of . . . interactive, multi-media communications."*

spending billions of dollars to develop a host of new technologies that promise to deliver a vast assortment of services—including interactive capabilities—to individuals, businesses, schools, hospitals, and other institutions.

But Mr. Gore is undaunted by reality in this crusade. "This Administration intends to create an environment that stimulates a private system of free-flowing information conduits," he says. "It will involve a variety of affordable and innovative appliances and products, giving individuals and public institutions the best possible opportunity to be both information customers and providers."

"But how do we get from there to here?" asks Mr. Technoveep. "That is the key question facing government." Indeed it is. "It is during the transition period that the most complexity exists and that government involvement is most important," says Gore. And then he gives the Administration's bottom line: "We want to manage the transition." Of course. The Clintonistas are big on "managing" and on government-business "partnerships." They realize full well that in most such "partnerships" there is a built-in tendency for the "transition" to become permanent and for government control to increase rather than decrease. National industrial planning is another name for it. Corporate-state fascism (government control without outright government ownership) is another.

> *"Government is ill-equipped to make any worthwhile market decisions, let alone those affecting cutting-edge technologies."*

There are plenty of statists in Congress who support this Clinton-Gore "vision." According to Senator John D. Rockefeller IV (D-WV), government has "a unique, essential role in making sure that the private sector is involved in developing new technologies, turning them into commercial products, exporting and selling those products, and putting people to work in jobs that pay good wages." He made that statement in 1994 in announcing his support for the Clinton-favored National Competitiveness Act. "This legislation will help our future Thomas Edisons," he asserted. Rather, it will help our technological dinosaurs who can't convince private investors of the worth of their products and services, but who have sufficient political clout to force taxpayers to fund their projects.

Free-Market Battle

Government is ill-equipped to make any worthwhile market decisions, let alone those affecting cutting-edge technologies with potential global markets. Titans of the computer industry such as IBM and Apple have faced several years of tough times with staggering financial losses and loss of market share to more aggressive, nimble, and market-savvy upstarts. Armies of electronic engineers, computer wizards, and financial geniuses are pulling out their hair over decisions on which technologies to invest in. Some of their decisions will be wrong and many entrants into the "information superhighway" race will be weeded out by consumers who will reject their products and services for one reason or another. That is the way of the marketplace.

The Clinton-Gore-Rockefeller way, by contrast, would have government bureaucrats, not consumers, pick the winners and losers. This is a sure prescription for havoc, bureaucratic inertia, and total frustration of the potential benefits offered by new technologies. An excellent example of this is the federal government's subsidies to manufacturers of flat-panel display screens for computers, one of the critical areas now dominated by the Japanese. The federal government continues to pour hundreds of millions of dollars into producers of flat-panels using the nearly 30-year-old liquid crystal display, or LCD, technology, when there are other American companies that have developed entirely new technologies far superior to—and less costly than—the Japanese flat-panel screens.

But besides intervening to make sure that industry provides consumers with the products they want and need, says Mr. Gore, it is fedgov's responsibility to guarantee that *all* people have equal access. The sacred cow of *equality* goes under the title of "universal service" in telecommunications jargon. In building the "national information infrastructure," Gore explains, we want to avoid creating "a society of information haves and have-nots." And he correctly notes that "the most important step we can take to ensure universal service is to adopt policies that result in lower prices for everyone." "But," he goes on to say, "we will still need a regulatory safety net to make sure that virtually everyone will be able to benefit." Which is a little like saying that unless the federal government controls and manages food production and distribution we will end up as a society of food "haves" dining on caviar and "have-nots" surviving on dog food.

Dr. George A. Keyworth II of the Hudson Institute tells those fretting about the information "have-nots" to just "look at the PC [personal computer] revolution." "The PC revolution happened at an absolutely explosive rate," he reminds us, "taking place in approximately six years. It went from around 10 percent market penetration to perhaps 50 percent practically overnight, and it penetrated down deeply into American society." And it continues to penetrate deeper, as technological advances and market forces drive down prices of computers, software, and online services.

> *"Predictions now are that by the year 2000 there will be 60 million mobile telephone users."*

The same can be said for cellular phone technology. When AT&T launched its venture into the infant cellular phone universe, it hired a consulting firm, McKinsey & Co., to research the potential cellular market. The consultants predicted that by the year 2000 there would be 900,000 cellular phone users. Another research firm, Herschel Shosteck Associates, predicted 1.5 million by the end of the century. They slightly misjudged the market; by the end of 1993 there were already *13 million* cellular customers, and predictions now are that by the year 2000 there will be 60 million mobile telephone users, not 900,000.

Technological Advances

Technology and market forces are throwing just as many uncertainties into the interactive, multi-media arena. Fiber optics are giving us virtually unlimited communications capabilities for voice, data, and video transmissions. The drawback with fiber is cost; laying fiber-optic cable to every community is labor- and capital-intensive. Which is one big reason wireless technologies are so hot. Another reason is portability. Huge advances in microchips and software have freed phones, faxes, and computers from wires, allowing telecommunications technology to move from conventional analog transmissions to digital, which converts speech and data to a stream of ones and zeros understood by computers. Digital transmissions are less susceptible than sound waves to static interference and can be compressed or transmitted in bursts to make greater use of the broadcast spectrum. New computer software programs have made new transmission technologies such as cellular digital packet data (CDPD) feasible. Existing cellular systems work at only 60 percent efficiency, say CDPD developers, leaving a large amount of unused "dead" time. CDPD breaks voice and data transmissions into bits that can be squeezed into the "dead" spaces between sentences, words, or even syllables in the electronic stream—and then reassembles the transmission at its designated destination.

New cellular telephone technology is also freeing up the previously jammed frequency spectrum. The United States is now covered with thousands of cells, many of them miles in diameter, using the same spectrum frequencies. By making the cells smaller—say, thousands or even hundreds of feet across—and covering the country with hundreds of thousands of these cells, it is possible to dramatically increase transmission capacity through the re-use of currently crowded frequencies and the use of very high frequencies that presently have few users. In fact, with emerging technologies making frequency spectrum a much less precious and crowded commodity, and making signals much less vulnerable to interference, the federal regulation of spectrum is becoming harder and harder to justify.

Bureaucratic Obstacles

Unfortunately, the regulators and the politicians are unwilling to yield any of their power. Instead, they are throwing road blocks onto the information highway. Industry giants and new entrepreneurs alike are being stymied in their efforts to bring consumers the technologies the Clinton Administration says it is all for. In February 1994, a $26 billion buyout of cable television giant Tele-Communications Inc. (TCI) by Bell Atlantic Corp. fizzled largely because of the Federal Communications Commission's (FCC) 17 percent rate roll-back of cable television rates, which caused TCI's stock to fall. In April 1994, Southwestern Bell Corp. and Cox Enterprises called off a proposed $4.6 billion partnership, citing the FCC's new cable television rate cutbacks as the culprit responsible for souring the deal. At the same time, AT&T's planned $12.6 billion purchase of McCaw Cellular Communications was nixed by Federal Judge Harold Greene, who presided over the breakup of AT&T in 1982 and still holds tight control over nearly every move AT&T and the "Baby Bells" make toward interactive communications.

> *"The federal regulation of [frequency] spectrum is becoming harder and harder to justify."*

The *Wall Street Journal* reported on April 8, 1994, that the FCC's bureaucratic morass has created a "logjam." "The agency has approved just five trials for interactive video services. Another 17 requests are pending, and some of them have languished at the agency for more than a year," said the *Journal*. According to *Journal* reporters John J. Keller and Leslie Cauley, "the FCC uses an approval process that dates back to the early 20th century and originally applied to railroad requests to extend their tracks. Today it is a fractious affair. One Bell Atlantic filing alone has had more than 50 pleadings, as consumer advocates, potential competitors, incumbent cable operators, and municipal officials weigh in with their conflicting views." So much for Mr. Gore's cutting-edge government.

Even when the FCC tries to be helpful to industry, it gets it wrong. In 1994, the agency sent cable television operators computer disks with the new mandated rate reductions. "But the agency used the Excel spreadsheet program instead of Lotus, which is used by almost every accounting department in the industry," the *Journal* reported. "The FCC is now working on a Lotus version." Nice, but a little late to do much good.

Get Out of the Way!

The best thing for the federal government to do is simply *to get out of the way* and let the consumers, inventors, innovators, and producers—rather than bureaucrats and politicians—build the information *autobahn* [highway]. There is no shortage of interested private parties willing to undertake the task. Long-distance phone giant MCI has unveiled plans to invest $2 billion to build "the nation's first transcontinental information superhighway." In Orlando, Florida, Time Warner said it would have its Full Service Network (FSN) up and running to 4,000 homes by the end of 1995. Customers will be able to call up movies on demand, carry out electronic banking and shopping, and have access to government agencies. In Omaha, U.S. West is test-marketing a similar service. Cable operators are seeking permission to compete with local phone companies in offering access to computer databases and services. Hundreds of companies are forming alliances and consortiums to pool resources for the effort.

The Information Highway Should Develop According to Consumer Demand

by Walter G. Bolter

About the author: *Walter G. Bolter is the director of the Bethesda Research Institute in Bethesda, Maryland, and is a business professor at Flagler College in St. Augustine, Florida.*

In examining the economic aspects of the government's plan to artificially quicken the pace of building an "Information Superhighway" (ISH), one cannot but conclude that the perspective taken should be macroeconomic, with an orientation toward enhancing efficiency, and that accelerating deployment of the ISH (beyond even the most optimistic forecasts of consumer need) is unjustified and risks a grievous misuse of resources. At this vital juncture, the pace of construction of these electronic pathways for information services should be subject to a market test, rather than political directives. Where there's demand, here or overseas, ISH facilities will be built to meet it. Government should be content to referee disputes and insure public access to information. Otherwise, it should stay out of the way.

Development Implications

The lead taken by the Clinton Administration in hastening deployment of fiber optic transmission, digital switching, and other communications network components has important implications. For instance, development of full competition is unlikely, since only a relatively small number of companies can participate at the noneconomic pace of construction expected. ISH security, privacy, and privilege of use respecting sensitive information have hardly been addressed. If, as the government tells us, America's international comparative advantage lies in its intellectual property, pushing forward without fully considering this aspect of our "information assets" is disturbing.

Walter G. Bolter, "Deployment of the Information Superhighway? Let Markets Decide," *Challenge: The Magazine of Economic Affairs*, September/October 1994. Reprinted by permission from M.E. Sharpe, Inc., Armonk, NY 10504.

Yet, the key economic issue is the degree to which the timing and level of demand for information services will match the capacity and features of an artificially accelerated deployment schedule. It simply won't. Demand doesn't exist yet (and may never exist) for the $450 billion expenditure for the capacity and features that are being contemplated. Were they allowed to work, market forces would make that apparent. The industry has had its "nose bloodied" in the past when it has ignored demand. Now the government believes that the mere act of building the ISH will engender its economic use. Thus, the judgment of politicians and the philosophy that "supply will create its own demand" seem to have transcended consumer sovereignty. Economists believe the reverse to be true.

Product Value and Marketing

In recent years the gullibility and patience of the public have been put to the test. Media and government report that a new electronic era is upon us. Everything must change. But skeptics abound as well. Investors, consumers, and others who wish to see hard evidence have not stampeded. They have resisted the "spin" being put on events by Washington and Madison Avenue.

This tension raises a fundamental issue in economics. Is there a difference between real need and the perception of need? Must providers offer what people want, or can they produce that which best suits their engineering capabilities (or strategic or political objectives), and then "create need" in order to clear their inventory through marketing gimmicks?

Most economists would like to believe that the true product value is primary. However, marketeers concentrate on appearance—or "apparent value"—instead, believing that the actual utility of a product is of much less consequence in buying decisions. Resolution of this conflict is fundamental in determining the merit of policies designed to take advantage of the dawning of the "Information Age" (IA). If marketeers are right, then the

> *"Must providers offer what people want, or can they produce that which best suits their engineering capabilities?"*

public can be convinced that IA is upon us (whether it is or not), and demand can be induced for new services *whenever* network facilities are built to make them available. On the other hand, if economic theory is sound, then advertising will not overcome consumer reluctance to plunge headlong into usage of IA services, and attempts to artificially accelerate deployment of network equipment to make IA "a reality" are just bad policies. Sleight-of-hand has been the approach taken in the past.

Selling the "Information Age"

The notion that the "Information Age" is fast approaching has been bandied about at least since the 1960s. But, until the last few years, for most people, the

IA fuss had the essence of "smoke and mirrors." Today, given all the resources and energy being poured into the enabling telecommunications facilities, it had better be on its way—at the very least.

In the United States, hardly a week passes without disclosure of some new development concerning these IA pathways or "infrastructure." Taken together with entertainment, educational, database, and other applications, we have what is commonly referred to as the "Information Superhighway" (ISH). Currently, this highway is a small collection of interconnected networks known as the "Internet." Eventually, when the contemplated

> *" 'Infrastructure' and 'information superhighway' have been transformed from esoteric terms of art to the common vernacular."*

services are added, and worldwide integration is achieved, we will have an ISH "network of networks."

If one believes the press reports, the ISH is cascading to inescapable, near-term deployment. Pathway construction is certainly quite tangible; key commitments are in place. Some of the world's largest companies, important governmental figures, educators and academics, and practically all other representatives of vested interests are on board. Thus, making the ISH a reality is "just a matter of time" (or so it would seem). Indeed, no one who expects to be taken seriously questions its coming anymore. Even the aforementioned jargon is in place. In just a few years, "infrastructure" and "information superhighway" have been transformed from esoteric terms of art to the common vernacular. Their usage has increased exponentially. Everyone, from politicians to late night television personalities, speaks "knowledgeably" of the ISH. Yet, if the Information Age is really upon us (or soon will be), these shorthand descriptions mask what promises to be a really far-reaching and complex array of impending social and economic developments. *Someone* should be worried by now.

Instead, congressional hearings and the media are all embroiled in technical issues or in writing futuristic "gee-whiz" articles. Notably, even the Administration's "Clipper Chip" proposal, which could be portrayed as the ISH's "big brother" spying mechanism, received few headlines and scarcely a mention by investigative television (or talk show comedians). America does not appear to be taking ISH hype or its implications seriously, even as multi-billion-dollar network construction programs plunge ahead. This could connote a lack of understanding, interest, or demand for what the ISH (and IA) have to offer.

The Problem of "Forced Technology"

Cynics seem to have sensed this anomaly. They advise that there is plenty of time for the country's transition to a new era of instant information and omnipresent communications, whatever the effects may be. The ISH is obviously not in place, at least to any degree, because there are no complaints from those who have had to live with it. Anyway, just putting in pathways and cobbling up a few services will not make the Information Age a fact, any more than stuffing electronic switching, coaxial cable, and "futuristic" services (such as defunct Picturephone) into the national consciousness could make it a reality in the 1960s.

Some believe that détente with the "human element" *must* precede the IA's coming. How quickly technology is utilized depends on anticipating and resolving forthcoming clashes between engineers' (and politicians') dreams of what people should want and what they actually do. John Naisbitt addressed this problem in the discussion of "forced technology" in his book *Megatrends*:

> Technology and our human potential are the two great challenges and adventures facing humankind today. . . . We must learn to balance the material wonders of technology with the spiritual demands of our human nature. . . . When high-tech and high-touch are out of balance, an annoying dissonance results. . . . High-tech dissonance infuriates people. It's even worse when you use the technology of the telephone to call a warm friend and instead get more technology. . . . Many of us instinctively feel the metric system is too high-tech. To make matters worse, it was imposed on us top-down by some Metric Council or other (presumably in Washington, D.C.).

The Road to Governmental Intervention

Does it help to have the government—e.g., some "Information Infrastructure Council" or task force—involved in making ISH decisions? Would central direction prove to be a better tonic for Naisbitt's dissonance than the ebb and flow of market forces?

In the late 1980s and early 1990s, the extensive network construction plans of the regional Bell operating companies (RBOCs) and local telephone companies (LECs), cable television (CATV), and other communications-providers were becoming manifest. During this period, traditional reliance on market-based facility-deployment schedules remained the orthodox approach. Opposition to governmental intervention included not just figures of industry, but ranged from such extremes as Orwellian [after author George Orwell] sociologists to neoclassical economists. This reliance on market processes constituted the conventional wisdom even as the electorate of the United States elected a Democratic president.

"Some believe that détente with the 'human element' must precede the [Information Age's] coming."

Intrusive intervention to further the building of the ISH was not a major issue during the 1992 presidential campaign. Indeed, there is some doubt that the Administration could have been elected had its future plans been disclosed. For instance, its aforementioned initiative for required use of a special computer Clipper Chip, which permits the federal government to decode any telephone, computer, or facsimile communications, would have caused an uproar. Just the noneconomic concerns regarding governmental intrusion into America's business and personal dealings, had they been addressed during the campaign, would most likely have raised the dander of the electorate irreparably.

After the election, there were no electronic town meetings, no national debate about whether government should actively promote the process of making over the nation into an information society. Contemporaneous with the furious debate over the free flow of goods to Mexico and Canada, the Administration's proposal to unleash the free flow of knowledge over the Internet was announced practically as a foregone conclusion. No serious

"There is some doubt that the [Clinton] Administration could have been elected had its future [information highway] plans been disclosed."

objections were raised, even though institution of its encompassing "Agenda for Action" (AFA) promised to affect ready access to America's priceless information assets. Construction of the network for the information services of the distant future, which was still a private venture that was largely beholden to demand and local needs, was put on a fast track. The heretofore cautious ISH effort was rechristened as the "National Information Infrastructure" (NII).

The AFA was promoted as a program to coordinate ISH private-sector and governmental activities and investment. The ISH was to be created in the shortest possible time. It was to include a guaranteed revamping of the present "narrowband" or telephone-based system to provide universal and affordable communications and "wideband" information services. High-capacity fiber optic or comparable cable was to find its way into every household. This would apply, regardless of a user's locational, personal economic, or demand characteristics. Provisioning would be accomplished via a "network of networks"—i.e., a user-driven, interactive, and efficient platform for information transfer. Somehow, intellectual property would be safeguarded, even as the NII took on international dimensions.

The AFA initiative was marketed less as the product of new leadership than as a need to respond to international pressures. The weight of U.S. economic prowess was not being employed as a catalyst for stimulating world developments; the reverse was the case. Previous allegiance to market-driven results was only weakly addressed. Apparently, private and local initiatives were believed to be insufficient to restore America's industrial power, internationally or at home. Instead, within six months of the election, 100-year-old policies of federal intervention and investment were given new life as fundamental NII program elements.

The Key Issue

Is there demand for the NII's capabilities? The Administration was surprisingly cryptic when it identified *demand* for the "myriad of services" that presumably justify accelerated ISH construction, despite likely commitment of a huge portion of America's near-term investment resources to building its NII. The emphasis was on *capabilities*. But the existing network facilities of the RBOCs and other LECs could already handle needs for competitive equal access. Integrated or multimode voice, data, and video-requirements features, introduced experimentally in the 1980s as integrated switched digital network (ISDN) offices, were appearing in numerous areas of the network as well. Advanced local "CLASS" (or customized) offerings, such as call waiting, caller ID, and call forwarding, were in place.

Moreover, pre-NII terrestrial and satellite network facilities were alleged to be capable of "eliminating geography" as a limiting factor for performing research, shopping, financial transactions, and even some health functions (e.g., patient monitoring). Simultaneously, they could enhance the productivity of those using the network by providing intelligence, data, and feedback. The features and capacity of the industry-initiated ISH program appeared staggering. What more could be needed?

For one thing, subscribers are required (i.e., customers who are willing and able) to pay the full costs of the many uses to which an NII (or the new industry network) could be put. When the AFA made its appearance, it was not at all clear that the services which the NII might proffer would engender sufficient (or timely) consumer interest and thereby prove to be economically viable. Logically, if greater demand were evident, the industry's ISH construction schedule would have been equivalent to that of the accelerated network (NII).

If it were not, then more rapid deployment is pointless (and wasteful)—unless one believes that the mere creation of features will cause demand for them to emerge. That is, all that needs to be done is to put the proper "spin" on the coming of the

> *"Apparently, private and local initiatives were believed to be insufficient to restore America's industrial power."*

Information Age. Thus, having a little faith in the capabilities of IA merchandisers easily translates into the view that accelerated construction of capabilities by engineers will be met by equivalent creation of demand. This is a variation of a *Field of Dreams* reasoning—namely, "if we build it (now), they will come (now)."

Key Administration officials apparently have long held this view. For instance, in 1991, while in the Senate, the Vice-President [Al Gore] advocated considerable governmental investment—technical aid and other subsidies to support construction of an ISH, regardless of the presence or absence of demand. Similarly, the Chief of the FCC's [Federal Communications Commission] Office of Plans and Policy has been convinced that there will be "unanticipated" functions or uses that emerge as a result of building the ISH. In 1990, he noted: "History shows that building new capacity tends to attract new, unforeseen functions and users. . . . Beyond this general prediction, . . . we cannot estimate with precision."

Other Investigations of Consumer Needs

Unfortunately, demand considerations do not seem to have been a major criterion for others who support the headlong push to put network facilities in place, according to artificial schedules. These include state authorities, media providers, and the telephone companies themselves. For instance, the recently outlined "California First" plan, which calls for network expenditures of $16 billion, emphasizes ISH capabilities and uses, rather than having any customer clamoring for its applications. Nor does it acknowledge that many applications can be satisfied while using existing facilities, or by extending plant [facilities and equipment] only to those willing and able to pay.

> *"In 1991 . . . [Al Gore] advocated considerable governmental investment— technical aid and other subsidies to support construction of an ISH."*

While technically sophisticated, the California plan includes unsubstantiated references to future applications, such as the "many things no one has thought of yet." The program does recognize the failures of CATV operators, who seem to concentrate on the number of channels available rather than on content or customer needs. But it has less insight into the difference between offering capabilities ("choices") and researching demand.

Reminiscent of the federal arena, in California, Connecticut, Tennessee, and many other jurisdictions, there seems to be a willingness to commit huge sums to construction without a firm view of the uses for which the serving capacity is being built. They assume that, somehow, the network will adapt. This is confirmed in part by the selections being made of ISH equipment suppliers. For instance, AT&T was chosen by the local California company (Pacific Telesis) to provide facilities for California's "mini-ISH" network. It has had similar success in other areas of the country having their own designs, including the New England and Middle Atlantic regions. The expert view is that one of the big advantages of selecting AT&T as contractor for such networks is that "its systems are very flexible. . . . That's important when building networks for a multimedia market that doesn't yet exist and will evolve in unforeseen ways," writes *USA Today* business writer Kevin Maney. Clearly, flexibility can take care of some situations where facilities are designed "in a vacuum," but perhaps not always. Even if engineers could, somehow, divine what functions consumers will want (without their help), the level of demand and its growth rate would still prove elusive.

Assessments of Demand

Where consumer needs for ISH services have been investigated, unexpected aspects of demand have been uncovered. This was the case for the Cerritos,

California, field trials of GTE Corp.—the second largest local telephone company in the state. GTE discovered that the local municipality would not allow participants to use the company's interactive fiber optic–based service to make reservations for city facilities, because it would give them an advantage over the "have-nots" in the community. Moreover, GTE's forecasts of revenue from "winner" offerings—such as movies-on-demand—were found to be limited by participants' willingness to pay charges no more than $1 over rental-store prices. Finally, despite *availability* of the most trumpeted ISH options—including home shopping; ticket ordering; news, library, and financial services (stock quotes and buy/sell features)—GTE concluded that only slow growth for the market could be expected.

Telephone company assessments of demand are still, unfortunately, in their infancy. While experiments with ISH-type services by media providers, merchandisers, and others have a much longer history, these have had typically dismal results. For example, in the early 1980s, Knight-Ridder's interactive videotext experiment in Florida was an abject and expensive failure. J.C. Penney lost over $100 million on "Telaction"—an interactive shopping system—before eventually ceasing operations in 1989. Similar problems with consumers' resistance to shopping online have been encountered by the IBM/ Sears Prodigy service—which is still unprofitable despite more than $800 million invested by the two partners. CATV operator Viacom concluded: "The technology is all there. What's missing is the consumer and exactly what the consumer wants and what they'll pay for."

For services that America supposedly will pay for—such as entertainment shows and movies, there is still some question of availability of the "content" that superhighways will transmit. Reports on Viacom's 1993–94 multibillion battle to win control of Paramount Communications' software/entertainment assets attest to the bottleneck nature of this aspect of the ISH, and to the prime returns (economic rent) such assets can command when put up for "auction." "[M]ost of the drama in the dawning communications age has focused on high-tech hardware and networks. Now the plot has taken a twist. . . . Content is king on the information superhighway. . . . Bidding for Paramount drove the final price of the deal to $9.5 billion—far beyond what some Wall Street analysts thought the entertainment giant was worth," according to *USA Today*.

> *"There seems to be a willingness to commit huge sums to construction without a firm view of the uses."*

Speculation over acquisition of Time Warner's assets centered on similar attributes of this media conglomerate. Industry experts believe that there simply isn't enough programming to "go around." If content availability is questionable before the industry's ISH is fully deployed, it is, perhaps, indicative of the idle capacity that will befall an accelerated construction schedule. . . .

The Extraordinary Case of ISDN

[Regional Bell and local telephone companies] probably shouldn't be advised to put in capabilities any more quickly than they have in the past. The case of technically advanced, integrated voice/data/ video services (referred to as "ISDN") is instructive. As the Electronic Frontier Foundation, an industry organization, observed:

> [D]espite the fact that ISDN has been under development since 1968, applications have been slow to develop. Although every RBOC (and many non-Bell companies) . . . offered ISDN . . . starting in the mid- to late 1980s, . . . growth of applications was stymied by the lack of standard protocols and the resulting small markets. In a classic "chicken and egg" conundrum, the service languished because potential subscribers could not identify useful applications, and applications developers saw little opportunity in ISDN because the market was not yet in place.

In 1993, this was still the LECs' view of ISDN's market failure. It was remarkably "supply-sided." The LECs apparently believed, after 25 years of experimentation, that they were just experiencing problems in engineering the perfect product. They thought that, if ISDN can just be made easier to use, "at last, customers will flock to our doors." This may reflect an astounding stubbornness on the part of engineers.

ISDN is perhaps the most extreme example of Naisbitt's forced technology syndrome in action. Even though ISDN was designed by their technological peers for what a very sophisticated segment of demand *should* want, it still flopped. This "technology push" innovation—dubbed the "great economic hope of most telephone companies" by a British Telecom marketing director—has been incredibly slow in

"There is still some question of availability of the 'content' that superhighways will transmit."

winning approval of users. For instance, a *Networking Management* survey of telecommunications managers of 250 large companies found that ISDN was only being used by 5 percent of respondents, while 62 percent still were not evaluating implementation of, or didn't plan to implement, ISDN. Relief to permit recovery of investments made long ago is still not in sight.

While keeping the focus on the consumer, it is also well for industry and governmental officials to remember how demand manifests itself in the marketplace—through "dollar votes." Simply put, it is not enough to have needs; the ability to fund those needs also comes into play. Industry is learning this lesson, as vigorous competition appears. But politicians may lack the experience and incentive to heed *both* of these necessary conditions.

Chapter 3

Will the Information Highway Benefit Society?

CURRENT CONTROVERSIES

The Impact of the Information Highway: An Overview

by Andrew Kupfer

About the author: *Andrew Kupfer is an associate editor for* Fortune, *a biweekly business and finance magazine.*

Imagine, if you can, a small room, hexagonal in shape, like the cell of a bee. An arm-chair is in the centre, by its side a reading-desk—that is all the furniture. And in the arm-chair there sits a swaddled lump of flesh—a woman, about five feet high, with a face as white as a fungus.

An electric bell rang.

"I suppose I must see who it is," she thought. The chair was worked by machinery, and it rolled her to the other side of the room.

"Who is it?" she called. She knew several thousand people; in certain directions human intercourse had advanced enormously . . .

The round plate that she held in her hands began to glow. A faint blue light shot across it, darkening to purple, and presently she could see the image of her son, who lived on the other side of the earth, and he could see her.

—E.M. Forster
"The Machine Stops," 1914

"Come on, honey. Remember those IBM machines. Let's get at it before people go out of style."
—Bobby Darin pickup line in *State Fair,* 1962

Technology and Apprehension

Ever since protohumans with sloping foreheads learned to set things on fire, people have feared and hated technology as much as they have been in its thrall. They have eyed with suspicion the printing press, the automobile, the telephone, and the television as solvents of the glue that binds people together. Each new technology brings a warning: To fall under its spell will be to sacrifice not only simplicity but also community, to metamorphose into alienated, isolated, sedentary blobs. In Forster's story, when the machine stops, everybody dies.

This kind of trepidation is sometimes overdrawn—even the advent of the washing machine produced expressions of yearning for simpler times—but it isn't really misplaced. The printing press vanquished the knowledge oligarchy, yet popular culture seems ever more trivial and debased. Modern medicine often prolongs life beyond all reason or desire.

Now information technology is poised to alter the scope of human intercourse, and the familiar combination of promise and dread makes itself felt once again—with an urgency seldom seen in the two centuries since the Industrial Revolution. The new technology holds the potential to change human settlement patterns, change the way people interact with each other, change our ideas of what it means to be human.

> *"The familiar combination of promise and dread makes itself felt once again—with an urgency seldom seen in . . . two centuries."*

Information technology will have the power to reverse what may have been an aberration in human history: the industrial model of society. While people in agrarian societies had for millenniums worked the land around their homes to the rhythm of the sun, industrialization created the time clock and the separate workplace. Wired technology already is assaulting the industrial concept of the workday; as technology brings greater realism to electronic communications, the workplace for many will become untethered from geography, letting people live anywhere. The fear is that in liberating us from geography and the clock, networks will destroy intimacy, both by making solitude impossible and by making physical presence immaterial to communication.

Information Technology's Magic

One reason we are wary about information technology is that it is still strange to us, new enough that we notice it all the time. We still marvel at what computers can do, and how we can carry in our laptops enough computing horsepower to have filled an entire laboratory not so many years ago. We view information technology as special, almost magical. Vincent Mosco of the Harvard Center for Information Policy Research, who has written extensively on the history of technology and the way electrification changed population distribution, says people felt the same way about electricity when it was introduced in the 19th century. "Companies used electricity to flash advertisements off the clouds," much in the way that Gothamites summon Batman in times of trouble, says Mosco. "I like that image of people gathering outdoors and watching lights flashing in the sky and seeing that as the spectacle of communications."

Today computers, the Internet, and the information superhighway are the magical elements, and even the basic rules of etiquette are unformed, reminiscent of the early days of the telephone. Paul Saffo of the Institute for the Future in Menlo Park, California, says: "Alexander Graham Bell proposed a greeting of 'Hoy! Hoy!'—a variation of 'Ahoy!' It didn't catch on." Instead his great rival Thomas Edison stole a bit of the jam from his crumpet by inventing, as a telephone salutation, the word "hello," a variant of the British exclamation "hallo."

Eventually, though, computer communications—like electricity and telephony—will quite literally fade into the woodwork. When that happens, wired technology will obliterate the significance of two of the great symbols of the Industrial Revolution, the train and the clock, and along with them the idea that society can organize everything to run on set schedules. The temporal shift this technology permits—even demands—is likely to be its most profound and enduring effect.

With an economy that straddles many time zones, the nine-to-five workday will disappear for those for whom it hasn't already. People will become accustomed to flitting between their different roles of work, recreation, and repose, constantly prey to interruption, even addicted to it. "The rush and flow of events is like electronic heroin," says Saffo. "And once you get it into your veins it's really hard to stop. You'll figure out a way to interrupt yourself." People may live in bucolic and pastoral settings but not live a pastoral life, competing via cyberspace for work against thousands of others, finishing each job in days or hours, then moving on to the next, like electronic versions of Charlie Chaplin's assembly-line worker in *Modern Times*.

Family Interaction

Many assume that people who can leave company headquarters will choose to work in their homes, and wired enthusiasts anticipate a resurgence of familial togetherness. But at least one expert on how the home reflects changes in American society says we may well see less family interaction than we do today. Clifford Clark, an American studies professor at Carleton College in Northfield, Minnesota, predicts: "We will see different family members sitting around different screens in different rooms."

> *"People will become accustomed to flitting between their different roles of work, recreation, and repose."*

That could touch off domestic turf battles: Our houses aren't suited to these purposes, having evolved over the past century from a large number of little spaces to a small number of big ones. The kitchen was once isolated in the back of the house to keep a continuously fired-up stove from overheating the living quarters, but with the invention of the gas range it moved forward and became a social room as much as a workplace. Today it sometimes flows right into the so-called great room, where families sit in front of the jumbotron to watch surround-sound movies. A shortage of solitary workspace may become just one more source of family disharmony.

Knowledge workers, selling their labor to new species of business that will flourish in the wired economy, may need to be ready to go at a moment's notice. Employers already seek workers via computer networks. But in the future the process will be more pervasive and almost automatic. Professor Thomas Malone of the Center for Coordination Science at MIT [Massachusetts Institute of Technology] says such wired workers will form "overnight armies of intellectual mercenaries."

"A shortage of solitary workspace may become just one more source of family disharmony."

Imagine a company with a task that needs urgent attention—say, designing a lawnmower or writing a computer program. The company might not maintain a cadre within its ranks to do the job. Instead, it trolls the net for talent, sending out a bulletin that describes the tasks to be done and the skills required of team members. The notice might go directly to qualified applicants, based on résumés filed online. Specialists anywhere in the world instantly submit bids to do a piece of the job, simultaneously triggering a query to their personal references. Winning bidders work together via video hookup, each at his or her home base. The project might last a few weeks or a few days or a few hours. Afterwards the team disbands and the members melt back into the talent pool to bid on new jobs.

Online Behavior

Socially, the wired society is likely to bring flip-flops in behavior like the changes wrought by the telephone, which made it acceptable for a man to talk to a strange woman without a formal introduction by a third party. The Internet is making it acceptable for a man to exchange explicit sexual fantasies with a strange woman—or with someone who claims to be a woman but who may really be a trio of male cross-dressers sitting around their screen laughing. At times people breach the bounds of decency and stray into the realm of the allegedly criminal: A college student was jailed in February 1995 for distributing via the Internet a depraved story in which he imagined the rape, torture, and murder of a woman he knew, and whose name he disclosed. Another young woman soon replied with an online revenge fantasy of her own.

Many fear that wired communications, by permitting a unique combination of intrusiveness and anonymity, will make people even ruder than they are today. Already people communicating online are rethinking what kind of information they feel comfortable sharing. Mark Weiser, principal scientist at the Computer Science Lab in Xerox's Palo Alto Research Center—and an inventor of the technology that let the Rolling Stones transmit a live video concert over the Internet in November 1994—says that at a business dinner we are likely to talk about our spouses and children but would not usually exchange résumés. On-line, though, people are guarded about their personal lives since they feel less able to size up, or even identify, their correspondents. Yet they can, in many cases, call up *curricula vitae* that disclose everything their Internet friends have done since high school.

"People are starting to put up different barriers to their interactions," says Weiser, speaking as one who doesn't like barriers very much. He usually has eight video windows open on his computer screen at work, showing his engineering colleagues' offices. Weiser also confesses to being the drummer for a band called Severe Tire Damage that sneaked onto the Internet before the Stones concert as an unscheduled opening act.

In time both the guardedness and the anonymity will evanesce, Weiser says: "As more and more business is conducted online, it will become more of a real place, and real-life expectations will take over. One is that I know who you are. We will stop talking to people we don't know." The wired connection will no longer seem like a strange way of meeting people—which won't be the first time a method that once seemed mad became a part of quotidian routine. And the change in attitude might not take as long as you think. A decade ago, if you telephoned a friend and reached an answering machine, you probably thought, "How rude!" Today you are more likely to be miffed by your thoughtless friends who refuse to buy one.

Unclear Effects

Despite its potential to free people from geography, the likely effect of wired technology on where people live is murky. While some will be able to leave cities, others won't, and still others won't want to. True, some jobs have already headed for the sticks, particularly back-office operations of financial firms, intensifying a long-term trend that began earlier in the century with improvements in transportation. But many potential movers seem to have sticky feet. Blame this partly on that hobgoblin of managerial minds, force of habit. People might love the idea of sending E-mail to their grandchildren, but as supervisors the same folks don't have the stomach for remote management. People want to see their employees and want to watch them work.

> *"Many fear that wired communications . . . will make people even ruder than they are today."*

They can't do that via video yet because existing technology is too crude: The picture transmitted by a typical desktop computer videoconference system is a low-resolution, herky-jerky postage stamp. Within the next ten years, though, better devices will be able to send crystalline images with lifelike color and perfectly fluid motion, conveying words, body language, expression. What will it mean when gazing at a face on a video screen is no different than looking at a face through a window? Will the cities empty and the people disperse like leaves in a fall wind?

If history is any guide, wired technology will create forces that pull in the other direction as well. Successive waves of technology, from the telephone to the automobile to rural electrification, have brought predictions of the emptying of cities. Yet the cities endure, and so they will a century from now. The telephone, for example, led to both dispersion and concentration. Not only did it open up remote areas

> *"By permitting dispersion, information technology promotes the globalization of the economy."*

to commerce, but it also helped make possible the most highly concentrated form of living and working space that we know: the skyscraper. Without the telephone to deliver messages, occupants of upper stories would be cut off unless the architect devoted the entire core of the massive structures to elevators and stairways for messengers.

In the information society, expect to see similar pushes and pulls. Most mobile will be the knowledge workers: people whose jobs largely involve talking to others and handling information—in other words, white-collar office workers. For them, electronic links will mostly suffice; they will be able to choose to live by the seashore, say, or near family and friends.

But as if to obey Newtonian laws of motion, information technology will also pull people to the center. By permitting dispersion, information technology promotes the globalization of the economy, guaranteeing a raison d'être for international cities like New York, London, and Tokyo that serve as the nodes for world communications networks—a major reason New York has shown much more resilience than city-bashers predicted. The economic vibrancy of these cities will attract the many people who thirst for amenities like theater, concerts, restaurants, and the continuous paseo of cosmopolitan life.

As they do today, the city dwellers of the information society will depend on a tier of lower-level service workers like barbers and burger flippers, whose work, involving physical contact with other people, cannot be liberated from place by communications technology. (Some higher-level professionals like surgeons will also remain tied to population centers.) Not all the people will be able to follow their bliss to the mountaintops.

Electronic Agents

Wherever we live, the nature of routine intercourse is likely to be changed by electronic agents—drudges, really, programmed to take over the tedium of interconnectivity. The first commercial prototypes of these agents have recently appeared, including one called Wildfire that acts as an electronic secretary, answering the phone, taking messages, obeying simple verbal commands, and routing phone calls to users wherever they happen to be.

As they become more sophisticated, these software agents will do our shopping, buy our plane tickets, and make our appointments for us, traveling through cyberspace like ghostly echoes of the self. "They won't be intelligent enough to make the clerics nervous," jokes Saffo of the Institute for the Future. "But they will exhibit whimsy and humor, and be interesting enough to convince people to interact with them." Not only will people be talking with these soulless beings, but agents will be interacting with other agents as well. The Hollywood patter of the future may remain "Have your agent call my agent," but people won't be talking about ten-percenters.

Our ghosts may come to haunt us as well. One nightmare scenario not yet on many worry lists is location tracking. With the auctioning off of vast swaths of the radio spectrum for new wireless services and the promise of cheap, lightweight cellular phones, the cellular industry is poised to sweep into the mass market. New low-powered cellular systems will blanket the country with great numbers of closely spaced transmitters. Nearly everyone will be carrying some sort of wireless communications gadget. Whenever they are on—and they are likely to be left on all the time—a signal will travel to the nearest transmitter, letting the network know where to send each user's messages and phone calls.

Cellular companies will be able to use their fine-meshed networks to pinpoint nearly everyone's location and track their movements. This is how the police, with the help of the phone company, tracked down O.J. Simpson as he was driven along the highway in the infamous white Bronco. [In June 1994, police pursued suspected murderer O.J. Simpson on freeways near Los Angeles.] Anyone with a cellular telephone scanner could also keep tabs on people's locations, even when new digital cellular systems make our conversations secure from eavesdroppers. (Only our words will be encoded; our identification numbers must stay unscrambled so the network can authorize our calls.)

> *"Nearly everyone will be carrying some sort of wireless communications gadget."*

If you don't think anyone really cares where you go from moment to moment, be assured that plenty of companies would pay to find out. Marketers, for example, would love to know who visits which stores, and when, and for how long. They could legally buy this information from the telephone company as easily as they buy mailing lists today. And as with mailing lists, we would have no control over who gets access to this information.

Seductive Technology

If our ever cozier relationship with wired technology makes us fear for our souls, perhaps that is because the stuff is so seductive. Unlike TV, the new technology requires our participation, drawing us in. As such it is insidious. Management professor Alladi Venkatesh of the University of California at Irvine, an expert on the impact of technology on the household, says: "Television is easy to dismiss. Its limitations are obvious. The danger of the computer is that it gives us the impression that it can do for us what TV has not: make us better people."

It is true that the power to make instant connections anywhere in the world, at any time, can bring inestimable comfort. For the millions who are stuck at home because of age or infirmity or because they are caregivers for young children, for insomniacs who need someone to commune with in the blue hours past midnight, for people who want to find out if their car is a lemon, or how to buy a house, or how to cope with a child's asthma attack, being wired may be the fastest way to connect with others who are willing to share their feelings and knowledge.

But with these gains there is loss. While people may feel just as intensely about friends they make via cyberspace as they do about their face-to-face confreres, the ease with which they form these links means that many are likely to be trivial, short lived, and disposable—junk friends. We may be overwhelmed by a continuous static of information and casual acquaintance, so that finding true soul mates will be even harder than it is today. And the art of quiet repose and contemplation may one day seem as quaint as the 19th-century practice of river gazing—staring at riverscapes to discern their coloristic and picturesque attributes.

MIT's Malone is worried about these risks but tries to remain an optimist. He says he feels closer to some people he has met over the net than he did even to the friends he made growing up in a small town in New Mexico. Those relationships were mere accidents of geography; he and his new friends chose each other through common interest. In an eerie echo of the cautionary tale that E.M. Forster wrote more than 80 years ago, he says, "There must be thousands of people I know personally . . ."

This machine will not stop. In time we will no longer ponder its existence, or be able to imagine a world without its constant hum.

A Global Information Infrastructure Can Benefit the World

by Al Gore

About the author: *Al Gore served as a U.S. senator for seven years before becoming the forty-fifth vice president of the United States in 1993. He is the author of* Earth in the Balance.

In 1993 I wrote in *Discover*'s October issue that technological innovation was a powerful engine driving our national economic growth. I called for continued research, development, and investment in the new technologies that will lead us into the twenty-first century, and I outlined President Clinton's vision for the National Information Infrastructure—a seamless web of communication networks, computers, data bases, and consumer electronics that will put vast amounts of information at users' fingertips and will forever change the way we live, learn, work, and communicate with each other.

Technological innovation continues to be a priority for our nation. In fact, with the countries of the world becoming increasingly interdependent, the need to create an information superhighway has reached beyond our borders. In the future, a global "network of networks" will be essential for expanded business and trade opportunities, improved education and health care, preservation and promotion of democracy, and the sustainable development of all countries in our family of nations.

The Example of South Africa

Let me explain with an example.

In 1994 I was privileged to witness the inauguration of the first freely elected majority president of South Africa, Nelson Mandela. It was an incredible, tremendous turning point for the human race. An extraordinary range of emotions filled my heart and millions of other people's as we watched a moment in history no one will ever forget.

Al Gore, "Technology Democracy," *Discover*, October 1994. Reprinted with permission.

With that election came the end of apartheid. It forever changed the country, opening doors of opportunity that had been closed for decades. The election swept in not only a new majority leader but a new partnership between the United States and South Africa—one of renewed diplomatic and economic relations.

In the coming decades, as South Africa struggles to improve its economy, house its people, educate its children, and care for its sick, the country will turn to the world for support that can be provided in large part through a Global Information Infrastructure.

A GII could, as President Nelson Mandela envisions, help create a South Africa where people's energies and talents can blossom in a free society: entrepreneurs could buy or sell their products in a global information marketplace, enhancing the country's economic and business development; building materials for housing could be ordered at the lowest cost from anywhere in the world; schoolchildren could access information in the finest libraries; and the sick could be treated right in their homes.

The concept of a GII was unveiled in a speech I gave to the International Telecommunications Union in Buenos Aires in March 1994. I called on legislators, regulators, and business leaders to build and operate a GII that would circle the globe with information superhighways, transcending the barriers of time and distance, of wealth and poverty, of developed and developing countries, and on which all people could travel.

> *"I called on legislators, regulators, and business leaders to build and operate a GII that would circle the globe."*

Like our National Information Infrastructure, a GII would consist of hundreds of different networks and use many different technologies, including satellite, fiber optics, video, and telephone. The goal would be to transmit information with the speed of light from the largest city to the smallest village on every continent in every part of our world. The GII would be built according to an ambitious agenda that would help all governments, in their own sovereign nations and through international cooperation, take part in this revolution—a democratic effort not dictated or built by a single country.

Enhancing Democracy and Economic Growth

In a sense, the GII will be a metaphor for democracy itself. Representative democracy does not work with an all-powerful central government, arrogating all decisions to itself. That is why communism collapsed and apartheid fell. Instead, representative democracy relies on the assumption that the best way for a nation to make its political decisions is for each citizen to have the power to control his or her own life. To do that, people must have available the information they need. They must be allowed to express their conclusions in free speech and in votes that are combined with those of millions of others. That's what guides the system as a whole.

The GII will promote the functioning of democracy by greatly enhancing the participation of citizens in decision making. And it will greatly promote the ability of nations to cooperate with one another.

Just as the GII will enhance democracy, it will also promote economic growth. Already the information infrastructure is to our 1990s U.S. economy what the transportation infrastructure was to our mid-twentieth-century economy. A global information superhighway will revolutionize the world economy, too.

For example, the integration of computing and information networks in the U.S. economy makes our companies more productive, more competitive, and more adaptable to changing conditions. The economies of other nations will experience the same effects. By enabling service sectors to expand their range of products and their ability to respond to customer demands, the GII will expand business and economic opportunities worldwide.

This revolution is already taking place; the GII is being built, although many countries have yet to see any benefits. Digital telecommunications technology, fiber optics, and new, high-capacity satellite systems are transforming telecommunications. All over the world, under the seas and along the roads, pipelines, and railroads, companies are laying fiber-optic cable that carries thousands of telephone calls per second over a single strand of glass.

Five Key Principles

As the GII progresses, the basic tenets by which to guide its development must be set forth. Here in the United States, the development of the National Information Infrastructure is based on five key principles: to encourage private investment; to promote competition; to create a flexible regulatory framework that can keep pace with rapid technological and market changes; to provide open access to the network for all information providers; and, finally, to ensure universal service so that everyone can benefit from the network. But these principles are not unique to this country. Many are accepted internationally, and they should inform and aid the development of the GII.

For example, the president and I believe strongly that every classroom, library, hospital, and clinic in the United States must be connected to the National Information Infrastructure by the end of the century. As a nation we cannot tolerate—nor in the long run can we afford—a society in which some children become fully educated and others do not, in which some pa-

> *"The GII will expand business and economic opportunities worldwide."*

tients benefit from shared medical expertise and others do not, in which some people have access to lifetime learning and job training and others do not.

One of the first objectives of the GII should be to determine how every school and library in every country can be connected to the Internet, the world's largest computer network, in order to create a Global Digital Library. Each library could maintain a server containing books and journals in electronic form, along with indexes to help users find other materials. This will allow millions of students, scholars, and businesspeople to find the information they need, whether it be in Albania, Ecuador, or South Africa. It will help insure that the gap between rich and poor and between developed and developing countries is bridged, and that all people of the world can benefit from the information superhighway.

The Global Information Infrastructure offers instant communication to the great human family. It can provide us the information we need to dramatically improve the quality of life around the world. By linking clinics and hospitals, it will guarantee that doctors have access to the best possible information on diseases and treatments. By providing early warning of natural disasters such as volcanic eruptions, tsunamis, and typhoons, it can save the lives of thousands of people. By linking villages and towns, it can help people organize and work together on local and regional issues ranging from improving water supplies to preventing deforestation.

> *"Every classroom, library, hospital, and clinic in the United States must be connected to the National Information Infrastructure."*

To promote, to protect, to preserve freedom and democracy, we must make technological advancement an integral part of every nation's development. Each link we create strengthens the bonds of liberty and democracy around the world. By opening markets to stimulate the development of the GII, we open lines of communication. By opening lines of communication, we open minds.

Internet Bulletin Boards Create a Sense of Community

by Evan Schwartz

About the author: Evan Schwartz is a contributing writer for Wired *magazine and a research fellow at the Edward R. Murrow Center for International Communications at Tufts University in Medford, Massachusetts.*

Can a truly vibrant community exist in cyberspace? Can a bunch of individuals at isolated computer stations achieve warmth, caring, and a shared set of values? Is the Internet becoming a pipeline for surrogate communities in an age of technological omnipresence?

Community is not the image of the Internet promoted by government or industry. If you ask the telecommunications giants and media conglomerates racing to build the infotainment pipeline of the future, they point to a world of interconnected business people, students, e-mailers, and government workers, all operating with breakneck efficiency and without leaving their desks. But this image might have little meaning for the numberless millions of actual Internet users, who might have a starkly different collective vision for tomorrow's advanced communications technologies. In *The Virtual Community*, author Howard Rheingold dismisses the now popular notion that the public demands a great stream of interactive entertainment and information. What the people really want, he argues, is a chance to form meaningful relationships with their far-flung neighbors in the global village. Dale Dougherty, publisher of the *Global Network Navigator*, an electronic magazine on the Internet, agrees. The Internet, he says, is filling a deep need: "We want a feeling of connectedness, of having things in common."

Connected by the "Net"

The "Net" is an amalgam of electronic bulletin boards, on-line information services, and computer conference sessions—all connected by the same global

Evan Schwartz, "Looking for Community on the Internet," *Responsive Community*, Winter 1994/95. Reprinted with permission.

telecommunications networks to which our phones are attached. Linking about 20 million people in 100 countries, the U.S. government–subsidized Internet originated in the Department of Defense in the 1960s and expanded into elite corporate labs in the 1970s, into American universities in the 1980s, and finally right into many living rooms in the early 1990s. For now, communication is mainly confined to written text, but that is changing as the Net gains the ability to handle voice, video, and other multimedia information. Already some cable companies are providing Internet linkups, and there will soon come a day when people with cheap digital video cameras can transmit their footage to the masses.

> *"The virtual community idea approximates much more closely the real Internet than does the popular metaphor of a superhighway."*

The virtual community idea approximates much more closely the real Internet than does the popular metaphor of a superhighway running into people's living rooms. The Internet is a spirited web of conversation that you can weave yourself into by tapping on your personal computer's keyboard and powering up your modem. A virtual community, according to Rheingold, is a group of people who have in all likelihood never met face to face, but who enjoy spending time in cyberspace with one another debating politics, discussing their hobbies, conducting business, spilling their guts, or just flirting and playing games with one another.

Bulletin-Board Communities

Rheingold's book provides a tour of the Internet—a tour that begins from inside the specific virtual community to which Rheingold belongs. Based in San Francisco and known as the WELL (for Whole Earth 'Lectronic Link), Rheingold's local virtual community began in 1985 as an experiment. The idea was to give people access to new tools for group communication, letting them decide on their own how it should all be used.

Not surprisingly, the WELL has experienced its greatest growth as a forum for discussing the Grateful Dead. But significantly, the Deadheads on the WELL translate their on-line interactions into face-to-face meetings. Occasionally the Deadheads and other interest groups hold picnics or concerts. For the most part, the Internet acts as a social leveler: Once on-line, no one can tell if you're black or white, old or young, male or female, sick or well. Perhaps most important, no one can tell how unattractive you are—looks have never played a smaller role in human affairs than they do on the Net.

For Rheingold, the WELL is a place to discuss the joys and problems associated with raising kids. One time, when his daughter got a tick caught in her scalp, he sat down at his PC, typed in his question, and learned from an on-line fellow named Flash Gordon, M.D., exactly how to remove it. The tick was gone by the time a real pediatrician returned a phone call from the author's wife.

Another bulletin board, Baud Town, also emphasizes community by building itself around the analogy of a town, complete with social norms. New joiners receive a lengthy etiquette message explaining that the bulletin-board community allows no X-rated discussion groups, nor messages in capital letters (the latter are the equivalent of shouting on-line). The bulletin board community even has its own "Neighborhood Watch," in which users police one another against abuse of the system. All of these efforts help to reduce anonymous harassment on-line and make for a safer electronic community.

The "citizens" of Baud Town have created an environment in which they give and receive support. Users receive comforting messages from fellow users during difficult times, such as divorce, illness, or death in their families. Much like WELL users, Baud Townies "date" on-line, taking advantage of the low-pressure atmosphere of the Internet that allows users to get to know each other's personality before meeting in person.

The Net's Influence

The Net's capacity to function as a vehicle for community lies in the differences between it and all previous communications media. While telephones are primarily a one-to-one medium and television a few-to-many medium, the hypergrowth of the Net marks the beginning of many-to-many communication. Greater possibilities lie just over the horizon. By 1997, one expert predicts, there will be more users on the Net than there are people living in California. Before 2000, the on-line populace will exceed the number of citizens of any single country except India or China. With the Net's ability to transcend time zones and national boundaries, it could contribute to greater understanding between cultures. On the other hand, the free-flowing dialogue could bring on social upheaval, especially in places like Japan, where communication with outside cultures is tightly controlled by the powers that be.

Like physical communities, virtual communities can exert strong pressure on members to conform to behavioral norms and conventions. In April 1994 a pair of lawyers in Phoenix, Arizona, placed an ad for legal services on the Internet.

> *"The 'citizens' of Baud Town have created an environment in which they give and receive support."*

(Noncommercialization of the Internet is one of the cardinal, if unofficial, rules of the Net.) In response to this transgression, users from around the world "flamed" the couple with 30,000 hostile messages. The barrage, according to the *Phoenix Gazette*, caused the local Internet node, Internet Direct, to overload and temporarily shut down. Internet Direct posted apologies for the ad and suspended the lawyers' access to the system. Internet Direct systems administrator Geoff Wheelhouse told the *Gazette*, "[The incident] has given us a bad reputation."

Most actual communities work no more effectively.

The United States might be poised to benefit most from virtual communities. Since the convivial atmosphere that still exists in Italian piazzas and Parisian bistros has largely died in the United States, Americans hunger for a new way to connect with each other. One of Rheingold's sources attributes the decline of public meeting spaces in the United States to the nation's "suburbanized, urban-decayed, paved, and malled environment." Others attribute the breakdown of intelligent public discourse to the fact that "the public sphere," particularly the airwaves, have been commoditized and sold off to media moguls and advertisers. The Internet, by contrast, still has a chance to be run by and for the grassroots.

Accommodating Many Interests

Internet enthusiasts sometimes see virtual community as a panacea for all sorts of social ills. They go a bit far, for example, when they hold out the possibility that the Net could be a forum for electronic democracy. The people conversing on the Internet and other on-line services are by and large not a bunch of civic leaders. The untamed, freewheeling nature of cyberspace means that it's often filled with every skinhead, Trekkie, religious zealot, and Rush Limbaugh–wannabe with a new theory on how the world should work. The Net is not, at least not yet, much of a town hall meeting. . . .

The question is how real these communities actually are and to what extent they really fill the needs of more traditional communities. The answer isn't entirely clear. The Net is uncharted territory both for individuals and for communities. "It's like a boomtown in the old West," says Dougherty. "The rules aren't written yet. With TV, people are controlling you. Here you are on your own."

Reservations About Community

Even Net enthusiasts acknowledge that cyberspace may never be a replacement for true communities. Rheingold, who is clearly caught up in channeling virtual communities as a force for good, expresses openly his reservations about the Net as a surrogate community: "Perhaps cyberspace is precisely the *wrong* place to look for the rebirth of community . . . offering a life-denying simulacrum of real passion and true commitment to one another." And he asks, "If a lonely person chooses to spend many hours a day in an imaginary society, typing witticisms with strangers on other continents, is that good or bad?"

The key word in the cyberspace community lexicon is "virtual." Like an elaborate, electronic flight simulator, the technology is breathtaking and the simulation appears perfect. Only when the users find themselves in the cockpits of real airplanes (or in the midst of real communities) do they realize how limiting "virtual" can really be. Still, for many people, the choice seems to be between a very good simulation of community and no community at all; that choice makes virtual community look attractive indeed.

The Information Highway Can Promote Environmental Networking

by Mickey Mercier

About the author: *Mickey Mercier is the associate editor of* Connecticut Town and City *magazine and a specialist in computer communications.*

Environmental cyberspace is a very busy place these days. New services are coming online practically every week as nonprofit groups and entrepreneurs stake out territory and try to develop services that will attract users and best serve their constituencies. This is great news for computer users and environmentalists, because there is something for everyone, from vast Internet-based environmental services with virtually infinite information and resources down to grassroots local bulletin board systems.

Expert computer users and novices alike will be able to find an online service that will match their needs, interests, budget and level of computer skill.

While there is no lack of environmental resources in cyberspace, there are decisions for users to make, especially for those on a budget. If you have a modem-equipped computer and want to try your hand at online environmental networking, plunge ahead and log on. You will need some patience and will probably run up some telephone or connect charges. And if you can get free Internet access through school or work, you're ahead of the game.

The Green Internet

The environmental resources of the Internet are readily available through several large information providers on the Internet, which also provide their users with the 'Net's basic tools for logging on to other computers, such as *Telnet*, *Gopher*, *Web* and e-mail.

Probably the closest thing to one-stop shopping for environmental information on the Internet is *EcoNet*, a large, well-organized Internet service that offers

Excerpted from "The Green Net" by Mickey Mercier, *E: The Environmental Magazine*, January/February 1995. Reprinted with permission.

global environmental news and action alerts, access to numerous databases, bibliographies and library catalogs, and online publications. The nice thing about the EcoNet is that a lot of the global information that can be gathered through the Internet is already located in one place. You can venture out to other Internet sites on the EcoNet's Internet connection if you want, but a lot of the work is already done for you.

> *"EcoNet . . . [has] more than 4,000 grassroots groups holding memberships."*

EcoNet, operated by the Institute for Global Communications (IGC), is also a particularly good choice for activists, with more than 4,000 grassroots groups holding memberships. Services under the IGC umbrella include specifically targeted networks like *PeaceNet*, *LaborNet* and *ConflictNet*, as well as *INTER-ACT*, which enables members to dispatch mail and FAXes to government officials and the media. . . .

A second large environmental information service on the Internet is *Enviro-Link*, which shares some functions with EcoNet, with the added advantage that it is free. EnviroLink founder Josh Knauer describes the fast-growing service as a "Cinderella story of the Internet." In 1991, Knauer, then a freshman at Carnegie Mellon University in Pittsburgh, started the service. In four years, EnviroLink has grown from an electronic mailing list of 20 college students to a huge Internet network with a claimed 550,000 users in 96 countries.

EnviroLink's extensive offerings include environmental news, databases, a large catalog of environmental publications, discussion groups, mail, online environmental action capabilities, and a chat mode that allows users to gather in electronic conference rooms and converse online. It even offers "Enviro-Products" online shopping. . . .

One of the most established gathering places on the Internet is *The WELL* (Whole Earth 'Lectronic Link), founded in 1985. The WELL is not strictly an environmental online service. It's more like the alternative culture's version of *CompuServe*, billing itself as a "virtual community" that emphasizes independent thinking and intellectual content.

The WELL's strength is its diversity—the environment is only one of more than 250 conferences on everything from social responsibility, virtual reality and the Grateful Dead to firearms, filmmaking and the First Amendment. The online publications list includes *Wired*, *Details*, *bOING bOING*, *Mondo 2000*, various fanzines and, of course, the *Whole Earth Review*.

Within the WELL's environmental conference, you will find several hundred ongoing discussion groups that tend to be a little more offbeat and intense than what you find on a dedicated environmental service. A few recent discussion group titles: "My Search for a Libertarian Biologist," "Three Solar Box Cookers," "Green Burnout," "Styrene Goodnight" and "Environmental Scams." The only downside of the WELL is that its richness is difficult to appreciate. The menu system is difficult and arcane, even by Internet standards, although regular users say they have come to love it over time. . . .

Bulletin Board Systems

For modem users on a budget, or those who do not have or want Internet service, bulletin board systems (BBS) are an economical alternative. There are thousands of BBS's located in communities across the nation, and perhaps 100 dedicated to environmentalism.

Bulletin boards are online systems that can run on a single PC or Macintosh. For that reason, they are economical to operate, and many grassroots organizations and amateurs have them. Membership fees range from free to $50 per year. Bulletin boards tend to be much easier to use than the Internet, and most well-run local BBS's include basic Internet mail services for members. While you won't be able to "surf" the Net, you will be able to exchange free letters with people all over the planet.

You can get a list of environmental bulletin boards across North America and Europe—"The Green BBS List"—by downloading it from the *Earth Art BBS*, where the list originates. Also keep an eye peeled for it on any other boards you log onto. The *Green BBS List* provides modem numbers for dozens of environmentally oriented boards, everything from *The Abalone Alliance* and *Body Dharma Online* to the *U.S. Environmental Protection Agency Library* and the *American Hydrogen Association*.

"EnviroLink has grown from an electronic mailing list of 20 college students to . . . a claimed 550,000 users."

Of particular note among green BBS's is Greenpeace's *Environet*. It's a free, full-service bulletin board that's well worth the toll call, and you can download the Green BBS List from there, too. Daily postings include Greenpeace news releases and locations of the organization's ships.

Another terrific environmental BBS, particularly for environmental educators and students, is *Classroom Earth*.

Graphic Interfaces

Everyone wants easy-to-use, mouse-driven online services with icons, pictures and color. They were once available only from big, commercial services like *CompuServe*, but this is changing.

A number of networks have begun to employ a software package called First Class, which provides both Macintosh and Windows users with a full-color graphic environment. But you first have to obtain special software from the network and load it into your computer. *TogetherNet* is an example of a hybrid service that provides a graphic interface for users who want it. It uses a specially adapted version of the First Class software to access databases, provide Internet conferencing and key into textual archives.

TogetherNet, which focuses on the environment and sustainable development, is particularly strong on United Nations information. It is accessible through a full Internet account, through SprintNet X.25 or direct dial through its worldwide hosts. . . .

Another example of an environmental bulletin board with the First Class graphic interface is *Earth Spirit* in Santa Monica, California. This BBS has an educational bent, providing an online curriculum, environmental news, databases and events.

Commercial Services

The big commercial online services such as *CompuServe, America Online, Prodigy, Delphi* and *Genie* all offer environmental information and Internet resources in one form or another, with *CompuServe*'s being especially extensive. Prodigy's *Green Connection* forum focuses on "the business of the environment." The idea behind this joint venture of the Environmental Product Information Center and Prodigy is to help people and companies find environmentally sound products, network, and advertise to one another. It's all part of the increasingly green scenery on the new data highway.

The Information Highway Can Benefit Blacks

by Alison Gardy

About the author: *Alison Gardy is a freelance writer who writes frequently about community activism.*

After Newt Gingrich suggested in 1995 that Congress tackle inequality in the information age by giving "a tax credit" for the poorest Americans to buy a "laptop" computer, he quickly backpedaled from the idea, dismissing it as "nutty."

The episode indicated that the Speaker of the House hadn't devoted much thought to specific ways of giving the nation's have-nots an opportunity to participate in the information-age economy. But many people who have devoted considerable time to the topic—particularly black professionals in computing and telecommunications—aren't so sure that Washington is the place to look for solutions, anyway.

"This technology needs to be a bridge, not a barrier; we can't afford not to make the investment," said Larry Irving, who is the Assistant Secretary of Commerce in charge of information-technology policy, and happens to be black.

"But we don't have the money in Washington for this," Mr. Irving continued, "so it's going to have to happen on a local level."

A National Movement

In fact, a national movement led by black executives and entrepreneurs in the information-technology fields is already under way.

Maybe it should be called digital activism. Through donations of time and expertise, and through business contacts, these black professionals are trying to make sure that low-income blacks—especially young people—have access to the hardware, software and networks of the digital economy.

According to national estimates, fewer than 40 percent of black schoolchildren have access to computers at school, compared with nearly 60 percent of white students. And in some predominantly black inner-city neighborhoods, one in four households have no phone line—much less a modem.

The digital activists know that people without access to information technology today might not have jobs in the twenty-first century, while those with such access could enjoy virtually color-blind opportunity.

Some of the activism is organized as in the New Interactive Niagara Movement, initiated in 1994 by Timothy L. Jenkins, publisher and chief executive of a magazine about black affairs, *American Visions*. The effort aims to coordinate and update the information-technology strategies of various black organizations.

Other efforts in digital activism involve less formal, though no less dedicated, types of outreach and volunteerism, like the activities of the following three black executives.

Getting Blacks On-Line

Sanyakhu-Sheps Amaré, principal owner, Sphinx Group. The Sphinx Communications Group, founded in 1987, operates one of the nation's oldest black-owned commercial on-line computer services, despite being based in a Bedford-Stuyvesant brownstone with such antiquated local-telephone service that high-speed, high-capacity Internet connection is still not possible.

But the low-tech locale, and a shoestring budget, hasn't kept Sphinx's principal partner, Sanyakhu-Sheps Amaré, from donating time, training and the company's computer-consulting services to the black community. "In 1988, we realized African-Americans were not aware enough to take advantage of our services," he said, "so we decided to give them away."

Since then, in conjunction with Medical Computer Systems, a company in Washington, where Sphinx has an office linked to the Internet, Mr. Amaré has helped the National Black Women's Health Project to electronically link their sixty-two chapters and the Harlem Churches H.I.V./AIDS Network to set up an electronic information clearinghouse on AIDS. When the National Urban League sought to develop a conferencing system, Sphinx provided free consultations and demonstrations.

> *"In 1988, we realized African-Americans were not aware enough to take advantage of our services, . . . so we decided to give them away."*

Mr. Amaré, who is 43, grew up in Harlem and went to high school at the Cardinal Farley Military Academy, a Catholic school in Rhinebeck, New York. He studied finance at Loyola University of Montreal for a year, but returned to New York to pursue a series of jobs.

Mr. Amaré was buying and selling real estate in 1984, when he bought his first personal computer. It came with a modem he did not order. He began playing with it and soon had taught himself enough on-line skills to begin his current career.

In 1994, Mr. Amaré began teaching Internet skills at the Higher Education Development Fund Career Advancement Program in the South Bronx, which has but a single computer. Each semester, around thirty students, most of them black or Hispanic, ages 17 to 21, learn to use the Internet. He gets paid to teach, but provides the Internet services free over a phone line linked to his Washington office.

> *"Black folks aren't buying as many computers, because they don't value computers as much as other things."*

"If we're going to do anything proactive," he said, "then black business people have to get into partnership with us."

Corporate Encouragement

S. Kay Gibbs, public relations, AT&T New England. Kay Gibbs is a self-described "child of the civil rights era" who came to the corporate world by way of politics.

After serving as Assistant Secretary of Transportation for Michael Dukakis when he was Governor of Massachusetts, she became legislative assistant on housing issues to Representative Barney Frank, the Massachusetts Democrat. In 1992, she joined AT&T's regional headquarters in Boston.

"Government was the instrument of change in the 60's," said Ms. Gibbs. "Now corporations are."

AT&T allows Ms. Gibbs a good deal of autonomy in her efforts to extend information technology's reach into the poorer neighborhoods of metropolitan Boston.

"They have encouraged me to go out into the community," she said. "I make the contacts and supervise a budget."

Through Ms. Gibbs, AT&T gave $100,000 to various local education, training and recruiting programs. One nonprofit social services agency in Boston, United South End Settlements, for example, is using a grant from AT&T to update its computer literacy program and another—Freedom House—is conducting an attitudinal survey about technology in predominantly black Roxbury, Massachusetts, to assess demand for computer education there.

And AT&T has helped black alumni of the Massachusetts Institute of Technology to promote an interest in math and science among young blacks and encourage them to attend the school or pursue careers in technology.

"Access is not just a matter of hooking people up to technology and the information superhighway," Ms. Gibbs said. "It's about educating and training them to empower themselves through technology.

"It doesn't profit us as a corporation to have ignorant consumers," she said. "People won't be interested in buying our products and services if they don't understand what they can do for them."

Chapter 3

An Entrepreneurial Activist

Ken Granderson, owner and founder, Inner-City Software. Ken Granderson was all set recently to teach a course in computer skills at the predominantly black Roxbury Community College in Roxbury, Massachusetts. But the class was canceled because too few students had registered.

"The fundamental problem is that blacks aren't interested," he said. "Black folks aren't buying as many computers, because they don't value computers as much as other things."

Mr. Granderson, 32, a self-described "technology evangelist," grew up in Bedford-Stuyvesant and graduated from M.I.T. in 1985 with a degree in electrical engineering. After a decade in the computer industry, in 1994 he founded Inner-City Software of Dorchester, Massachusetts, a business-productivity software and computer-consulting company. But he also set out "to do something to create a technology-based industry within our inner cities."

Inner-City's first project is an interactive CD-ROM version of "350 Years of Black History," a book published by the Boston Library. Mr. Granderson plans to sell the CD-ROM commercially. But in a project financed by the Shawmut Bank, he will also provide copies to any school, youth program or library in the Boston metropolitan area that has the equipment to use it. He plans further joint efforts with libraries.

Mr. Granderson helped Boston public high schools update their computer curriculums and donated technological expertise to the Mo Vaughn Youth Development Center in Dorchester. Mr. Granderson met Mr. Vaughn, the Boston Red Sox first baseman, while working on "350 Years of Black History."

Mr. Granderson says that more black businesspeople should become entrepreneurial activists. "Our parents didn't work two or three jobs and clean people's toilets just so we'd be middle-level managers somewhere," he said. "That's not why black history's heroes died.

"I imagine a future," he added, "with fewer big gold chains and more computers."

The Information Highway Benefits Rural Areas

by Bill Richards

About the author: *Bill Richards is a staff reporter for the* Wall Street Journal *daily newspaper.*

For years, travelers in Ainsworth, Nebraska, were greeted by a billboard that said, only half in jest, "Welcome to Ainsworth, the Middle of Nowhere." So when a gust of wind blew the sign down in 1994, it seemed like an omen of change.

While Ainsworth is far from the nearest interstate, it and many other tiny towns find themselves located right on the information superhighway. For the rest of the nation, the multimedia, megabit future may still be mostly hype and hope, but small-town America is starting to get an inkling of what it means, as the new technology blurs distinctions between rural and urban areas.

Ainsworth's public library boasts a two-way, video-conferencing unit. Sidney Salzman, the town's 67-year-old mayor, says when state officials installed the system in 1992, he figured it would be an electronic gadget gathering dust. But by now, just about everybody in town has tried it—including him. Local ministers, hospital officials, a lawyer and insurance agent use it regularly. The Over-50 Club even squeezed in front of the set to discuss their arthritis with the staff of a nursing school in far-off Omaha.

"With this thing," the mayor marvels, "we're just another suburb of Chicago."

How and Where to Live

Like the coming of the railroad a century ago and the arrival of the interstate-highway system in the 1950s, telecommunication is dramatically rearranging rural life. Such developments as fiber optics and data compression are shaking up everything from business to rural education to medicine. And perhaps as important as its influence on how people live, the new technology is starting to affect *where* they live.

During the 1980s, farm consolidations, plummeting land prices and declining

Bill Richards, "Linking Up: Many Rural Regions Are Growing Again; A Reason: Technology," *Wall Street Journal*, November 21, 1994. Reprinted by permission of the *Wall Street Journal*; © 1994 Dow Jones & Company, Inc. All rights reserved.

services drove many people out of rural areas like Ainsworth. Almost unnoticed are recent census figures showing an abrupt turnabout in the rural diaspora: more than 400 rural counties whose populations shrank during the 1980s are now growing. Hundreds of others have either stabilized or slowed their population loss since 1990.

In all, during the first two years of the 1990s, rural counties gained nearly 900,000 new residents. That is a sharp contrast to the previous decade, when the future looked so bleak that some planners suggested turning the Great Plains back over to the buffalo. So rapid and unexpected has the population turnabout been that U S West Communications, which services 10 states in the Great Plains and Northwest, now blames the rural influx for swamping its installers.

The "Wire" Brings Jobs

While some of that influx is caused by retirees or companies seeking lower-cost environs, technology not only is enabling those trends, but exerting a pull of its own, says Calvin Beale, a senior demographer at the U.S. Department of Agriculture. Mr. Beale says advanced-communications technology is starting to allow small towns to hold on to existing jobs and attract new ones.

"Every survey shows more people want to live in small towns than can find jobs there," he says. "If you wire them, they will come."

Nowhere is this field of dreams phenomenon more evident than in Nebraska, where nearly half the 1.8 million residents still reside in pinprick communities scattered across the state. The 1980s hammered Nebraska, with 83 of its 93 counties losing population. Since 1990, however, all but 20 counties are either gaining residents or have stabilized.

John Allen, a rural sociologist at the University of Nebraska, says it is no coincidence the state's population turnaround tracks the growth of communication technology here. "After the 1980s," says Dr. Allen, "we looked around and said we have a decision to make: We can do nothing and just watch our population drain away, or we can try some creative things to hold on to our people."

Nebraska officials began prodding local telephone companies and other businesses to invest in fiber optics, digital switches and other high-tech gear. "We told industry, 'You build it, and we'll be the anchor tenant,' " says William Miller, director of Nebraska's division of communications.

> *"Every survey shows more people want to live in small towns than can find jobs there. . . . If you wire them, they will come."*

Some 6,700 miles of fiber-optic cable has been laid across Nebraska cornfields, providing a pathway for large amounts of digitized data used by corporations and high-resolution, two-way video. State officials are using the system to sponsor a host of small-town experiments in telemedicine and "distance learning." All but five of the state's county seats are linked now to the fiber-optic network.

"Nebraska has excelled at adapting to the communications revolution," says Colleen Murphy, a rural-policy specialist at the Center for the New West, a Denver-based, public-policy think tank. Ms. Murphy says a handful of states including Nebraska, North Carolina and Iowa are "really on the cutting edge in using these technologies in everyday life."

> *"Access to 'the fiber'... sometimes can spell the difference between life and death."*

For example, Aurora, Nebraska, with about 3,800 residents, has become something of a case study in high tech's impact in the state. During the 1980s, more than a dozen empty storefronts lined the town's courthouse square, and population had begun to dwindle. "There was a time when there were only two choices of jobs if you stayed here," says Phillip Nelson, president of Hamilton Telecommunications, the local telephone company. "You could farm, or you could clerk in the Coast to-Coast store."

Payoff for Business and Education

Nowadays, Aurora's unemployment is under 1.5 percent, and there are no vacancies on the town square. Three transcontinental fiber-optic cables cross surrounding Hamilton County, enabling Iams Co., the pet-food manufacturer, to link its heavily automated Aurora plant with corporate headquarters in Dayton, Ohio, as well as with shippers and major customers around the country. That network allowed Iams to boost production and increase its local work force to 125 from 20.

"Ten years ago, fiber optics wouldn't have been among our top-10 reasons for opening a plant here," says Daniel Murphy, Iams's plant control–systems analyst in Aurora. Now, Mr. Murphy says, "It's in the top three."

Mr. Nelson's telephone company has also boosted its work force to more than 200, up from 30 in the mid-1980s when it shelled out $28,000 for its first seven miles of fiber-optic cable linking two local grain cooperatives. The company's fiber now loops across its 700-square-mile service area, and Hamilton operates a telemarketing center, a cable-television system that is tying together three towns on the fiber-optic network and a long-distance operator service handling 24 local telephone companies in Nebraska and South Dakota. Mr. Nelson is debating whether to invest in a million-dollar, state-of-the-art piece of equipment called an asynchronous transfer mode switch that would sharply boost his system's data capacity.

The 55-year-old scion of the family-owned telephone company seems a bit awed by this technology explosion. "I'm sitting here in Aurora, Nebraska, and I'm competing head-to-head with AT&T, MCI and Sprint," Mr. Nelson says. "You don't need a plant with 5,000 parking spaces to do this anymore."

In the delicate ecology of small-town survival, access to "the fiber," as Nebraskans call their high-tech transmission lines, sometimes can spell the difference between life and death.

Take Dunning, Nebraska, a community with about 135 residents, whose Sand Hills High School is one of five rural schools wired into a "distance learning" network the state set up in 1992. Dunning can't afford a foreign-language teacher, says Michael Teahon, Sand Hills' principal. Instead, 35 of Sand Hills' 65 students take Spanish from a teacher in Merna—30 miles away—by interactive television, communicating over the monitors on their classroom wall and a fax machine.

Without the system, Mr. Teahon says, Dunning's students who want to take Spanish would have to transfer to Merna. "Eventually," he says, "the smaller high school shuts down. And once a community loses its high school, it's doomed."

Donald Vanderheiden, the school superintendent in Broken Bow, another of the five towns in the network, says some school-board members balked at the annual cost of operating the video gear—about $12,000. "They saw it as just another big-spender project," he says. "I don't think very many people here understood what this system could do."

They do now. "It used to be that football was the first thing they showed visitors here," says Crystal Cole, a senior at Ansley High School, one of the schools on the network. "Now it's the fiber-optic room."

Practicing Telemedicine

Halfway across the state, in Cambridge, change is coming in the form of telemedicine. On a recent afternoon, the town's three doctors sit stiffly in front of a pair of interactive video screens in Cambridge Memorial Hospital, preparing the state's first telemedicine patient—a local man whose leg pain is too severe to allow him to travel. Instead, a neurosurgeon at the University of Nebraska Medical Center in Omaha arranges to examine the man on the video unit. The specialist delivers an opinion on the spot and faxes a more complete diagnosis two days later.

"We didn't even know what we could do when we put in our order for a lot of this equipment," says James Jackson, Cambridge Memorial's director of ancillary services. Now, Mr. Jackson says proudly, "any scope inserted in any orifice can be monitored at the other end of the cable."

"They're pushing the information superhighway because it will put them on a par with bigger states."

Cambridge Memorial is hoping to extend its reach even further. The 29-bed hospital is negotiating to hook up with Minnesota's Mayo Clinic: Mayo specialists would consult by two-way video while a Cambridge Memorial doctor examines a patient hundreds of miles away.

"We can do Mayo's initial workup or any follow-ups right here by telemedicine,"

Mr. Jackson says. The prognosis: "New patients and new jobs," he says.

Telemedicine experts say just about every large medical center in the country is experimenting with similar two-way outreach programs for patients living in rural parts of states like Nebraska, Idaho, Montana and Alaska.

"There's a lot of dirt between light bulbs in these states," says Eric Tangalos, a Mayo Clinic community-medicine consultant and a board member of the American Telemedicine Association. "They're pushing the information super-highway because it will put them on a par with bigger states."

Researchers are just beginning to study the impact of communications technology on rural areas. They say the nation's traditional economic development patterns may be in for a dramatic recasting. "We are right on the edge of a new form of social and economic organization," says the University of Nebraska's Dr. Allen. "We are rapidly approaching the point where technology empowers people to change their living patterns in the United States. People will be able to take their family and their skills and settle somewhere based on quality of life, not on how close they'll be to the big-city job market. That's a departure from the traditional form of social organization in this country."

Does that mean Ainsworth can forget about replacing its "Middle of Nowhere" sign? Perhaps, says William Beyers, chairman of the University of Washington's geography department.

Dr. Beyers's research team recently interviewed 240 service-industry employers in rural areas, asking them why they located where they did. What he found, he says, was a proliferation of accountants, management consultants and architects moving to small towns. "These people are deeply into computers and telecommunications," Dr. Beyers says. "They can work in small towns and sell the information to clients elsewhere."

A Two-Edged Sword

But Dr. Beyers says his team also found jobs flowing down the fiber-optic cable away from small communities. "We found telecommunications pulling jobs out of small towns by eliminating branch offices for insurance companies and banks," he says. "This is a two-edged sword."

Mr. Salzman, Ainsworth's mayor, says he isn't worried. Things are looking up here since the 1980s, when the town lost 15% of its population. Ainsworth's Chevy dealership has reopened, adding a dozen new jobs. Kelly Cobb, the manager, says he has used the dealership's computer, which scans inventories across nine states, for about 20% of his new-car sales. In 1992, Jerry Koszut moved his computer-designing business, Up-'n'-Running, to Ainsworth, his wife's hometown, after burglars trashed his home in Phoenix two years ago. "I said I don't need this. And you know what, I didn't," says Mr. Koszut, who plans to hire two new employees.

After five years without a new house, four have been built here in 1994. "We're getting healthy," says the mayor. "We're the envy of the area."

Virtual Reality Can Help Disabled Persons

by William Kelly and Patrick Kinsella

About the authors: *William Kelly is a writer and Patrick Kinsella is a researcher specializing in virtual reality. Both authors live in Derry, Northern Ireland.*

Virtual Reality is based on the fact that humans do not directly experience reality. What we receive is information through the senses which is interpreted by the brain as reality. Information therefore is what reality is for us; and if we can tailor information to the brain we can generate a reality which is indistinguishable from the 'real' thing.

Opponents fear that the new technology may end up serving as a mere escape from reality becoming, as it were, an electronic narcotic. So it is important to state what Virtual Reality actually is. It is a computer-generated mind-space with input and output devices that enable the user to interact with it and experience it. What is in that space depends on the programmes in the computer's memory. These may be lifelike or fantasy objects. They can be anything the imagination can conceive, ranging from important files to harmless baubles—you can play tennis or fly through galaxies.

Sensory Devices

The input and output devices currently in use are gloves that sense the movements of hand, fingers and arm; body suits that monitor body movements; Head Mounted Displays (HMDs) that show the three-dimensional environment; and stereophones that relay three-dimensional sound. In a 3D 'virtual world' what you do and how you do it depends on a hand gesture, or a nod, or even a sound. It is this enablement technology that is the focus of much serious research geared to people with disabilities. You do not use a computer: you wear it. The implications for those with physical or mental disabilities are tremendous.

In the 'virtual office' a severely disabled worker can enjoy equal status with anyone else. Blind people or those with sight deficiencies will be able to relate to information more audibly or tactually. Deaf people will be able to manipulate information visually. Voice-recognition and speech-synthesis devices are already available. Walter J. Greenleaf of Greenleaf Medical Systems, California, has created a prototype using a Dataglove and a Macintosh computer to control a telephone receptionist station. Using hand gestures the receptionist can instruct the computer to answer and route telephone calls or to activate pre-recorded messages. This highlights the specific nature of Virtual Reality. In cyberspace one is not merely a voyeur but an actor. Disabled people have the opportunity to accomplish tasks and have experiences which would otherwise be unattainable.

> *"In the 'virtual office' a severely disabled worker can enjoy equal status with anyone else."*

For those with severe disabilities, systems like BioMuse are being developed that use the biological signals generated by the eyes, the muscles and the brain. For example the user's eye movements can manipulate the cursor on the screen. The point to which she directs her gaze is the point to which the cursor moves. In this way she can navigate her way around the menu of a word processor. By using additional input of jaw muscle tension she can write complete documents. In the same way she can move through a three-dimensional Virtual Reality space using muscle tension to access files or dialogue with objects in general.

Advances in this field are now centering on brainwave detection devices that will allow the user to interface with the computer simply by thinking. The combination of electroencephalogram (EEG) pattern recognition and muscle movements will greatly help disabled people use new technology.

Sight and Sound

People with sight impairment can have the visual content of their screens tailored so as to be visible whether by altering colours of objects or accentuating borders. Audio-based games are being developed that will enable blind people to interact with fantasy worlds every bit as exciting as those enjoyed by the sighted.

Researchers are working on many other projects that will enable disabled people to express themselves more easily. A system called SLARTI, for example, will translate sign language into any spoken language. By bending fingers or wiggling a stick in the mouth, a disabled person can learn and play a musical instrument. Using other techniques for representing sounds visually she can be taught to see musical notation. Such sounds can also be rendered as tactile stimuli, so that the disabled person can create musical forms that are beyond the abilities of the so-called 'able-bodied' person. Meanwhile, psychologists are also looking to Virtual Reality to help treat mental afflictions such as depression and phobias of all types.

These and other developments promise to open up the world to those who hitherto have been barred from what the majority take for granted. If you look at it from this point of view Virtual Reality looks not like an escape from reality but a way into it.

The Information Highway May Not Benefit Society

by Reed Karaim

About the author: *Reed Karaim, who was a newspaper journalist for fifteen years, now writes fiction and magazine articles.*

Early in 1995 Kirkpatrick Sale, co-founder in the 1980s of New York's short-lived Green Party, was among 26 "visionaries" gathered on the stage of Manhattan's Town Hall by *Utne Reader*, commonly referred to as the *Reader's Digest* of the counterculture. When Sale's turn came to share his vision with the audience, he was concise.

The 57-year-old activist and writer took a sledgehammer and, swinging it over his shoulder like a lumberjack, smashed a personal computer set up on-stage. The first blow connected with the monitor, which bounced and exploded in a puff of shattered glass. The second crushed the keyboard into shards of plastic. "It turned out to be incredibly satisfying," Sale said afterward. "I was surprised, really, how good it felt."

Critics' Caution

Americans are told almost daily that we have entered the "information age" or even the "second industrial revolution," a time of endlessly unfolding technological wonder. *Newsweek*, in a recent special issue, went so far as to declare that we are in the midst of a kind of second Creation, the Big Bang followed by the "Bit Bang." From *Army Times* to MTV, the country is rushing to go on-line, digitize, dive down the virtual rabbit hole. But there is a little-noticed circle of social critics who beg to differ. Metaphorically at least, they are hammering away at our enthusiasm for the high-tech future.

This movement, if it can be granted the force of that word, ranges from neo-Luddites [people who oppose technological change], like Sale, who see our souls trickling away every time a fluorescent light flickers on, to Internet jockeys who wish to raise a few caution flags about where we are headed. Neil Postman, a

Reed Karaim, "Technology and Its Discontents," *Civilization*, May/June 1995. Reprinted by permission.

communications professor at New York University whose book *Technopoly* is one of the movement's touchstones, captures the ambivalence that characterizes many critics when he calls himself a "loving resistance fighter."

The technology-resistance movement clearly operates in occupied territory, but it may have more sympathizers than are apparent. When Bill Henderson, a New York publisher, wrote an Op-Ed piece in the *New York Times* in 1994 announcing the neo-Luddite "Lead Pencil Club," he received more than 600 letters of support.

Declaring his intention to "create a pothole on the Information Superhighway," Henderson took the pencil as a symbol of the virtues of old-fashioned communication and declared [American naturalist] Henry David Thoreau the club's honorary founder. "I did it with a sense of humor," Henderson says. "But these letters I've gotten are impassioned. People are very upset, particularly by computers, the info net. They thought nobody else felt this way."

A sign of the pervasive triumph of technological culture is that most critics approach it gingerly. It's as if the PLO [Palestine Liberation Organization] felt compelled to label itself "the Greater Israel Improvement Society" just to get people to listen. For what the resistance proposes is no less than a remaking of the map, a change in world view. It asks us to contemplate the possibility that we are shredding our society on the bright, shiny edge of our own cleverness.

Humans and Machines

The enigma of humankind's relationship to its machines has always been how much we are remade by the things we make. The Wright brothers, for example, gave birth not just to the airplane but also to the pilot and, finally, the bombardier. And so, is it fair to ask if the spark of imagination on which humanity takes wing ultimately lights the fires of Dresden?

The first response is that new technologies are simply tools, and whether they help or harm society depends on the wisdom of those who use them. The airplane leads no more inevitably to the fire-bombings of World War II than a hammer does to a bludgeoning. "Machines themselves are not good or bad, relationships between people are good or bad," says Phil Agre, a professor at the University of California, San Diego, whose on-line Internet news service, "The Red Rock Eater," examines issues central to the information age. "Technologies don't do things. People do things."

> **"Technology . . . is never *neutral.*"**

But in the eyes of the resistance, this is the fundamental error. Technology, they say, is *never* neutral. "Embedded in every tool is an ideological bias," writes Postman, "a predisposition to construct the world as one thing rather than another." He notes an old adage—"to a man with a hammer, everything looks like a nail" (apparently, even a keyboard). He then adds, "To a man with a computer, everything looks like data."

The 20th century has been distinguished by transforming technologies: the automobile, the airplane, the atomic bomb, the television. The computer leads the way into uncharted ground. Voice-activated programming, robotics, artificial intelligence, mechanical implants, biotechnology—all of these "advances" blur the distinction between human and machine. Already our computers greet

> *"The computer is an excellent tool for rote memorization, but the essence of learning remains learning to think."*

us with more courtesy than most salesclerks, have more facts on hand than our teachers and are more fun than half the people we meet at parties. On the other hand, it is not unknown for programmers to dream in computer code.

In this world, we have elevated the computer in status until it has become a kind of squared-off Buddha squatting at the center of our culture. It is the first machine that "thinks" and, until 1994, when the Pentium chip unexpectedly proved unable to do certain calculations, was widely accepted as thinking flawlessly. "The computer doesn't make mistakes" has become an offhand way of comparing the rickety structure of human reasoning with the sleek precision of silicon-chip logic. Among artificial-intelligence engineers, consciousness is often considered to be only a particularly thorny software challenge. Once we can harness sufficient processing capability with the right program, it is assumed computers will quickly leave us behind. In the oft-quoted words of Ed Fredkin, an artificial-intelligence specialist formerly at M.I.T. [Massachusetts Institute of Technology], "If we are lucky, they will keep us as pets."

How can the mind, a clumsy apparatus that forgets where it has left the car keys, hope to compete with a device that can regurgitate the complete works of Shakespeare? Theodore Roszak, a professor of history at California State University, argues that we have fallen into a trap in measuring ourselves by the machine, a trap exalting the limited, linear, data-processing capabilities of silicon chips over the intuitive nature of human consciousness.

In Roszak's view, human thought is a marvel of intuition and epiphany. The difference between man and machine, Roszak says, is understanding that "the mind thinks with ideas, not with information." In his book *The Cult of Information*, Roszak argues that the "data merchants" have endlessly hyped the significance of bits of information as they hurried us down the road to the new age. But "master ideas"—the religious and philosophical teachings at the center of our culture and consciousness—"are based on no information whatever." An example: "All men are created equal." This idea cannot be proved through the accumulation, addition or subtraction of data, but nonetheless millions have found it to be self-evident.

Computers and Data

None of this has stopped educators from rushing to embrace computers as classroom tools, spurred on by manufacturers who have donated hardware to schools or sold it at greatly reduced prices. Roszak, however, notes that there is no empirical evidence that learning by computer is superior to learning through traditional methods. The computer is an excellent tool for rote memorization, but the essence of learning remains learning to *think*. Even as a tool for simple study, the computer cannot bypass the laborious process of mastering difficult subjects. As Princeton's Edward Tenner notes, "The trick isn't getting ancient Greek texts on-line, the trick is getting somebody to read ancient Greek."

Electronic databases have become common tools for academics, journalists and countless others who routinely sift through large amounts of information in their work. This reliance is also not without its problems. The most common are errors that refuse to die, rising like vampires from the grave to be reprinted in report after report. Still, electronic databases have made more information more accessible to a greater number of people. The Library of Congress's new on-line system, "THOMAS," for example, makes congressional data that used to be the province of Capitol Hill insiders available to anyone with access to the Internet. THOMAS, named for the Library's founder, Thomas Jefferson, provides the full text of bills, press releases and committee schedules in one location on the Net.

Remember the paperless office that was coming with the computer? Ever ponder how the push-button phone, which was supposed to speed up dialing, led to the automated systems that make simple calls last half a lifetime? (. . . *Dial 9 for more options . . . Dial 7 for accounts receivable . . . Please enter your account number now . . . Please hold . . . I'm sorry, the computer system is down . . . Thank you for calling Transworld MegaBank, your friendly neighborhood bank . . .)*

The curious way the world has of getting even, defeating our best efforts to speed it up and otherwise improve it, has been termed "revenge effect" by Tenner, who has written extensively on our interaction with technology. Tenner believes that the failure of technology to solve problems can often be traced to the interaction between machine and man. Freeways, intended to speed travel, lead to suburbs, which end up spreading urban sprawl out instead of up, so commuting times climb. Computers make it remarkably easy to copy and print files, so many more files are copied and printed, and the paperless office fills up with paper.

> *"If 500 channels mean 300 I Love Lucy reruns, . . . are we really richer as a society?"*

New technology can also add extra layers of complication to what were simpler tasks. The automated phone system is only one example. Computers have allowed airlines to create fare systems so complicated that they cannot be understood without the aid of another computer. In *Harvard Magazine*, Tenner writes that the airline industry has recorded as many as 600,000 fare changes in 24 hours. This phenomenon, which Tenner calls "recomplicating," also explains why the clock on your VCR is blinking at 12:00 right now.

On-Line Computer Networks

Now comes, at the heart of the information age, the on-line computer network, brought to you by your personal computer. The technologies are still awkward, but we can already shop, bank, read magazines, sample videos, make plane reservations and find a date through our computers. We can also "chat." The word has been remade to mean casual communication through typing.

Boy, can we chat. America Online, the country's most popular on-line service, with 2 million subscribers, resembles nothing so much as an electronic tower of babble. Log in and you can find electronic conversations rolling along about everything from comic books to Clinton. Television, sensing its reign over the electronic world threatened, is rushing to catch up. Soon, Vice President Al Gore and House Speaker Newt Gingrich tell us with the enthusiasm of 16-year-olds contemplating the ultimate car stereo, we will be able to get 500 channels, many interactive.

But if 500 channels mean 300 *I Love Lucy* reruns, if interaction means home shopping and a chance to play Mortal Kombat head-to-head, are we really richer as a society? Librarian of Congress James H. Billington, describing the Library's plans for putting materials on the information superhighway, offers a cautionary note: "Our democracy and, more than ever, our economic vitality depend on

> *"The idea that on-line debate represents a flowering of democracy also comes under attack."*

the kind of active mind that the print culture—the culture of the book and of the newspaper—has historically nurtured, and that television, feeding an essentially passive spectator habit, does not."

The benefits promised from the virtual world are virtually endless—more information, more entertainment, more choices. The on-line networks, supporters say, amount to a flowering of democracy, a million voices raised—*empowerment*. "On line it doesn't matter what color you are, how handsome you are, where you went to school," says Mike Godwin, an attorney who writes frequently about networks. "What matters is the quality of your ideas."

Escaping from the Real World

But what "revenge effect" will the virtual world have? The technology-resistance movement begins by pointing out that we are cobbling together virtual communities while our real cities crumble, at least partly because our sense of common purpose has frayed. Today, only about 5 percent of American households are on-line, but what happens, the critics wonder, when half the country is wired?

Will we escape the unpleasant complications of the world outside our locked doors by opting for communities in "cyberspace," where we can enjoy the company of people who share our interests and our views? Where the streets never need to be cleaned and you don't have to keep an eye on your neighbor's house? What happens if the sirens outside become too distracting? Will we simply buy insulated drapes?

"Prescribing greater mobility—whether automotive or electronic—as an antidote to society's fragmentation is like recommending champagne as a hangover remedy," says Tenner.

Richard Sclove, founder of the Loka Institute in Amherst, Massachusetts, which studies society's relationship with technology, has drawn fire from on-line enthusiasts by suggesting that we will need to find ways to temper the effects of virtual communities on everyday life. One possibility, Sclove says, is raising on-line access rates one night a week, levying a tax that would be used to promote genuine community activities. The idea is that Tuesday nights, for example, might become "community nights," when Americans unplug themselves and wander out goggle-eyed to vote, attend town meetings, relax and involve themselves in the things that need doing in the real world.

Smaller businesses, the neighborhood hardware and grocery stores already hurt by discount chains, may need similar help to fend off on-line shopping services, Sclove says. If not, "cyberspace will finish what Wal-Mart started."

The idea that on-line debate represents a flowering of democracy also comes under attack. Critics say we are mistaking the ability to voice an opinion for the ability to influence decisions. You can contact the White House through e-mail, but your message has no better chance of reaching the eyes of the president than it ever did.

"Everybody always talks about how [every advance in mass communication] is going to help the little guy," Tenner says. "But then the powers that be see how they can use the technology and they wind up using and controlling it quite well."

The *littlest* guy, the person at the bottom of the economic ladder, may simply be left out. The quality of your ideas doesn't matter very much if you can't get online. Tenner notes that the information "revolution" is unique in requiring an entrance fee of $1,200 or more for a computer. Godwin and others argue that you can buy a used system for much less. You can, but you'll find precious little software to run on it.

Those who see a flowering of democracy in computer networks

> *"The new problem is information glut."*

generalize from their own middle- or upper-class experiences and assume the skills needed to go on-line are universal, observes Sonia Jarvis, a communications professor at George Washington University. She cites the finding of a Department of Education study that nearly half the U.S. adult population has difficulty dealing with complex information. In the poorest urban areas, she says, up to 25 percent of the homes do not even have phones. "How much sense does it make for the Speaker of the House [Newt Gingrich] to talk about putting lap-

tops in the ghetto, when the rest of the infrastructure there makes that meaning-
less?" she asks. "When they can't read? When their schools are falling apart?"

A Glut of Information

So many images, words and other items are being cataloged and stored electronically that some librarians worry about our ability to retrieve what we need.
"The great problem of the 19th century was how to get more information to
more people fast and in diverse forms," says Postman. "The new problem is information glut." One imagines future explorers digging into long-forgotten
databases the way archaeologists unearth lost cities, finding who knows what
buried in the deepening sediment of the information age.

John R. Stilgoe, a professor of visual and environmental studies at Harvard,
has noted the subtle degradation that occurs as information is microfilmed, digitized or moved on-line. The idea that something is preserved when it is transferred to the new technologies is an illusion, according to Stilgoe. What is preserved is a *facsimile*. The distinction
can be minor if it is a piece of text
but significant if it is an image or the
reproduction of an object.

> *"Throughout history, there
> have been those who saw our
> doom approaching with
> every new contrivance."*

Stilgoe, who refuses to have a computer in his office because he says it inevitably ends up the center of attention,
led a battle at Harvard against a plan to put much of the university library's archives
of old magazines and other periodicals on microfilm. In his research, Stilgoe has
examined old advertising to compare the fortunes of the automobile and railroad industries. There is a point in the early 20th century, he thinks, where advertising reveals the shift in the industries' fortunes—the train ads go from color to black and
white while the automobile ads spring into glorious color for the first time.

"That tells you a tremendous amount," Stilgoe says. But it would have been
lost with the transfer to microfilm, which records only in black and white. (Recognizing the legitimacy of the issue, Harvard decided to allow continued access
to the original publications in storage.) The Library of Congress has moved to
make its wealth of materials more broadly available through digitization. But
Billington says the Library recognizes the distinctive value of the printed word
and will continue to collect and make generally available books, magazines,
newspapers and the rest. "Only a small fraction of humanity's vast paper record
will be—or should be—digitized in the foreseeable future," he says.

The ability of computers to "enhance" images goes to the core of the resistance movement's objections to the virtual world. When we look at pictures of
distant galaxies clarified by computer, are we looking into the far corners of the
universe or the mind of the programmer? When we have redefined words such
as *chat, community, visit* and *presence*, they ask, haven't we yielded some part
of ourselves in the process?

Throughout history, there have been those who saw our doom approaching with every new contrivance, from the written alphabet to the television. When some cave dweller first lit his own fire, a guy dressed in skins sitting two rocks down probably turned to his buddy and said, "Oh man, I'm not sure *this* is a good idea."

Socrates worried that the written word might cripple learning. The medieval gristmill, the crossbow and the printing press were so threatening to the established order that political and religious leaders tried to ban or restrict their use. By the time the original Luddites came on the scene in the early 19th century, they were, at least indirectly, the inheritors of a tradition.

Kirkpatrick Sale, who happily smashed a computer in the opening of our story, has published *Rebels Against the Future*, a history of the Luddite movement and its relevance to today. The Luddites were a product of England's transformation into an industrial economy, which sharply lowered income and employment among the working class. The shift was particularly painful in cloth manufacturing, which had been a cottage industry until new mills and looms made it the business of factories. Suddenly, fewer weavers were required, and those who were working found themselves toiling in brutally primitive factories.

The people of England's industrial heartland reacted by breaking looms, burning factories and waging a war on the machine that lasted roughly from 1811 to 1816. They took their name from Ned Ludd, an early protester who was probably mythical. The British government responded by dispatching 14,000 troops to put down the protests and by making the act of destroying factory equipment a crime punishable by death.

"It seems so symbolic that the industrial revolution is won when the idea of killing a machine becomes a capital crime," Sale says. "There was only one voice raised against it in Parliament—George Gordon, Lord Byron . . . the great Romantic poet."

Effects on Workers

It ought to be noted that historians are divided about how much English workers suffered from the industrial revolution. There are those who argue that the cottage system of production has been falsely romanticized, and that life improved in modest ways for some workers who moved from the countryside to cities.

"For every software designer and laser surgeon, there will be more waiters, janitors and nurse's aides."

There have been no angry mobs taking hammers to the robots in auto plants, but the second industrial revolution has paralleled the first for many workers. Manufacturing jobs have fallen from about 30 percent to about 15 percent of the labor force. Job loss to computerized automation—the robot arms that toil tirelessly in so many factories—has been estimated at roughly half a million a year from 1988 to 1994. Wassily Leontief, a Nobel Prize–winning economist, has suggested that people's role in manufacturing may go the way of the horse's in farming. Those of us too young to be put out to pasture will seek work in a changed world. Peter Drucker, a social scientist and writer, estimates that a third of us will be "knowledge workers." But for every software designer and laser surgeon, there will be more waiters, janitors and nurse's aides toiling in lower-paying service industries. . . .

Rethinking Technology

Huddled in our homes amid neglected cities, our brains numbed into a stupor while our hearts race like engines popped into neutral because of television, turning late at night to the illusory companionship of strangers in electronic worlds where those who disagree with our prejudices can be dispatched with a keystroke, unable to relate to the leisurely reality of a sunset or trees creaking in the wind, surrounded by gadgets, yet more alone than ever—Is this really to be our future? There is a kind of apocalyptic, end-of-the-millennium gloom, a distaste for the world we have made, that permeates the thinking of the neo-Luddites. Maybe the world is being swallowed up by the technological spider, but it is also undeniably true that moose are drifting back into the Great Plains, most children are still amazed by a dandelion, and a good lightning storm can reduce even jaded urbanites to mute awe.

It seems clear that our machines and our technological society need to be remade to adhere more closely to the spirit of humanity. We should view with greater skepticism the latest electronic wonders paraded before our eyes. The rush to computerize our schools and our lives needs more debate. Smashing computers may be extreme, but turning one off can be good for the soul.

> *"We should view with greater skepticism the latest electronic wonders paraded before our eyes."*

Still, we are tool-making creatures. It is hard to see, absent a neo-Luddite theocracy, how this can be changed. Or why we should deny the creative spirit that finds expression not only in Pablo Picasso but also in Edison. In his novel *Player Piano*, Kurt Vonnegut conjures up a future in which technology has left people useless and unemployed. The disenchanted rise up and destroy the machines. Yet in the last scene, some men come across a broken orange-drink machine and begin fiddling with it. "We'll fix that, won't we, Bud?" one of them says excitedly. And the strange, often troubling compulsion humanity has to make and remake its world sparks anew.

The Information Highway Will Not Connect Most of the World's People

by Leonard Marks

About the author: *Leonard Marks is an entertainment lawyer and a former assistant U.S. attorney general.*

Travelers beware! If you are planning to use the Global Information Superhighway (GIS), be prepared for potholes, barriers and detours.

When Vice President Albert Gore announced the Clinton Administration's plans for this project, his remarks were acclaimed by a world conference in Buenos Aires. The headlines featured the opportunities for world communications, but made no mention of the formidable obstacles that lay ahead.

The vice president's speech heralded a new age, pointing out that,

> Telecommunications is an essential component of political, economic, social and cultural development. It fuels the global information society and economy which is rapidly transforming local, national and international life and, despite physical boundaries, is promoting better understanding between peoples.

No Telephone Access

While the Western world routinely enjoys direct dialing, receives faxes and television programs from remote points of the globe and looks forward to computer hookups via Internet and other whiz kids' inventions, the developing world yearns for a Plain Old Telephone (POT). When the telephone is installed, they pray daily that there will be a dial tone and that the receiver on the other end will be in service. Here are the grim facts:

- Two-thirds of the world's population have no access to telephone service.
- Over one-half of the world's population live in countries with less than one telephone for every one hundred people.
- Three-fourths of the world's population live in countries with ten or fewer

Leonard Marks, "Detours Along the Information Highway," *Washington Times*, October 16, 1994. Reprinted with permission.

telephones for every one hundred people.

- Low-income countries have less than a 5 percent share of global telephone lines but have 55 percent of the world's population.

When the International Telecommunications Union [ITU] reviewed this issue in 1984, it commented:

> While telecommunications is taken for granted as a key factor . . . in industrialized countries and as an engine of growth, in most developing countries the telecommunications system is not adequate even to sustain essential services. In many areas, there is no system at all.

As a goal, they proposed that by the year 2000, all mankind should be within easy reach of a telephone—i.e., within walking distance.

Telecommunications Barriers

Efforts are being made to remove these barriers. However, the financial outlays would be enormous. The World Bank has estimated that $40 billion a year will be needed in the five-year period from 1995–99 to build the networks in developing countries to meet international standards. In addition, some $10–15 billion needs to be spent to modernize the networks in Eastern Europe. This would amount to a grand total of $250 billion, which is four times the level of spending of the 1970s and three times the level of the 1980s—needless to say, a formidable barrier.

Even though telecommunications operations have been very profitable and have shown returns on capital of 10–20 percent, telecommunications entities often have difficulty finding investment capital. Investors have been discouraged by management ineptness in many developing countries, compounded by glaring problems in procurement. One horrible example in West Africa disclosed a cost of $20,000 to add one extra telephone line for reasons which the ITU says are "unclear." These factors make a $250 billion investment for new construction more than a pothole.

"Three-fourths of the world's population live in countries with ten or fewer telephones for every one hundred people."

International travelers are aware of the existing telecom barriers throughout the developing world. Telephones are usually out of order and take a long time to repair. Even when the telephone does work, difficulties are encountered because of the shortage of equipment and inadequate maintenance. In peak periods, this situation becomes critical and frequently more than half of the calls fail to connect. Recognizing this problem, sophisticated users, when they are successful in getting a line connection, keep it open all day even though they may use it only sporadically, denying everyone else the opportunity to communicate. During peak periods, all too frequently it becomes impossible to call anywhere.

In addition to these technological potholes, which could be cured, formidable man-made obstacles still exist because of political or social differences. As an example, for years the neighboring states of Israel and Jordan would not allow the use of existing telephone lines to connect these two points. When they diplomatically shook hands, they removed these "obstacles" and today, direct telephone communication is possible. However, in many parts of the world, areas are isolated because of political and social differences.

Advocates for the GIS proclaim the wonders of satellites, fiber optics, data networks, cellular phones, interactive video and the miracles of the computer age. Their enthusiasm is justified but should be confined to a small part of the globe— the United States, Western Europe, Japan and pockets of industrial growth. Two-thirds of the world's population—the telecom "have nots"—will continue to read about these developments while they yearn for the good old POT.

Corporate Control of the Information Highway Threatens the Public Interest

by Herbert I. Schiller

About the author: *Herbert I. Schiller is a visiting professor at American University in Washington, D.C., and the author of* The Mind Managers, Mass Communications, *and* American Empire *and* Culture Inc.: The Corporate Takeover of Public Expression.

President Clinton was elected to restore prosperity to the American economy. From the beginning, high tech has been the chosen instrument to achieve this end. Computerization and high-speed telecommunications are the promising routes, in Washington's view, to economic revitalization. How justified this linkage is, we leave aside for the moment.

What is becoming clear is that in pursuit of the goal of economic stimulation through high-powered information technology, the democratic character of American society is at risk. Well on the way to extinction is the public sector of American life—the space where social purpose takes precedence over private gain. Increasingly, public schools, public libraries, and the public arts are endangered species.

Much of what is happening is centered in the production and distribution apparatus for images and messages. The nation's informational-media-cultural sphere is the terrain of the sweeping but relatively unexamined changes. The White House and other prominent voices see an expanded, state-of-the-art electronic information system as the key to general economic improvement, individual well-being and substantial profitability.

The NII Agenda for Action

In September 1993, the federal government laid out these expectations in a comprehensive report entitled "The National Information Infrastructure:

Herbert I. Schiller, "Electronic Highway to Where?" Reprinted from *National Forum: The Phi Kappa Phi Journal*, vol. 74, no. 2 (Spring 1994), © 1994 Herbert I. Schiller, by permission of the publishers.

Agenda for Action." The proposed "Agenda for Action" is "the construction of an advanced National Information Infrastructure (NII), a seamless web of communication networks, computers, databases, and consumer electronics that will put vast amounts of information at users' fingertips."

When this infrastructure is developed, the government claims, it "can help unleash an information revolution that will change forever the way people live, work, and interact with each other." More specifically, the new information "highway" "will enable U.S. firms to compete and win in the global economy, generating good jobs for the American people and economic growth for the nation. . . .

> *"[The radio spectrum] will become the property of those who can bid the most for slices of it."*

[T]he NII can transform the lives of the American people—ameliorating the constraints of geography, disability, and economic status."

Powerful expectations! How will this happy state come into being? The President's advisers see the physical components—cameras, scanners, keyboards, telephones, fax machines, computers, switches, compact discs, video and audio tape, cable, wire, satellites, optical fiber, transmission lines, microwave nets, television, printers, etc.—integrated and interconnected "in a technologically neutral manner, so that no one industry will be favored over any other."

The Private Sector and the NII

At the same time the presidential document repeatedly emphasizes that "The private sector will lead in the [development and] deployment of the NII." "Agenda for Action," in fact, acknowledges that "the private sector is already developing and deploying such an infrastructure." This may be the understatement of the year!

Vast corporate mergers and acquisitions, which show no signs of abating, are transforming the domestic informational-media-cultural landscape. Telephone, computer, cable, and entertainment companies, already dominant in their fields, are combining and making alliances that will ensure their near total envelopment of the anticipated future electronic environment.

These mergers herald a powerful corporate move to pre-empt the informational-cultural realm. Who will emerge triumphant in the current corporate rivalries for controlling position is still obscure. What is clear is that the corporate stakeholders will be few, their resources enormous and concentrated, and their concern riveted to their balance sheets.

Abandonment of the Public Interest

At the same time, the public interest faces abandonment alongside the (electronic) road. One of the telltale signs of this abandonment is a key policy set forth in the President's NII report, already on the way to implementation. It is the announced sale to private users of a chunk of frequencies in the radio spectrum—the natural (and national) resource which is used for all wireless communication. From the beginning of radio in the early days of the twentieth century, the radio spectrum, however poorly managed, has always been regarded and treated as the inalienable property of the American people. No longer! Now it will become the property of those who can bid the most for slices of it. The super communications corporations that are being feverishly created will be the major bidders.

Though the auction arrangements appear to guarantee a large number of bidders, the final outcome is hardly in doubt. The released part of the spectrum will wind up in the clutches of a few mega-corporations. This is noted in an 18 October 1993 *Business Week* commentary by Mark Lewyn titled "A Boon for Telecoms, A Break for Taxpayers" which states, "The likely outcome will be a vigorous market in licenses, with the MCIs and the AT&Ts buying the rights of the smaller, successful bidders."

The public, failing government intervention—which is hardly likely since the program is governmentally supported to begin with—is shut out. This dismaying development is given a benign gloss in the President's report. It states that the allocation and use of the radio spectrum will be "streamlined," and that the application of market principles in spectrum distribution "will promote greater flexibility."

Hokum aside, with governmental support and encouragement, message and image generation, transmission, and dissemination are being handed off to the clutch of giant corporations.

The Fate of the Internet

Selling off a parcel of public property, however, is but a modest depredation compared with the corporate appropriation of the public sphere in the offing. The stated aim of the Clinton administration is to create a National Information Infrastructure—essentially a comprehensive electronic highway that will carry voice, data, and video in digital form. But a far-flung electronic network already exists. It is the Internet.

The Internet, begun in 1969, was originally an experimental computer network organized and financed by the Department of Defense (ARPAnet). It was made available to facilitate the research of a small number of scientists, engineers, and researchers. The National Science Foundation (NSF) also contributed funds. In this period, commercial usage of the network was prohibited.

"Some view the Internet as the embodiment of a new form of (electronic) democracy."

Over time, the number of users of Internet multiplied greatly, although it remains mostly a university and research tool. Currently, however, it is estimated that there are more than 15 million users, mostly in the United States but also in 134 other countries, among which are increasing numbers of commercial enterprises. In early 1993, more than half of the registered networks were private businesses.

Still, to date, the Internet continues to be an assemblage of networks that offer relatively uninhibited expression to its many users, with individuals exchanging views and messages in a non-hierarchical system. It has been the closest approximation, in the emerging electronic information age, of an open forum for ideas and untrammeled expression. Some view the Internet as the embodiment of a new form of (electronic) democracy. Mitchell Kapor, for instance, the founder of the Lotus Development Corporation—a very successful computer software company—offers this by no means atypical assessment of the Internet in an issue of *Wired*:

> *"The democratic promise of the Internet is fading rapidly."*

> Life in cyberspace seems to be shaping up exactly like Thomas Jefferson would have wanted . . . founded on the primacy of individual liberty and a commitment to pluralism, diversity, and community . . . openness, freedom and diversity . . . is the true promise of this technology.

However hyperbolic, the Internet's initial non-commercial character and the relatively free exchange of messages it supports lend a certain plausibility to Kapor's (and others') enthusiasm. Its expansion as a national public utility would justify the belief that democracy could be strengthened with electronic communication.

But the NII outlined in the President's report, and, more tellingly, the steps under way in the corporate information technology–entertainment spheres, foretell a very different development. Public concerns are being elbowed out of the way to suit the goals of cable, telephone, and entertainment combines.

And not surprisingly, the Internet itself—which could serve as the core of the new superhighway with its initial non-commercial characteristics intact—is being pushed toward commercialization. Its subsidy from the National Science Foundation, which allowed it to remain independent of the private sector, is being [phased out]. Its commercial users are multiplying while hungrily eyeing the network's millions of users as potential advertising targets. According to Steve Stecklow of the *Wall Street Journal*, advertisers "are beginning to view the global network as a potential electronic gold mine."

Pressed from within, and almost certain to be outflanked from without, by a corporate-financed and managed electronic superhighway, the democratic promise of the Internet is fading rapidly. The "high tech vision of Jeffersonian democracy," writes Steve Lohr of the *New York Times*, "would have to be paid for by private enterprise; . . . it is big corporations that will invest the many billions of dollars over the next several years to build the information highway. Some worry that they will have no incentive to offer anything but the most profitable services."

The nation's social-informational needs that are so desperately deficient are quite likely to be submerged in a flood of entertainment and electronic gadgetry services that the corporate players are readying. On 13 October 1993 the *Wall Street Journal* reported that "After spending most of the past decade fighting tooth and nail, cable companies and phone companies are joining up to deliver an array of interactive TV and telephone services so vast that it isn't yet clear Americans are even ready for it." No matter! Ready or not, the services are on their way.

Corporate Control

Given these "realities," that is, acceptance of corporate ownership and control of the new electronic highway, Mitchell Kapor, the prophet of electronic democracy, is reduced to wistful reflection. He writes:

> The critical public choice regarding the information highway is this: If industry builds it, how happy will we be with the result? . . . The optimist in me thinks we should give telephone and cable companies every opportunity to get it right. In fact, we should seek to educate and enlighten, while developing contingency plans.

Enlightening billion-dollar corporations may be an oxymoron. At the very least, it makes the problems of teaching within the nation's public schools seem trivial.

In the new and improved electronic network, the ownership and the direction, however they are defined and presented by Washington, are corporate. It is worth recalling, therefore, that for more than one hundred years, Americans have mistrusted and sought to limit economic monopoly. The Sherman Anti-Trust Act of 1890, and a variety of state and federal measures since, were enacted to rein in the power of big money and the Trusts.

"The new economic overlords are those active in the informational-media-cultural spheres."

In the 1990s, this concern seems to have disappeared, and vast agglomerations of private resources and power have been tolerated, often encouraged. More disturbing still, the new economic overlords are those active in the informational-media-cultural spheres. Railroads, banks, and steel complexes threatened the economic well-being of nineteenth and early twentieth century citizens. Today's cultural barons threaten our minds.

A popular movement in behalf of a non-monopolistic cultural environment seems a reasonable and urgent goal in the new electronics age.

The Information Highway May Harm the Environment

by James H. Snider

About the author: *James H. Snider is a political science fellow at Northwestern University in Evanston, Illinois, and the coauthor of* Future Shop: How New Technologies Will Change the Way We Shop and What We Buy.

Over the years environmentalists have cautioned us against threats to the environment—the population explosion, nuclear radiation, pesticides, aerosols, nonrecyclable garbage, and automobile exhaust, to name just a few. But what they haven't noticed yet is the environmental menace posed by the information superhighway.

If you look at the literature of some of the organizations concerned with preserving the land, such as the Wilderness Society or the Sierra Club, you don't see the information superhighway listed as a threat. On the contrary, the information superhighway is supposed to help the environment by reducing the need for automobile and airplane travel and all the pollution they bring. In fact, some of the most ardent environmentalists also happen to be ardent advocates of the information superhighway.

Telecommuting on the Information Highway

U.S. Vice President Al Gore is a prime example. In his book *Earth in the Balance*, Gore attempts to recount the present dangers to the environment. In the chapter "A Global Marshall Plan," he advocates building an information superhighway to facilitate telecommuting as a partial solution to our problems. This, he believes, will reduce the demand for cars and the pollution that cars inevitably bring. He notes that, for "a dozen years, I have been the principal author and advocate of a proposal to build a national network of information superhighways."

James H. Snider, "The Information Superhighway as Environmental Menace." Reproduced with permission from *The Futurist* (March/April 1995), published by the World Future Society, 7910 Woodmont Ave., Suite 450, Bethesda, MD 20814.

More recently, the Clinton administration has directed the U.S. Environmental Protection Agency and the Department of Transportation to promote telecommuting, largely to improve air quality, reduce future environmental risks, and conserve energy resources. High-population centers such as New York City, Los Angeles, and Chicago are among the areas targeted. Among the many policy proposals are tax incentives for employers and individuals to change to home-based telecommuting arrangements, as well as "flexiplace" incentives similar to current "flexitime" ones.

> *"Unbeknownst to the advocates of telecommuting, the coming information superhighway portends an environmental disaster."*

Yet, unbeknownst to the advocates of telecommuting, the coming information superhighway portends an environmental disaster of the first magnitude. In the United States, where population growth is relatively subdued, it may lead to the massive destruction of the remaining forests, open land, and wild flora and fauna over the next few decades.

Rural vs. Metropolitan

Despite the huge increase over the last few hundred years, the world's population has been highly concentrated on a limited landmass. Only about 2% of the earth's land surface is covered by cities and towns. Though human beings affect much landmass through farming, tree growing, pollution, or other means, the mass of humanity has tended to congregate in metropolitan (urban or suburban) areas. Even now, the ratio of people living in metropolitan vs. rural areas continues to increase, substantially reducing the pressure on open spaces that would otherwise ensue from population increases.

In the United States, the population is also highly concentrated. About 80% of Americans live in metropolitan areas, which cover just 16% of the contiguous states. The number of Americans living in rural areas has decreased not just because of population increases in other areas, but because of changing job opportunities. In 1800, more than 90% of U.S. jobs were agricultural. Today, that figure is under 2%, and the vast majority of the remaining jobs can only be done in metropolitan areas.

Thanks to the information superhighway, this hundred-year-old trend toward metropolitan areas is about to reverse. In fact, a *Wall Street Journal* article argues that,

> Like the coming of the railroad a century ago and the arrival of the interstate highway system in the 1950s, telecommunications is dramatically rearranging rural life. . . . Almost unnoticed are recent census figures showing an abrupt turnabout in the rural diaspora. . . . In all, during the first two years of the 1990s, rural counties gained nearly 900,000 new residents.

Transportation and Population Dispersion

Throughout history, transportation technology has largely determined where people live. Before the Industrial Age, when boats dominated the movement of people and goods, major population centers were located next to major bodies of water. During the nineteenth century, railroads opened up the hinterlands and led to a vast dispersion of towns and cities clustered around railroad stops and junctions.

As transportation historian Stephen Goddard says in *Getting There: The Epic Struggle Between Road and Rail in the American Century*, the West was worthless until the railroads

> opened up the West to settlement. Pioneers rode the rails into the wilderness and seemingly overnight built new towns with supplies manufactured in the East. Towns called Omaha, Tulsa, and Wichita grew from tiny settlements to cities overnight.

In the twentieth century, the automobile led to the massive growth of suburbs surrounding traditional urban areas, as well as the growth of new cities along the interstate highway system. The interstates, says Goddard, altered

> beyond recognition where and how Americans lived. They allowed a breadwinner to commute double the distance in the same time. Sleepy farming villages at the outskirts of cities doubled their population within a decade as their cornfields gave way to row upon row of tract houses.

The information superhighway could potentially spread people out much farther than the train or automobile ever could. People may have created new urban areas or moved to suburban areas, but the difficulty of driving to "civilization" has kept them within relatively narrow distances. By eliminating the remaining transportation barriers, the information superhighway threatens a massive migration out of metropolitan areas to the relatively unspoiled hinterlands.

The Death of Rural America

Public officials representing rural areas throughout the United States (including Alaska, Idaho, Iowa, Maine, Montana, Nebraska, North Carolina, and Vermont) are advocating the information superhighway in order to stimulate business in their states. For example, U.S. Senator Conrad Burns of Montana explains in the *Congressional Record* his rationale for accelerating its building:

> Workers will travel to work on the information highways instead of our traditional highways. The cars on these information highways will be bits of information which can travel anywhere in the world instantly. . . .

> Think of it, a stockbroker could live in Circle, Montana, with a population of 931, and be in instant contact with anyone, anywhere, anyway. That person wouldn't have to burn thousands of gallons of fossil fuel each year to drive to and from work. . . . And, best of all, that person will be able to live and work in rural America.

Burns also expects the information superhighway to stem the historical out-flow of population from rural Montana to metropolitan areas in other states:

> In Montana, many of our graduating seniors want to stay in our beautiful state where the skies are blue, the water is crisp, the air is healthy, and the quality of life is good. But they are forced to leave the state to find jobs. We need to keep our best and brightest at home.

Until now, a large number of jobs have only been available in metropolitan areas. Occupations such as accounting, law, advertising, management consult-ing, and architecture tend not to thrive in more rural areas. In occupations such as movie production, book publishing, and international finance, only a few metropolitan areas hold the vast majority of jobs.

Similarly, most cultural activities have only been available in metropolitan areas. Movies, theaters, playhouses, video stores, sports events, concerts, high-quality schools, and pools of potential friends are still heavily concentrated geographically. In the future, the information superhighway will make high-quality entertainment and education increasingly available in the home or anywhere else on the planet. And as "virtual" communities sprout, the need to be physically close to friends and relatives will continue to dimin-ish. At the same time, the allure of open spaces is unlikely to diminish.

> *"The information superhighway could potentially spread people out much farther than the train or automobile ever could."*

In *A Fierce Green Fire*, a history of the environmental movement, author Philip Shabecoff says, "The migration to the suburbs was, for many if not most of the families who moved, an environmental choice for open space, greenery, cleaner air, less noise, and a generally healthier place to live." More than ever, environ-mental quality is seen as an integral part of a search for a higher standard of liv-ing. With economic and cultural restrictions removed from the quest to live in open spaces, such a quest is likely to reach a new and environmentally destruc-tive phase.

"Every survey shows that more people want to live in small towns than can find jobs there," says Calvin Beale, a senior demographer for the U.S. Depart-ment of Agriculture. "If you wire them, they will come."

"The New Yorkers Are Coming!"

So what will happen if the information superhighway is built and the popula-tion can disperse evenly throughout the land? Let's take Vermont, the self-described "Green Mountain State." The *Wall Street Journal* rated metropolitan Burlington, Vermont, as the best place in the United States to raise a family. What would happen if the relatively nearby inhabitants of New York City could find good work in Vermont (whose current population is 560,000)? Would this attract millions of people to not just visit but live in Vermont?

No definitive answer can be found. I did ask this question to half a dozen of my friends in Manhattan. All of those with families told me that they'd readily move to Vermont if only they could find good work and a solid career. Whether justified or not, it certainly can be said that Vermonters live in constant fear of an onslaught of "flatlanders" from the south. Vermont is widely perceived as a highly desirable place to live. Much of its 50% increase in population since 1950 has resulted from out-of-staters seeking the quality of life that Vermont's environment makes possible. By 1994, a majority and ever-increasing proportion of Vermont's voting-age population were out-of-staters. Vermont's governor and U.S. representative are both transplanted New Yorkers.

If we allow the information superhighway to be built, it does seem reasonable to believe that it could absolutely blight this little gem of a state. Already the few suburban areas in Vermont are chock full of expatriates from nearby metropolitan areas such as New York City and Boston. But that is merely a trickle compared with the millions who are likely to come if the information superhighway flourishes. The best and brightest will leave the urban blights and turn Vermont into one huge and spread-out suburb. They will spoil Vermont, but it will still be far better than where they came from. They will telework from their home or nearby office. Maybe Vermont will become one of the premium telelifestyle locations, but the destruction visited upon its land will not be unique.

If all Americans succeed in getting their dream homes with several acres of land, the forests and open lands across the entire continental United States will be destroyed. Even if the U.S. population were to quadruple to 1 billion, the havoc wrought on the land would not be as great as from a more even dispersal of its present 250 million. Today's one-acre apartment building with 200 families will turn into 200 five-acre homesteads spread out over 1,000 acres. Even if the average home lot only increases from a quarter of an acre to an acre, the environmental destruction would be huge.

In the past, environmentalists have not been oblivious to the environmental impact of new communications technologies. Many, for example, have bemoaned the tendency of the car to destroy open spaces and ecosystems. Shabecoff recounts Lewis Mumford's warning that "the swelling size and power of the cities was overwhelming the countryside." For Mumford, "the automobile filled in the last open spaces and was the true Frankenstein's monster of the twentieth century,

> *"The allure of open spaces is unlikely to diminish."*

surpassed only in its destructive potential by the hydrogen bomb, but more dangerous because more complacently indulged." More recently in *Healing the Planet*, Paul Ehrlich calls for "a near absolute ban on the building of new freeways and roads." But environmentalists have yet to discover that the information superhighway might not only be destructive, but far more so than the physical highways of the past.

Chapter 3

Preserving Open Spaces

The emerging information superhighway offers the potential to dramatically improve education, consumer information, democracy, entertainment, and economic growth. But it also has the potential to be the most environmentally destructive technology of the early twenty-first century.

Is there any way to gain the benefits of the information superhighway while preserving the earth's open spaces? The ideal solution would be to strengthen land-conservation incentives and laws. The government could buy or protect more land. Zoning laws could be tightened and more strictly enforced. Many such efforts are currently under way in the United States, but the pace will have to be dramatically accelerated to ward off the new onslaught on the land.

The paradox is that the very reason the land is threatened is because having open space around one's home is equated with a high standard of living. People's environmental values lead them to want to leave crowded cities and suburbs. But in doing so, they destroy the environment that attracts them there in the first place. The tendency to want a homestead with at least an acre is deeply rooted, and efforts to preserve open spaces will come into conflict with this powerful drive and the economic forces that cater to it.

> *"The best and brightest will leave the urban blights and turn Vermont into one huge and spread-out suburb."*

This leads to pessimism that traditional land-conservation measures will be enough to hold back the flood of spreading humanity. The only way to stop the flood might be to dam it at its source—to prevent information superhighways, just like interstate highways, from being built in environmentally important areas. This is the path I urge upon land conservationists—at least until traditional land-conservation measures are significantly strengthened.

The Information Highway May Not Benefit Minorities

by Libero Della Piana

About the author: *Libero Della Piana is the editor of* RaceFile, *a bimonthly journal on race relations published by the Applied Research Center in Oakland, California.*

Imagine it's the year 2005, only a few years into the future. Juana is a new public school graduate, a young woman of color, whose community and others like it have been either bypassed by, or run over on, the Information Super-highway. Her older sister graduated from high school and got a job processing orders for the phone company, but Juana can't do that: the new communications company has replaced clerks with automated voice mail processing. A couple of years ago, Juana might have been able to work part-time for her uncle who had a storefront which rented videos. But when the new communications company started transmitting copies of digitized movies on a pay-per-view basis, the video storefront went out of business.

Computer Skills

Even though she likes to read and did well in English classes at school, Juana can't even get a job shelving books at the local library without computer skills. The main library downtown has put most of the system's books and resources on-line and the local branch is only open one afternoon a week. If she was used to using computers, maybe she could get a job downtown. Since her school only had a couple of ancient Apple Macintoshes which she got to use for half an hour a week, she is scared to try to work somewhere with one of those new operating systems that don't even use a keyboard or mouse to give commands to the machine. Meanwhile, kids in distant suburbs received only the best long distance video tutoring, preparing them for the new world.

This vignette is a fictional, but possible, glimpse into the future of ordinary people of color in a world where the important space is "cyberspace." The current

Libero Della Piana, "Race in Cyberspace," *RaceFile*, March/April 1995. Reprinted with permission.

hype would have us imagine the Superhighway bringing integrated phone service, utilities payment, interactive video games, 500-channel television, and hot and cold running pay-per-view movies into our homes. Admittedly, life in cyberspace will drastically change the way we think, consume, and interact with each other, but what might the future really look like, and what is the significance of new communication technologies to people of color in the United States?

Rather than a utopian future of electronic efficiency and computer meritocracy, the future of the Information Superhighway will more likely be one of heightened economic disparity. Juana and her friends will have fewer jobs, no voice in the deluge of electronic information, and little or no "home" in the electronic networks that may be real sources of power in the future.

No On-Ramps in Communities of Color

While millions of people each week use the Internet, a national network of interconnected computer servers which is the backbone of the Information Superhighway, a very small percentage of people actually have access to its services. Most people of color, in fact, don't even have access to computers, modems, and other tools needed to acquire even the most basic online information. The November 1994 issue of *Emerge* magazine offered some census statistics on computer availability and use by race. Significantly few African American children under the age of 17 have access to computers in the home or in school. Twenty-seven percent of white children, and 28.1 percent of other children of color have computers in the home, compared with just 10.6 percent of African American children. This disparity in computer access holds true for adults as well. The accompanying chart shows that in schools, the home, and

Who's Using the Computer?

The Bureau of the Census studied computer use in
the United States in 1989 (numbers in thousands)

Persons 3 to 17 years old

With Computer at Home

Race	Total	Percent
White	10,773	26.7
Black	806	10.6
Other	570	28.1

Uses Computer Any Place

Race	Total	Percent
White	20,662	48.9
Black	2,622	31.9
Other	932	42.5

Enrolled in School

Race	Total	Uses Computer	Percent
White	37,756	17,463	48.2
Black	7,387	2,416	35.1
Other	1,922	785	43.6

Persons 18 years and older

With Computer at Home

Race	Total	Percent
White	26,902	18.3
Black	1,573	8.4
Other	1,141	20.9

Uses Computer Any Place

Race	Total	Percent
White	45,264	29.4
Black	3,673	18.4
Other	1,732	29.5

With a Job

Race	Total	Uses Computer	Percent
White	100,074	35,977	37.8
Black	11,767	2,990	27.6
Other	3,828	1,278	36.4

US Census; Chart: Rod Little, *Emerge*

the workplace, African Americans use computers less than whites and other people of color.

Undoubtedly, educational attainment, economic hardship, and job discrimination all play a role in the game of "who gets to play with computers?" But now, the practice of "redlining," the discrimination against people of color by banks and insurance companies, has moved from the streets onto the modem lines.

Video Dialtone

For instance, low-income people of color are being excluded from plans to develop video dialtone networks. These are regional systems being developed by the Baby Bell companies [regional telephone companies created by a 1984 court-ordered breakup of AT&T] which provide a limited two-way connection between consumers and the service provider. There would be an interactive component, whereby individual households could order merchandise, vote electronically, or participate in any number of other activities.

There is potential for these networks, and other new technologies, to replace existing telephone, broadcast, and emergency network services. Critics of the move toward video dialtone have pointed out that initial experiments are being limited to affluent white neighborhoods. Jeffrey Chester, Executive Director of the Center for Media Education, says that video dialtone networks "could become the primary communications system for millions of Americans. [But] they must be made available in an equitable and nondiscriminatory manner." Denver, Colorado; Chicago, Illinois; Washington, D.C.; and other areas are already being wired with experimental underground cable that will be the backbone of local video call-in networks, and might be the on-ramp to the Information Superhighway for millions of consumers.

> *"The future of the Information Superhighway will more likely be one of heightened economic disparity."*

Mark Cooper of the Consumer Federation of America notes that the initial research in these three cities shows neighborhoods with the highest concentrations of poor people and people of color, and even entire counties, are being bypassed for infrastructure development. Some local groups have asked that the FCC [Federal Communications Commission] not approve applications by the regional Bell companies to expand the video dialtone services until the projects comply with the 1934 communications law forbidding discrimination in communications services.

As information technologies develop and become more central to the way many of us live and work, the disparity in access is likely to get worse. Unbridled by existing regulations, and in fact boosted by federal incentives, companies that are trailblazing the National Information Infrastructure will continue to place profit above all else. The majority of people of color will not benefit from this equation. Community-oriented usage, public access, and community control is more important than ever with technologies that may change the way we do everything from talk on the phone and pay our electric bills, to the way we vote and look for jobs.

The production of electronic information by communities of color is an essential component to making the Information Superhighway accessible and useful. On the one hand, Internet and other electronic networks could potentially provide more diverse resources. On the other hand, large corporations are already dominating information production on-line as much as they do through traditional means.

This monopoly of information will get worse as the Internet is swamped with millions of mostly useless entries. One example, Usenet, which is a network of thousands of discussion conferences called newsgroups, is loaded with annoying get-rich-quick schemes and corporate advertising, as well as thousands of pointless files posted by individuals. Cultural education resources and community-based information projects could become mired in the torrent of electronic information.

Existing Uses and Resources

Even though there are now relatively few on-line resources for and by people of color, there are some interesting tools that organizations, advocates, and individual people of color can use. The project garnering the most attention in recent years is LatinoNet, which received a grant from the U.S. Department of Commerce to develop experimental uses of communications technologies. Hosted by America OnLine, an enormous commercial access provider, LatinoNet offers electronic archives, discussion conferences on a variety of topics, Latin American and Latino news, as well as a regional and national calendar of events.

For several years, Native American activists have been conferencing across the country and the globe through a listserv, or electronic mailing list, called NativeNet. NativeNet also now has a site on the graphic Internet service called World Wide Web. There, one can browse through Native American news items, search an activist database, or sign up on the listserv. Increasingly, NativeNet has helped bridge geographic and cultural barriers among Native Americans in a quick and inexpensive way.

The organizations with the most experience and success in using new information technologies to the benefit of people of color are those in the environmental justice movement. Advocates, community groups, and individuals are using electronic databases, local free on-line access providers called "free nets," and government records to reveal the racist edge to polluting. In an example from Brooklyn, New York, residents have the use of the graphic information system (GIS), a computer program which

> *"Neighborhoods with the highest concentrations of poor people and people of color . . . are being bypassed for infrastructure development."*

combines government information with graphic mapping to monitor "block-by-block information about the area's biggest and smallest polluters."

NEWS (Neighborhood Early Warning System), another electronic database, was developed by the Center for Neighborhood Technology (CNT) in Chicago to help organizers monitor and fight absentee landlords and abandoned housing. Michael Freedberg of CNT stresses the need to get housing information out of city hall and into communities, saying, "community groups don't have the resources to do this kind of research for a single property, let alone a whole block."

> *"The Internet also is home to a number of sites that could be a huge benefit to . . . businesses owned by people of color."*

Internet Benefits

Besides providing information on housing and the environment, the Internet also is home to a number of sites that could be a huge benefit to organizations, activists, organizers, advocates of color, as well as businesses owned by people of color.

Information on government contracts, scholarships for higher education, congressional records, and census data are just a few examples of free and accessible information on the Internet.

There are even organizations fighting for access to on-line services from their desktops. African American Information Network (AAIN), which is housed on Apple Computer's eWorld network, developed a campaign called "95 in '95," with the goal of getting 95 percent of Black churches on-line by the end of 1995 as a strategy for increasing access for African Americans.

Recently, AAIN organized hundreds of members, supporters, and others to send e-mail (electronic mail) to *Newsweek* to protest the magazine's lack of acknowledgement of African American contributions to new information technologies in an issue on the Information Superhighway during Black History Month. Organizer Jim Davies stated in a phone interview that while AAIN wants *Newsweek* to acknowledge African Americans on-line, AAIN really wants the community to "wake up and realize the power of the technology," particularly the power to make change. Other organizations, particularly the Electronic Frontier Foundation, while not specifically addressing what Davies calls "digital racism," are also fighting for equal access to electronic services and community control over those innovative technologies.

Community Control

Jefferey Chester of the Center for Media Education said in the October 1994 issue of *Macworld* that "the idea that the design of the network should evolve from the needs of the community is absent from this debate."

The coalition believes that including the broadest selection of people on the front end is important precisely because the video dialtone systems and other aspects of the National Information Infrastructure "could compete with or even supplant telephone service, broadcast television, and cable television," which communities of color depend on for communication, education, safety, and entertainment. More disturbing is that while the communications utilities are obliged to provide low-cost services under current legislation, the new technologies, so far, are loosely regulated and have no such constraint.

Like other technological developments, new information technologies are tools that can either be used for and made by people of color or they can leave people of color in the silicon dust. Already it is clear that people of color have less access to existing technology, less computer job training, less money for private services, and fewer places to "call our own" on-line. While the media and advertising bring us endless hype about the improvements the Information Superhighway will bring to our lives, the realities of racial inequality cast a shadow on corporate promises. Most people meet these new technologies with an understandable mix of fear and excitement.

> *"People of color must learn to utilize new technologies and to view clearly their effect on our communities."*

People of color must learn to utilize new technologies and to view clearly their affect on our communities. If communities organize for accountability and community-oriented resources on-line, maybe Juana's future will not be as brutal as it is earlier depicted. The Information Superhighway could pave the road to an electronic future where Juana and her friends have free access to the Internet from local libraries, can use computer archives to help blow the whistle on polluters and slumlords, use on-line learning programs to help acquire valuable job skills, and produce their own electronic resources. Without input from communities of color into the way the Information Superhighway is developed, how it is accessed, where it goes, and how it works, the new technology will either pass us by or run us down.

Computers Occupy Too Much of Children's Time

by Nathan Cobb

About the author: *Nathan Cobb writes feature articles for the Living/Arts section of the* Boston Globe *daily newspaper.*

It's 9 p.m., and your kids are upstairs jockeying the family computer again, right? Maybe they're cruising the Internet, playing games or dashing off bursts of e-mail, downloading files or writing code or checking out an electronic bulletin board or two.

Whatever they're doing, they've likely lost track of time, and so have you. Has it been an hour? Three? Five?

The coming of the home computer has introduced yet another screen into the lives of children, bringing with it a brush fire of issues. Many of them are similar to those raised about television content, parental control, socialization, breadth of experience and so on.

Children Take to Computers

But computers are not TV sets. Unregulated and interactive, they also have the capability of taking on multiple personalities, including that of learning tool, amusement arcade, community center and homework machine. They present an uncharted and varied landscape over which parents are still finding their way—often several steps behind their children in terms of computer skills.

There are no age limits or barriers on the Internet. Pornographic images, computer "phone sex" and sexually explicit subjects are readily available.

Several bills have been introduced in Congress in the government's first attempts to regulate the Internet.

Kids across the country are using computers far more than adults. Of the 100 million Americans who use computers at home, school or work nearly 60 percent are 17 or younger, census figures say.

Beyond the highly publicized issue of "stranger danger" on the information su-

Nathan Cobb, "Kids Online, Parents on Edge," *Boston Globe*, February 22, 1995. Reprinted courtesy of the *Boston Globe*.

perhighway, many parents and their kids are grappling over how much and what kind of role the computer should play. The result can be a kind of digital generation gap. "I hate you!" a young girl announces to her father in a recent *New Yorker* cartoon. "You don't understand me, and you don't understand my software!"

What many parents do understand is that computers can teach, entertain and empower their youngsters. But they also are discovering that pulling children away from a computer screen is no easier than yanking them away from a video game or a TV show. In fact, it may be more difficult.

> *"Pulling children away from a computer screen is no easier than yanking them away from a video game or a TV show."*

Alex Randall, president of East West Educational Development Foundation, a Boston-area organization whose mission is to further computer access, is downright effusive about computers, even extolling their powers of seduction. "They're interactive, and as a result, they suck your brains up," Mr. Randall says. By that I mean they're engrossing and they're enthralling because they *respond.*"

He even uses the A-word: "They're addictive," Mr. Randall chirps.

The Prime Activity

Rick and Susan Tresch Fienberg agree, at least when it comes to their son John. Nearly four years ago they made an offer that the boy, 8 years old at the time, couldn't refuse. In return for ditching the mind-numbing video-game system that had become John's activity of first resort, the family would soup up its computer to better handle "educational" software. Goodbye, Super Mario Brothers. Hello, Carmen Sandiego.

The plan to change the quality and quantity of John's screen time worked for a while. But soon his parents noticed that John, the oldest of their three sons, was forsaking challenging programs such as Sim City for the likes of splatter games such as Wolfenstein 3-D. The software was coming into the house via friends or being downloaded from electronic bulletin boards. Meanwhile, John had reverted to his Nintendo posture: sometimes slack-jawed, sometimes tense, always riveted.

But it isn't only a matter of content. The Fienbergs worry that the computer has become too large a slice of John's young life no matter what's flickering across the screen. "He doesn't have a lot of other passions," his father, a magazine publisher, points out. "If we didn't actively go upstairs and yank him off, he'd fall asleep in front of it." Fittingly, they sometimes use an alarm clock to remind John that his computer time is up.

In soft and measured voices that reveal the depths of their concern, the Fienbergs talk about the changes that have come over their son. "He used to play chess, he used to like music, he used to sing a lot," Mr. Fienberg says. "He seems no longer interested in those things. The computer has displaced the other activities in his life."

John agrees. As his fingers fly across a computer keyboard—he is visiting a planet called Alpha Centauri BZ in a space-simulation game called Outpost—a visitor asks him what he likes to do.

"Well, this," John replies, his eyes locked on Alpha Centauri.

Anything else?

"Well . . . this, pretty much."

Social Interaction

The issue of socialization, of not mixing face-to-face with other children, is clearly starting to worry some parents about computer usage. Eugene Provenzo Jr., a professor of education at the University of Miami, thinks they have a point. Computers, he says, raise many of the same issues as video games (which are, after all, computer-driven too).

"Being at a computer is a singular, often isolating activity, and it blocks out social interaction," says Mr. Provenzo, author of the book *Video Kids: Making Sense of Nintendo*. "If children spend an unreasonable amount of time at it, it raises the question: What are they *not* doing?"

But nobody, especially parents, seems sure what constitutes an unreasonable amount of time. Parents believe computers have a kind of magic that is necessary to prepare their children for the 21st century.

"Parents of this generation are proud that their kids are getting more and more technologically sophisticated," says Steve Bennett of Cambridge, Massachusetts, a parent who limits his two young children's computer access with the help of a kitchen timer. "But the majority of parents don't have a clue as to what their kids are doing (on computers). They say, 'Oh, he's on the Internet, isn't that wonderful?' Or 'This program was written by smart people: it must be better than television.'"

> *"The issue of socialization, of not mixing face-to-face with other children, is clearly starting to worry some parents."*

Leslie Laredo is the mother of a 5-year-old son, Josh, as well as a self-described on-line junkie. After all, the information highway is her job: She's in charge of advertising products for on-line sites maintained by the interactive division of Ziff-Davis Inc., the multimedia giant. Yet as a parent Ms. Laredo worries about being able to raise "a more socially adept human being than someone who just wants to interact with a screen."

"My son goes over to a friend's house," she says

> and they play at the computer for hours, and there's no social interaction except fighting over who'll use the mouse.

> But people think it can't be bad because it's a *computer*. It's the future, right? Yet maybe it's not.

Chapter 3

Family Tensions

It certainly seemed like it would be for 12-year-old Leah Levin Beeferman of Cambridge, Massachusetts. In the fall of 1993, Leah became deeply engrossed in Multi User Simulated Environment, MUSE, an on-line activity in which participants create "virtual worlds" in text.

Adopting the screen name "Saturn"—Satty for short—she used the family's 12-year-old IBM computer to participate in 20 or so such "worlds" from Cambridge to Sweden. Her best friends had handles such as sARaH3, Uncle-John and opps. And why MUSE? "I like it because you get to meet people from everywhere," Leah replies.

"People think it can't be bad because it's a computer. It's the future, right? Yet maybe it's not."

Ann Levin and Larry Beeferman, Leah's parents, realized there was clearly an educational and creative upside to their daughter's passion. They also believed that a child's interests shouldn't be stifled. On the other hand, it wasn't uncommon for Leah to spend five hours a day seated at the basement computer. Her karate lessons stopped, and so did her piano lessons. Family tensions rose. Limits were set, but not adhered to. There were arguments. There were even times when the parents disconnected the computer's modem in mid-MUSE. "We were at our wit's end," Ms. Levin recalls. "And we were close to [starting] family therapy." Finally, in December, Leah agreed to a regimen of three computer-free days a week. "Since I couldn't get on the computer," she says, "it forced me to do other things. Play my guitar. Listen to music. Write. Draw."

The limits have worked. For now.

"I still don't understand what it is," Ms. Levin says of MUSE.

"Because you never take the time to look at it," her daughter answers quickly.

Losing Track of Time

Indeed, it is frequently the difference between low-tech parents and high-tech kids that causes the computer to become a family issue.

Consider Michael Castleman, a slim eighth-grader. He sits in an upstairs bedroom in his family's two-story ranch home in Sharon, Massachusetts, his fingers playing the keyboard of a Packard Bell like a piano.

Having taught himself at least part of five different computer languages, having programmed a number of games himself, having logged onto the Internet hundreds of times via his screen name, MCool1, Michael is the kind of adult-child who is not uncommon in the computer age.

Behind him, in a bookcase, are a number of kids' books by Dr. Seuss. Closer at hand is a copy of *Netgames: Your Guide to the Games People Play on the Electronic Highway.*

On this particular evening he is playing Ship's Ahoy, a game he wrote himself. "You have to acquire $100,000 in 100 moves by traveling to six sites and buying and selling five types of items," he explains.

"My mom can play a few games, but she doesn't know much about computers other than that," Michael says. "My dad, he knows a little bit about DOS [disk operating system]. But basically I've set the whole thing up myself. I taught myself. I got books from the public library. I'm usually alone, but sometimes I use the modem to call up my friend, Levente."

Downstairs, Michael's parents, Claire and James Castleman, explain that the house rule for both Michael, 13, and his brother, Daniel, 11, is that they must finish their homework—of which the computer is often a part—before firing up the Packard Bell for pleasure. The boys' weekday limit is then one hour of screen time per night, but . . .

"The other night, we went out at 7:30," Claire Castleman says. "When we came home at 10, Michael was still on the computer. He said he was doing his homework, but I know he wasn't. He just has no idea of how long he's been doing it. He has no concept of time."

Jim Castleman says he has mixed feelings about what's happening. "The computer represents a lot of Michael's time, but some of what he does is very creative," he says. His

"It is frequently the difference between low-tech parents and high-tech kids that causes the computer to become a family issue."

wife is decidedly less upbeat, in part because she feels her son has entered a world of which she can't be part.

"There have been several times when I've said, 'Why don't we just get rid of the thing?'" she says. "Because both boys are so obsessed with it. And I'm so unsophisticated. When Michael tells me what he's doing, it's like he's speaking Martian. I have no idea what he's talking about."

One floor above, MCool1 is logging on to his Internet account. He's flying solo, and it looks like a long trip. "If I'm up here too much, sometimes my parents tell me to get off," he says. "But mostly I'm on my own."

Chapter 4

Should Computer Content Be Regulated?

CURRENT CONTROVERSIES

Regulating Computer Content: An Overview

by Charles S. Clark

About the author: *Charles S. Clark is a staff writer for the* CQ Researcher, *a weekly news and research publication of Congressional Quarterly Inc.*

From somewhere in the community of cyberspace came an anonymous query to a computer "chatroom" for subscribers to America Online: "Anybody know what action's being taken to censor the Internet?"

What is driving the buzz is an amendment introduced in Congress in 1995 by Sens. Jim Exon, D-Nebraska, and Slade Gorton, R-Washington, that would attempt to update federal laws on telephone harassment to the computer age. It would toughen penalties for people who transmit indecent and harassing material by computer or fax to people who didn't request it, raising the maximum fine from $50,000 to $100,000 and the jail sentence from six months to two years.

The proposal, which cleared the Senate on June 14, 1995, as part of a massive telecommunications deregulation bill, was modified by Exon after on-line service providers complained that the original draft would have held such companies as CompuServe, America Online and Prodigy Services Co. responsible for objectionable material that their users originate. "That would have been a global nuke of the whole information infrastructure since the only way to [protect yourself] would be to pull the plug," says [executive director] Tony Rutkowski of the Internet Society. "The new version is more pointedly focused on individuals or organizations that actually make the material available."

Protecting Children

The amendment's goal of shielding children (who these days are often more computer literate than their parents) from sexual material is shared by the politically ascendant Christian Coalition, which included a plank about limiting indecency on the Internet in its "Contract With the American Family."

"Any 12-year-old surfing passively around with his mouse can now click on

Excerpted from "Regulating the Internet" by Charles S. Clark, *CQ Researcher*, June 30, 1995. Reprinted with permission.

material that can greatly undermine what's being taught in his own home," says Mike Russell, a spokesman for the coalition in Chesapeake, Virginia. Criminal law should be amended, he adds, to put the onus on the deliverer of soft- or hard-core pornography to children, even if that means that parents or on-line providers must pay extra to review transmissions or install a block-out device.

A *Newsweek* poll in February 1995 indicated that 85 percent of Americans are concerned about pornography being too available to young people through the Internet, and 80 percent are concerned about "virtual stalking" through unwanted messages.

Sexual Images and Text

What sort of material is so readily accessed? Though several cases of child pornography have surfaced, far better known to Internet frequenters are the risque World Wide Web sites operated by the major men's magazines and the sexually oriented "news groups" on the popular USENET network, accessed under such headings as "alt.sex."

Both *Penthouse* and *Playboy* offer nude photos of women along with text highlights from current and back issues of the magazines, though browsers are given ample advance notice should they opt not to call up the images. *Penthouse* claims to attract 2 million "hits" from visitors daily, while *Playboy* draws about 800,000, says a spokeswoman.

> *"Any 12-year-old . . . can now click on material that can greatly undermine what's being taught in his own home."*

The "alt.sex" news groups offer such fare as reports on strip clubs in Helsinki, Finland, "celebrity nudes" from which users can download unauthorized or pirated photos, and various discussion groups with restroom graffiti-caliber titles such as "men talking to breasts."

Though the sex groups represent a small percentage of the 14,000-plus news groups in the USENET, they are among the most popular. A 1994 count by Carnegie Mellon University graduate students found that over a six-month period, Americans on the Net called up 450,620 pornographic images and downloaded sexually oriented text files almost 6.5 million times.

Finally, there are the discussion groups in which unsuspecting conversationalists can be sucked into sexual banter with strangers. The free flow of suggestive comments fueled by the anonymity of Internet discussions has prompted many of the small percentage of users who are female to avoid unpleasantness by logging on with male or gender-neutral signatures.

Opposition to the Exon Plan

Though the sexual material may be controversial, efforts to keep the Internet clean provoke critics concerned about free speech. And that is the main reason the Exon amendment has drawn opposition from an array of organizations (many of them organizing on-line) ranging from the American Civil Liberties Union (ACLU) to the American Library Association (ALA) to People for the American Way to the National Retail Federation.

"This is like the federal government deciding that too many people use 'filthy language' in their private letters and phone calls and then proposing to prosecute, fine and imprison anyone who curses," said ACLU legislative counsel Donald Haines.

"Libraries and librarians should not deny or limit access to information available via electronic resources because of its allegedly controversial content or because of the librarian's personal beliefs or fear of confrontation," said the library association. "Information retrieved or utilized electronically should be considered constitutionally protected unless determined otherwise by a court with appropriate jurisdiction."

Because pornography is defined differently in different communities, passage of the Exon plan would mean that conservative parts of the country would become "Internet police," argues [Electronic Privacy Information Center director] Marc Rotenberg, adding that museums would be afraid to reproduce many classic paintings or books on the Internet.

Spokesmen from the computer industry point out that Internet users seldom encounter material involuntarily. The Exon approach "treats the Internet, interactive television and [phone-delivered] video dialtone systems as if they were one big radio station whose broadcasts are constantly assaulting unwilling listeners," says a critique from the Center for Democracy and Technology.

Daniel J. Weitzner, the center's deputy director, says the Exon proposal "puts the entire Internet community at an absolute Rubicon in terms of how the Internet will be treated. Will it be like dial-a-porn regulation or [looser], like print models? It's a long-term issue."

Terri Tomcisin, director of corporate communications at Playboy Enterprises, says it is up to parents, not Congress, to decide what children should be exposed to. "The Internet is like a library, and you wouldn't edit a library based on what's accessible to children," she says. "*Playboy* is for adults. Also, there is a big difference going from talking about *Playboy* to talking about child porn, which is already illegal."

> *"The Internet is like a library, and you wouldn't edit a library based on what's accessible to children."*

Software industry attorney Karen L. Casser acknowledges that, "I wouldn't let a 10-year-old on the Internet unsupervised." But she calls the Exon legislation a kneejerk reaction. "It would be better to impose a technological limit," even though it can be a burden to on-line providers, she says.

For example, in 1995 "Surfwatch Software," which blocks out some 1,000 risqué sites on the World Wide Web, was put on the market for $49.95, plus $5.95 per month for optional updates.

Blocked Out

Other on-line services are equipped with a "First Amendment privacy curtain," which requires the user to enter his age and sign a statement of consent before his password will permit access to adult material. During Senate debate on the telecommunications bill, three software companies announced that they would form an Information Highway Parental Empowerment Group to develop other filtering devices.

At CompuServe, "parents can send a note to a systems operator to block any account," says company spokesman Pierce Reid. He adds that his firm offers a health and human sexuality forum on-line, but that users may not enter it without advance approval from the systems operator to assure that they are there to "discuss serious personal health issues and aren't just looking for a laugh. And if people don't behave accordingly with its values and standards, they can get kicked off," he says.

CompuServe is pleased that Sen. Exon has consulted with the industry, Reid adds, "taking pains to craft a bill that protects children and makes the on-line world a clean place for all Americans but doesn't eliminate the positive aspect as a free communications forum where people are judged only by their ideas."

Objectionable Computer Content Should Be Regulated

by James Exon

About the author: *James Exon is a Nebraska Democrat in the U.S. Senate and cosponsor of the Communications Decency Act of 1995, an amendment passed by the Senate and included in the Telecommunications Reform Bill. The act was one of several similar proposals to be considered by Congress in the bill's final version.*

When a youngster logs onto a computer terminal, he or she is welcomed into a vast new world of information that will revolutionize how we all learn and work in the future.

This worldwide web of computer connections represents an information explosion unprecedented in world history. But there are some dark side roads on the information superhighway that contain material that would be considered unacceptable by any reasonable standard.

My proposal lays down some basic guidelines on the information superhighway. I want to make this exciting new highway as safe as possible for kids and families to travel. Just as we have laws against dumping garbage on the interstate, we ought to have similar laws for the information superhighway.

What the Legislation Does

My amendment to the Telecommunications Reform Bill will toughen penalties for people who actively "transmit" pornographic and harassing material, boosting the maximum fine from $50,000 to $100,000 and increasing the maximum jail sentence from six months to two years.

We need this added deterrent so that those who would pervert the network will think twice. We already have laws to prohibit obscenity over the telephone or pornography through the mail. My amendment extends to computer users the

James Exon, "Protection for Children," *Washington Times*, April 16, 1995. Reprinted by permission of Scripps Howard News Service.

very same protections against obscenity or harassment that now partially protect telephone users.

The legislation does not make innocent "carriers" of electronic messages liable for inappropriate messages, nor does it by any stretch of the imagination require system operators to "eavesdrop" on electronic messages. To do so would be the equivalent of holding the mailman liable for the packages he delivers.

> *"If anyone thinks this material is hard for youngsters to come by, they don't know youngsters."*

Many critics say that on the Internet, anything should go, no matter how outrageous.

I say the framers of the Constitution never intended for the First Amendment to protect pornographers and pedophiles.

Computers are a unique medium because children often have much more knowledge about how they operate than their parents. Does anyone really think parents can stand over their children's shoulders and monitor them all of their waking hours of every day?

If anyone thinks this material is hard for youngsters to come by, they don't know youngsters.

We have laws against murder, and we have laws against speeding. We still have murder, and we still have speeding. But I think most reasonable people would agree we very likely would have more murders and more speeders if we didn't have laws as a deterrent.

Safeguarding Children

In a recent newspaper article, a computer "hacker" who viewed some of this pornography on the Internet said 98 percent of it is no worse than you might find in an "adult video rental store."

That weird admission makes my point. Is material that is OK for an adult video store OK for kids to see on their home computers?

To those who are critical of my suggestions, I say come let us reason together. Nothing is etched in stone, and I am open to any constructive proposals. I have suggested, for example, a parental lock-out mechanism as a possible solution to make certain areas of the Internet inaccessible to youngsters.

We are talking about our most important and precious commodity—our children. We cannot simply throw up our hands and say a solution is impossible or the First Amendment is so sacrosanct that we must stand idly by while our children are inundated with pornography and smut on the Internet.

The public needs to be aware of the problem and direct its correction.

Computer Pornography Should Be Prohibited

by the National Coalition for the Protection of Children and Families

About the author: *The National Coalition for the Protection of Children and Families, in Cincinnati, Ohio, was founded in 1983 to eliminate obscenity, child pornography, and other material deemed harmful to minors.*

The problem of pornography in cyberspace is in the national spotlight. Of most concern to parents, educators, professionals and concerned organizations is the availability and impact of computer pornography on children. Following are some frank questions and answers intended to highlight the issues being debated and their potential impact on children.

Porn on the Internet

What types of pornography are freely available to any child on the Internet?

Everything explicit that can be imagined and many other types of material that are beyond the comprehension of most Americans. Types of pictorial/image pornography available on the Internet include soft-core nudity, hard-core sex acts, anal sex, bestiality, bondage & domination, sado-masochism (including the actual torture and mutilation of women for sexual pleasure), scatological acts (defecating and urinating on women for sexual pleasure), fetishes and child pornography. These computer images are usually very clear (like magazine photographs or videos) and can be displayed on any computer/color monitor sold today with the same quality and clarity. Types of textual pornography include detailed text stories on the rape, mutilation and torture of women, sexual abuse of children, graphic incest, etc.

Who can access pornography on the Internet?

Virtually anyone with an account or access to the Internet. Once "online," there are no truly effective safety measures to prevent children from accessing all of the pornography described above. For the first time in history we are giv-

Abridged from the National Coalition for the Protection of Children and Families brochure *Children Pornography, and Cyberspace: The Problem, Solutions, and the Current Congressional Debate,* October 1995. Reprinted with permission.

ing young children unlimited access to pornography, with no age check and no responsibility/verification procedures in place. This has never occurred in the print, broadcast, satellite or cable media before.

Where do children and adults find pornographic materials on the Internet?

Pornography is readily, publicly available through the Internet by accessing sections in the "alt.binaries.pictures" and "alt.sex" hierarchies of the Usenet and at a number of sites on the World Wide Web. It is also traded daily via Internet e-mail and "anonymous ftp" [file transfer protocol] sites set up for the exchange of pornography.

Are these groups popular or is this really a small problem?

Surveys done by online administrators indicate that the pornographic sites are among the most often used on the Internet. They are accessed thousands of times daily. This is a big problem and it is growing rapidly. Further, the size of the problem is not really the central issue being debated. Few would argue that because toxic waste sites don't represent an overwhelming portion of American real estate that the problem of toxic waste should be ignored. The same principle is true concerning children's access to pornography on computer networks.

The Online Community

Don't we need to study the issue more before we take action on a problem that affects the future of cyberspace?

Proposals to "study" the issue of computer pornography or pursue strictly market-based approaches are attempts by the ACLU [American Civil Liberties Union], Electronic Frontier Foundation (EFF), Center for Democracy and Technology (CDT) and other online groups to delay *ever* taking legislative action on this problem. They seem to believe that there should be no *legislative* restrictions whatsoever on anything distributed to children online, including hard-core pornography. They understand that the longer they can delay action, the easier it will become to claim that the problem cannot be solved, so nothing should be done. They want to dump *all* responsibility for action into the laps of parents, many of whom are far less technologically capable than their children. *The problem is clear:* children have widespread access to hard-core pornography for the first time in history through the Internet. No one is taking serious responsibility for this problem and they won't until they face potential legal liability for refusing to act. *Solutions need to be implemented now*, before millions of children are harmed and this *positive* technology is further abused for the perverse benefit of a few.

Isn't the online community against proposals for "decency" on the Internet?

Some users in the online "community" and many media are vehemently against any proposals to regulate the Internet or children's access to pornography. For months, electronic petitions have circulated online condemning legislative approaches to children accessing pornography on computer networks. Not surprisingly, although various online networks are estimated to have over twenty million users, less than two hundred thousand have "signed" various petitions. Further, apparently over half of those who have signed the petitions are from ".edu" e-mail addresses. In other words, they are college students and faculty receiving free access to the Internet through their universities and free access to Internet pornography. It is also worth noting that the online community, up to this point, is predominantly male.

Aren't there "technical fixes" or "market-based" approaches that are less restrictive/intrusive than a regulatory or criminal law approach?

No. While online advocates of maintaining the legal status quo (free pornography distribution) often claim that there could be *purely* technical means of restricting pornography access on the Internet, this is simply false. To date, only a few software programs have been released to regulate what pornographic groups a child has access to. They can be bypassed by those users with a good knowledge of the Internet and some technical sophistication.

Further, while it is laudable that some of our best technical experts are attempting to find technical solutions, this approach is (and will be) inadequate in and of itself. It does *nothing* for parents whose children can walk down the street to another computer. It does little for parents whose technical sophistication pales in comparison to their children's expertise. It does *nothing* to legally discourage pornographers from peddling their materials to children. In essence, parents are now being told by some civil liberties groups that if they want to keep hard-core pornography out of their homes and children's reach, the parents must go out and *pay extra* for special software programs (whose effectiveness is limited) and then continue to *pay extra* for regular updates to the software programs. It is offensive that the ACLU, EFF, CDT and others are suggesting that the new baseline for hard-core pornography access in our society should be:

> Pornography freely available for all, including children; if you don't want it in your home or your child to have access to the worst forms of pornography, either keep them off the computer networks or *pay extra* to try and keep pornography out.

. . . What is the deeper issue being debated here?

The deeper issue is whether there will be *any* standards of responsibility for online distribution of sexually graphic and violent materials *to children*. Existing obscenity and child pornography laws cover *commercial* distribution of illegal materials for adults. They are totally inadequate as solutions for what children are being exposed to. Either we will take action *now* or millions of children will be exposed to the equivalent of entire pornographic bookstores online, where *anything goes* and no material is too explicit or too violent or too degrading. A shift in the baseline for children's access to hard-core pornography would be remarkably callous and would mark a fundamental shift in our society's attitude. This problem requires a three-part initiative: 1) greater parental supervision and involvement, 2) industry designed technical blocking mechanisms, and 3) legal liability for making pornography available to children over computer networks.

Sexually Repulsive Internet Postings Should Be Prohibited

by Simon Winchester

About the author: *Simon Winchester is a foreign correspondent for the* Spectator, *a weekly British magazine covering current events.*

If in 1994 it was merely modish to be seen speeding down the information superhighway, in 1995 it is fast becoming essential, at least in America. Hitch your wagon to cyberspace, says the Speaker of the House, Mr Newt Gingrich, and your democracy will become absolute, with all America joined together for the first time into one vast and egalitarian town meeting.

Mr Gingrich made this all clear in January 1995 when he unveiled a new system for bringing Congress to the electronically connected populace, which in honour of President Jefferson is called 'Thomas'. Anyone with a computer and a modem at home or in the office (or even up in the skies, courtesy of USAir's new back-of-seat telescreens) may now, with only the click of a few buttons, find the text of any bill, any resolution, any government statement.

On the Internet

Mr Gingrich is hugely excited by this idea—going so far as to suggest, and not at all facetiously, that perhaps every citizen be given a thousand-dollar tax deduction to allow him to buy himself a laptop computer. Thus will all America be conjoined, he argues, and thus will its democracy be ever strengthened as in no other country on earth.

Fine, say I, and not just because I will become richer by $1,000. For the last three years or so I have been a dedicated and enthusiastic user of the Internet. (The Internet—'the net' to those in the know—began innocently enough 20 years ago as a vast worldwide network of computers linked together by government-funded telephone lines, with high-powered government-funded 'exchanges' to

Simon Winchester, "An Electronic Sink of Depravity," *Spectator*, February 4, 1995. Reprinted with permission.

speed calls on their way, which enabled universities and governments to swap information. Five years or so ago, its controllers opted to make it more democratic, and now anyone is able to connect to it; tens of thousands of new subscribers join every day, and the net is becoming truly global, with at least 20 million regular users.)

I am a typical enough user. I send electronic mail—e-mail—to everyone who is similarly hooked up (it is lightning fast and essentially free); and I browse through the world's libraries and data-bases to do research for whatever book I happen to be writing. I bask happily in the Panglossian [excessively optimistic] principle that the Internet seems to enshrine. By virtue of the net, I have complete freedom to explore and trawl for anything I want in what has become by custom an untrammelled, uncontrolled, wholly liberated ocean of information. The Internet seems and sounds to be something almost noble. One can understand why the US Congress named its own portion of the net after Jefferson: all knowledge there is is on hand for all the people—just the kind of thing the great man would have liked.

An Appalling Discovery

But this week, while I was peering into an area of the Internet where I have hitherto not lingered, I discovered something so appalling as to put all such high-minded sentiments into a quite different perspective.

I had stumbled, not entirely accidentally, into a sinkhole of electronic but very real perversion. The first thing I read, almost as soon as I entered it, was a lengthy, very graphic and in stylistic terms quite competently composed narrative that presented in all its essentials the story of a kidnapping, and the subsequent rape, torture, mutilation and eventual murder of the two victims. The author called himself by a code-name, Blackwind; and while it is quite likely that he is American, almost as certain that he is well-educated and quite possible that he is at least a peripheral member of the academic community, we know, and are allowed to know, nothing else about him.

His anonymity is faultlessly safeguarded by a system of electronics which has been built into the Internet, and which even the police and the other agents of the state are unable, technically or in law, to penetrate. This is, from their point of view, highly regrettable. Blackwind's offerings—and the very similar stories currently being published on the Internet by scores of men who are in all likelihood as deranged as he seems to be—should be subject to some kind of legal sanction, and for one very understandable reason: the victims of the story he has written are small children.

> *"I had stumbled . . . into a sinkhole of electronic but very real perversion."*

One is a six-year-old boy named Christopher, who, among other indignities, suffers a castration—reported in loving detail—before being shot. The other is a girl named Karen, who is seven years old and is raped repeatedly by no fewer than nine men, before having her nipples cut off and her throat slashed.

At the moment of my writing this, I find that there are perhaps 200 similar stories presently circulating and available on one of the so-called 'newsgroups' on the Internet. The choice of tales is endlessly expanded and refreshed by new and ever more exotic stories that emerge into this particular niche in the ether every day, almost every hour. You want tales of fathers sodomising their three-year-old daughters, or of mothers performing fellatio on their prepubescent sons, or of girls coupling with horses, or of the giving of enemas to child virgins? Then you need do no more than visit the newsgroup that is named 'alt.sex.stories' and all will reliably be there, 24 hours a day, for everyone with a computer and a telephone, anywhere on (or above) the face of the earth.

> *"The choice of [sexually obscene] tales is endlessly expanded and refreshed . . . every day, almost every hour."*

There are about 5,000 separate newsgroups on the net, each one of them presenting chatter about some scintilla of human knowledge or endeavour. I have long liked the system, and found it an agreeable way to discover people around the world who have similar interests. I used to tell others who were not yet signed up to the net that using newsgroups was like going into a hugely crowded pub, finding in milliseconds those who wanted to talk about what you wanted to know, having a quick drink with them before leaving, without once having encountered a bore.

And so, with an alphabetical list running from 'ab.fen'—which shows you how much fun you can have in Alberta—down to something in German called 'zer.zmetz.wissenschaft.physik', the enthusiasms of the world's Internet-connected population are distilled into their electronic segments. Alberta-philes can chat with each other, as can German physicists, and those who would bore these are left to chat among themselves. In theory, an admirable arrangement.

By Jeffersonian rights it should be uplifting to the spirit. In reality it is rather less so. In far too many groups the level of discussion is execrable and juvenile. Arguments break out, insults are exchanged, the chatter drifts aimlessly in and out of relevance. This is a reality of the electronic world that few like to admit. It is prompting many browsers to suspect, as I do, that a dismayingly large number of users of this system are not at all the kind of sturdy champions of freedom and democracy and intellect that Mr Gingrich and Mr Al Gore would like them to be.

From Unpleasant to Horrifying

More probably, to judge from the tone and the language in many of the groups, they are pasty-faced and dysfunctional men with halitosis who inhabit damp basements. And it is for them, in large measure, that the newsgroups whose titles begin with the code-letters 'alt.sex' seem to exist.

There are 55 of these, offering manna for all diets. Some are fairly light-hearted: 'alt.sex.anal', for example, contains much spirited chat about amusing uses to which you can put the colonic gateway; 'alt.sex.voyeurism' seems to contain reasonably harmless chatter between a whole worldful of civic-minded Peeping Toms, who like to advise one another which public loos in which national parks have eye-sized knotholes in their doors. There is also 'alt.sex.nasal.hair', into which I have not thus far been tempted.

There are a number of the groups, though, which are not so amusing. There is 'alt.sex.intergen', where the last letters stand for 'intergenerational', which is the current paedophile bulletin-board; and there is my current target, 'alt.sex.stories'. I came across it by accident, and I double-clicked my mouse to open it, briefly enthralled. It did not take many seconds before I realised I had been ill-prepared for what was on offer.

There is a kind of classification system. Each story entry lists a title, an author (invariably either a pseudonym, or posted via an anonymous computer that has laundered the words and made the detection of the author impossible), and a series of code-words and symbols that indicate the approximate content.

Blackwind's many offerings—there were about 200 stories in all, with Blackwind contributing perhaps 15 of them—usually fell into the categories that are denoted by the codes 'm-f, f-f, scat.pedo.snuff', meaning that they contain scenes of male-female sex, female-female sex, scatological imagery, paedophiliac description and the eventual killing of the central victim. You quickly get, I think, the drift. Others are more horrifying still—those that end with the invariable 'snuff' scene, but whose enticements on the way include 'beast', 'torture', 'gore' or 'amputees', and which refer to sex with animals, bloodlettings, sadistic injury, and the limitless erotic joy of stumps.

It is important to note that no one polices or, to use the Internet word, 'moderates' this group. (Some of the more obscure and non-sexual newsgroups do have a volunteer, usually a specialist in the field, who tries to keep order in what might, if unchecked, become an unruly discussion.) On 'alt.sex.stories' there is only one man, a Mr Joshua Laff of the University of Illinois at Urbana, who oversees the group, in a somewhat lethargic way. He helpfully suggests the code-words for the various kinds of perverse interests. He indicates to people who want to talk about sex stories, rather than actually contributing them, that they would be better advised to post their gripes on 'alt.sex.stories.discussion', next door, and so on.

Constitutional Concerns

But Mr Laff has no admitted scruples about what is permitted to go out over the air. So far as he is concerned, the First Amendment to the Constitution protects all that is said on 'alt.sex.stories' as free speech. What is demonstrated on these thousands of electronic pages is a living exhibition of the birthright of all who are fortunate enough to be born in the land that has given us the National Rifle Association, the Reverend Jimmy Swaggart, and Blackwind.

In truth, Mr Laff and those who support the published existence of such writings are technically right. No obscene pictures are published—these could be banned in law. No obscene truths are proffered, so far as we know—no confessions of real rapes, nor of actual acts of pederasty. And since all the stories are prefaced with warnings that those under 18, or those of a sensitive disposition, should read no further—devices that presumably attract precisely those they purport to deter—so, the authors seem to agree, their ramblings do no harm at all.

> *"So far no one has successfully prosecuted the Internet [for sexually explicit material]."*

Most individual states legislate firmly or less so against printed pornography: but so far no one has successfully prosecuted the Internet—not least for the reason that with so amorphous, so global and so informal a linking of computers, who out there can be held responsible? People like Blackwind simply open accounts at what are known as 'anonymous posting systems', and their words become filtered through two or three computers in such a way that the original source can never be known, and the perpetrator of any possible crime becomes impossible to find. And, anyway, those who endlessly cry First Amendment! here are wont to say that the publishing of mere words, even those from so clearly depraved an individual as Blackwind, can do no harm at all.

Commonsense would argue otherwise. A long and graphic account of exactly how and at what hour you wait outside a girls' school, how best to bundle a seven-year-old into your van, whether to tell her at the start of her ordeal that she is going to be killed at the end of it (Blackwind's favoured *modus operandi*), how best to tie her down, which aperture to approach first, and with what—such things can only tempt those who verge on such acts to take a greater interest in them.

Surely such essays tell the thinker of forbidden thoughts that there exists somewhere out there a like-minded group of men for whom such things are really not so bad, the enjoyment of which, if no one is so ill-starred as to get caught, can be limitless. Surely it is naive folly—or, at the other end of the spectrum, gross irresponsibility—to suppose otherwise.

Equally Available Newsgroups

Such material is not, I am happy to say, universally available. Some of the big corporations which offer public access to the Internet—America On-Line, CompuServe, Prodigy, Mr Rupert Murdoch's Delphi—have systems in place that filter out the more objectionable newsgroups. On America On-Line you may read the ramblings on 'alt.sex.voyeurism' and probably even 'alt.sex.nasal.hair', but you may read no 'alt.sex.stories', nor may you learn techniques for having real relationships, as paedophiles like to say they have, with young children.

But for those with the wherewithal to find more robust and uncontrolled access to cyberspace—and that means, quite frankly, most of the world's computer users, be they 90 years old or nine—all newsgroups are equally available, the evil along with the excellent. The question we have to ask is whether that should continue to be the case.

One might not mind so much if the material were being confined to the United States, where most of it originates. But in fact it manages to seep its electronic way everywhere, from Wiltshire [England] to Waziristan [Pakistan]. And crucially, no mechanism is yet in place allowing foreigners—whose laws might well be far less tolerantly disposed to it—to filter it out.

A computer-owner in Islington or Islamabad can have easy and inexpensive access to material over the net which would be illegal for him or her to read or buy on any British or Pakistani street. In China, pornographers would be imprisoned for publishing material that any Peking University students can read at the click of a mouse; and the same is true in scores of other countries and societies. The Internet, we smugly say, has become a means of circumventing the restrictive codes of tyrannies. But the reverse of this coin is less attractive: it also allows an almost exclusively American contagion to ooze outwards, unstoppable, like an oil spill, contaminating everyone and everything in its path.

We cannot, of course, prevent such things being thought. We may not prevent them being written for self-gratification alone. But, surely, science and the public can somehow conspire and co-operate to see that such writings as are represented by 'scat.pedo.torture.snuff' and the like

> *"Surely, science and the public can somehow conspire and co-operate to see that [sexually obscene] writings . . . are neither published nor read."*

are neither published nor read, and that they do not in consequence have the opportunity to spread outwards as an electronic contagion from the minds of those who, like Blackwind, first create them.

The Jeffersonian model for universal freedom which Mr Gingrich so rightly applauds could not take into account the barbarisms of the modern mind. Nor could it imagine the genius by which such barbarisms can be disseminated as they are today, in seconds, to the remotest and still most innocent corners of the world. Someone, perhaps even the Speaker of the House of Representatives, is going to have to consider soon the implications, for ill as well as good, of our venture out onto the information superhighway, or else there are going to be some very messy electronic traffic accidents.

America Needs a Secure Computer Encryption System

by Dorothy E. Denning

About the author: *Dorothy E. Denning is a computer science professor at Georgetown University in Washington, D.C., and a specialist in computer and communication security. Denning was consulted by the federal government to review its Clipper encryption system.*

Imagine you are the program manager for a new, energy-efficient airplane. You fax the design plans to the manager of an overseas plant that will manufacture parts of the plane. You also discuss the design by phone with engineers in the plant. A few months later, your company loses a bid for a fleet of planes to an overseas competitor who proposed a nearly identical design. The rival stole your plans by intercepting your voice and fax communications.

Fortunately, electronic communication can be protected against such industrial espionage with encryption—scrambling of data in such a manner that they are unintelligible to anyone other than the intended receiver. In today's digital world, communications are first converted into ones and zeroes. An encryption algorithm mathematically transforms these bits into a stream of digits that seems random. Performing the transformation requires a secret key—which is also a random-seeming string of ones and zeroes; the receiver uses this key to decrypt and recover the original message. The more digits there are in this key, the more secure the protection; each additional bit doubles the number of possible combinations that a would-be snooper must try.

The Use of Encryption

Encryption has been used in the United States primarily to protect classified state and military secrets from foreign governments. However, its use outside the government has been steadily increasing ever since the Data Encryption

Standard (DES) was adopted as a federal standard in 1977. DES, which is based on a 56-bit key, is now used extensively by the banking industry to protect money transfers and by some corporations to protect sensitive communications transmitted through company networks or the telephone system. As individuals and companies swarm onto the Internet, they are also beginning to encrypt electronic mail and computer files.

But encryption is a dual-edged sword. The spread of high-quality encryption could undermine the value of wiretaps—a technology that has helped ensnare organized crime figures and other menaces to society. With the government essentially locked out, computers and telecommunications systems would become safe havens for outlaws and terrorists. In one recent child pornography case in California, evidence was concealed in encrypted computer files that could not be broken.

> *"Almost everyone agrees that individuals and organizations need access to encryption technology."*

Encryption also could interfere with U.S. intelligence abroad, because it could allow a country like Iraq to operate behind a wall of electronic secrecy. Encryption technology is therefore subject to export controls: products that incorporate DES or other strong encryption methods cannot generally be exported. This has been a sore point with U.S. industry, which has argued that since DES-based products are manufactured overseas also, the controls have succeeded only in putting U.S. industry at a disadvantage. However, even though export controls have not prevented DES and other methods of encryption from being implemented elsewhere, the controls have protected valuable and fragile intelligence capabilities.

Encryption poses a threat to organizations and individuals, too. For effective secrecy, a minimal number of people should be allowed to know the encryption key. This practice invites disaster, though, as valuable information stored in encrypted files could become inaccessible if the key were accidentally lost or corrupted, intentionally destroyed, or maybe even held for ransom by a disgruntled employee or former employee. Encryption also could enable an employee to transmit corporate secrets to a competitor or to cover up fraud, embezzlement, and other illegal activity.

Despite such problems, almost everyone agrees that individuals and organizations need access to encryption technology. With the spread of computer networks, people are conducting more and more of their personal and business affairs through computer and telephone networks. Encryption is essential for erecting a wall of privacy around those communications.

The Clipper Chip

To resolve the encryption dilemma, the Clinton administration in 1993 proposed a new approach, called "key-escrow" encryption. The idea is to make broadly available an essentially unbreakable encryption scheme. The catch: to allow for emergency access to information, the keys to unlock the keys to unlock the encrypted data would be held by the U.S. government.

The idea is to allow the most secure encryption, but with a built-in emergency decryption capability that allows authorized officials, with the cooperation of one or more trusted parties who hold keys, to decrypt data. The initial embodiment of this system is a microelectronic device called the Clipper chip, and its escrow agents are the National Institute of Standards and Technology (NIST) and the Department of Treasury's Automated Systems Division. In principle, commercial organizations also could serve as escrow agents. [In August 1995, the federal government announced it would consider the adoption of encryption alternatives to Clipper technology.]

The Clipper chip uses an encryption algorithm called Skipjack and keys of 80 bits—24 bits longer than DES keys. The extra 24 bits provide 2^{24} or about 16 million times the security against trial-and-error guesses at keys. The Skipjack algorithm was designed by the National Security Agency (NSA) and is classified.

Some civil libertarians have adamantly opposed this plan, worrying that the key escrow system will put the communications of honest persons needlessly at risk. After all, they argue, criminals are not going to be dumb enough to use an encryption scheme to which the government holds the keys. The logical next step, they say, would be to outlaw other methods of encryption, striking a blow at citizens' right to communicate away from the government's eyes and ears. Thus, critics argue, Clipper heralds future erosions in privacy rights—Big Brother on a chip.

> *"The [Clipper system] is voluntary; nongovernment agencies have no obligation to use it."*

Actually, Clipper represents a more secure approach to encryption than the two other avenues that the government has considered. One approach would use an encryption method with short enough keys that it becomes practical for any eavesdropper to guess a key by trying all possibilities. The other would use long keys, but have a built-in "trapdoor" allowing someone familiar with the system to find the key. The problem with this approach is that someone else might discover the trapdoor. Clipper avoids these weaker methods, offering a high-security solution to the encryption dilemma.

Holding Keys in Escrow

The specifications for Clipper were adopted in 1994 as the Escrowed Encryption Standard for use with sensitive but unclassified telephone communications, including voice, fax, and data. The EES standard is voluntary; nongovernment agencies have no obligation to use it, and government agencies can choose between it and any other encryption standard, such as DES. With the U.S. government holding the keys, EES poses no threat to foreign intelligence operations and thus EES-based encryption products can be exported.

The first product to use the Clipper chip is a device that plugs into a standard phone between the handset and the base unit. Manufactured by AT&T, the device can encrypt any conversation as long as the party at the other end has a compatible device. After a call is established in the usual way, one party presses a button on the device to activate its "secure mode." The two devices then enter into a digital, behind-the-scenes conversation to establish a "session key" that is unique to the conversation. Each device passes this 80-bit session key to its Clipper chip; the Clipper uses this key to encrypt outgoing communications and decrypt incoming communications. Before encrypting any data, however, the chip computes and transmits a string of bits called the law enforcement access field (LEAF). The LEAF contains the session key for the conversation and is what enables authorized government officials to decrypt the data.

To protect the session key in the LEAF, it is itself encrypted. Each Clipper chip has a unique identifier (ID) and associated "device-unique key." The device-unique key is split into two components, each of which is given to a separate escrow agent. Using this device-unique key, the Clipper chip encrypts the session key. The encrypted session key is then put into the LEAF along with the chip ID. The entire LEAF is further encrypted under a common "family key" so that even the chip ID is not transmitted in the clear. These two layers of encryption provide a strong shield against an eavesdropper learning the session key and then decrypting the data.

Users of Clipper don't need to be aware of any of these details; they simply use their phones as always. The complexity surfaces when a law enforcement official encounters encrypted communications on a tapped phone line. First, the communications must be passed through a special device, known as a decrypt processor, to ascertain if they are Clipper communications. If they are, the processor locates and decrypts the LEAF, and then extracts the chip ID. (Because the same session key is used to encrypt both ends of the conversation, it is not necessary to obtain the chip ID for both parties.)

> *"Keys and key components are generated in computers and are never displayed or printed out in forms readable by humans."*

But knowledge of this chip ID alone will not allow the wiretap to be deciphered. What is needed are the two components of the device-unique key associated with this ID—and this information is what is held by the two key escrow agents. So the law enforcement officials, having obtained this ID, must request these components from the escrow agents. These key components are then entered into the decrypt processor, which combines them to form the device-unique key. This device-unique key, in turn, is used to decrypt the session key in the LEAF. Knowledge of this session key enables the conversation to be decrypted. If subsequent conversations on the intercepted line are encrypted, the decrypt processor can decrypt the session key directly, without going through the two escrow agents. This allows for real-time decryption.

Clipper Safeguards

Critics maintain that the very idea of a key escrow system raises the risk that encrypted messages will be decoded by the wrong people. Without proper safeguards, an intruder might break into a computer containing escrowed keys, download the keys, and use the keys to decrypt communications intercepted illegally. Alternatively, a corrupt employee of an escrow agent might use the keys to engage in illegal wiretapping or sell the keys to a foreign government or to the mafia.

Clipper's key escrow system is being developed with extensive controls to protect against such threats. One fundamental safeguard is key secrecy. Keys and key components are generated in computers and are never displayed or printed out in forms readable by humans. In addition, they are always stored and transmitted in encrypted form.

Physical security is used extensively to protect sensitive material. The computer workstations at NIST and the Department of Treasury that are used for key escrow functions are used for nothing else and are kept in secured facilities. The chips are programmed with their IDs and device-unique keys in a vault designed for handling classified information.

As the Clipper system develops, keys are stored on floppy disks in double-locked safes and carried manually, wrapped in tamper-detecting packages, from the facility where the chips are programmed to the escrow agents and from the escrow agents to the law enforcement facility that is tapping the call. Ultimately, the keys will be transmitted electronically—in encrypted form—between the chip-programming facility and escrow-agent workstations, and between those workstations and the law-enforcement decrypt processors. Separation of duties limits the power of a single person or agency. Different organizations operate the chip-programming facility (so far, Mykotronx Inc. of Torrance, California, runs the only one), the key escrow services (NIST and the Department of Treasury), and the decrypt processors (law enforcement agencies). Escrow officers are not allowed to program the chips, operate a decrypt processor, or even have a decrypt processor in their possession. Law-enforcement officers have access to a decrypt processor but not to keys (keys cannot be extracted from a decrypt processor). Escrow officers will attach a "self-destruct" date, corresponding to the end of the period of authorized surveillance, to keys transmitted to a decrypt processor. This measure precludes the use of keys after a wiretap order expires.

> *"The only way to make sure that an algorithm is any good is to let many people analyze it and try to crack it."*

To limit the power of a single individual to abuse the system, the key escrow system requires that at least two people be present whenever a critical function is performed or when sensitive data might be exposed. In fact, because each chip's device-unique key is split into two components, and each component is held by a separate key escrow agent, it is not possible for one person to act independently. Neither component by itself reveals any information about the key; to reconstruct and use the key, both escrow agents must supply their parts. Further, within each escrow agency, it takes two escrow officers to unlock the safes that contain the key components. Similar two-person control systems have worked successfully in the military to control nuclear-launch codes and in the banking world. . . .

> *"Critics say that the introduction of Clipper points national policy in a disturbing direction."*

Based on what I have seen so far of the design, I conclude that there is no significant risk of an insider or outsider acquiring unauthorized access to keys.

As the Clipper system proves to be strong and resistant to abuse, the technology will, I believe, become more widely accepted. The Department of Defense already uses Capstone—a more advanced chip that is built into a PC card named Fortezza—to provide security for electronic mail. Fortezza offers an attractive option for secure electronic commerce: it contains a mechanism for electronically "signing" a digital document so that the recipient can verify the sender's identity. The American National Standards Institute (ANSI) is developing banking standards that could use Fortezza technology.

Who Do You Trust?

These safeguards have not eased everyone's mind. One big concern is that the Skipjack encryption algorithm on which Clipper is based is classified. Because Skipjack is not open to public review, some people have questioned whether NSA might have intentionally sabotaged the algorithm with a trapdoor that would allow the government to decode encrypted communications while bypassing the escrow agents.

Critics also worry that this secret algorithm might harbor a design flaw that would leave it vulnerable to cracking. Such concerns have a legitimate base. Designing strong encryption algorithms is a difficult task. The only way to make sure that an algorithm is any good is to let many people analyze it and try to crack it over an extended period of time; many encryption schemes that appeared strong when first proposed later succumbed to attack. . . .

To address the concerns about weaknesses and trapdoors in Skipjack, the government invited outside experts to independently review the algorithm and report their findings. I participated in that review along with four other cryptographers in 1993. We examined NSA's internal design and evaluation of Skipjack and found them to be the same as used with algorithms that protect the country's most sensitive classified information. Skipjack underwent thorough evaluation over many years following its initial design in 1987, and the specific structures used in the algorithm have an even longer history of intense study. We also conducted some analysis and experiments of our own to determine if the algorithm had any properties that might make it susceptible to attack. Based on our analysis and experiments, we concluded that there was no significant risk that Skipjack contained a trapdoor or could be broken.

Although publication of Skipjack would enable more people to confirm its strength, NSA is unlikely to do so; declassifying Skipjack would benefit foreign adversaries and allow the algorithm to be used without the key escrow features. Even if Skipjack were made public, it would probably be years before skeptics would accept its strength. When DES was introduced in 1975, it was similarly distrusted because of some NSA involvement even though the algorithm was developed by IBM and made public.

Still, Clipper's use of a classified algorithm does limit its acceptability. There are many people who will never trust the NSA; for them, Clipper is tainted goods. In addition, many potential foreign buyers will not accept a classified algorithm or keys held by the U.S. government, although Mykotronx has reported that some potential foreign buyers are not concerned about these factors. Agreements might be reached that would allow some other governments to hold the keys or have access to the classified technology, but such agreements would likely be limited to a few countries.

Moreover, as long as the algorithm is supposed to remain secret, it must be implemented in tamper-resistant hardware. That's because there is no known way of hiding classified information in software. This precludes software implementations, which are generally cheaper. On the other hand, hardware generally provides greater security for keys and greater integrity for the algorithms than software, so some customers will want hardware products.

What Would Criminals Use?

Although key escrow is voluntary, critics say that the introduction of Clipper points national policy in a disturbing direction. The main premise here is that the criminals that Clipper is meant to uncover would be unlikely to choose an encryption scheme to which the U.S. government holds the keys. Many forms of unescrowed encryption are already on the market, and more are being developed. One file encryption package, called Pretty Good Privacy (PGP), is spreading as free software through the Internet and becoming popular for encrypting e-mail. Unescrowed encryption with time-tested algorithms such as DES and RSA [an algorithm invented at the Massachusetts Institute of Technology in 1977] is also being integrated into commercial products. The only way to accomplish the goals of Clipper, skeptics therefore maintain, would be to ban unescrowed encryption systems—a prospect that enrages some defenders of electronic privacy.

But it is not self-evident that criminals will shun Clipper. Whether they use the escrowed encryption system will depend in part on what else is available—and in particular what other forms of encryption are built into the most widely used commercial products. While PGP has a certain grassroots appeal, many organizations will be reluctant to trust their assets to software obtained over the Internet.

Over time, market forces could easily favor escrowed encryption. Some organizations might choose to use Clipper because the high quality of its encryption outweighs the slight risk that information will fall into the wrong hands. Vendors might favor key escrow because they will be able to build it into products that are exported. And the government's adoption of escrowed encryption will set a de facto standard; any company that needs to exchange encrypted information with federal agencies will need to use compatible encryption. If escrowed encryption becomes a business standard, many criminals will tend to use it—the convenience will outweigh the risk.

> *"While abuse of the Clipper system cannot be ruled out, it is unlikely."*

Even if criminals do not use Clipper, the government's voluntary initiative serves a useful purpose. If the government instead promoted strong encryption without key escrow, this would accelerate the spread of encryption that the government could not decrypt and the use of such encryption by criminals. The government decided that it would not be responsible to use its own expertise and resources to pursue encryption standards that fundamentally subvert law enforcement and threaten public safety and national security. . . .

Key escrow encryption offers the best hope for an international standard that would facilitate international communications. In fact, an encryption method that does not provide a capability for government access is unlikely to be accepted as an international standard; other countries share the U.S. desire not to be left in the electronic lurch. Each country could designate its own escrow agents, which could be either government or commercial organizations. Users might have the option of choosing an escrow agent from this list. Bankers Trust has outlined a proposal for just such an approach. Like Clipper, the Bankers Trust system would use hardware for its greater security; unlike Clipper, however, the algorithm would be unclassified and therefore more suitable for commercial and international use.

Will Clipper Catch On?

Much opposition to Clipper stems from the belief that the government has an insatiable and unsavory desire to gather information about its law-abiding citizens. Clipper, say critics, is a bad idea because it permits such activity. Despite the system's safeguards, some people are concerned that a future administration or corrupt police officer could obtain keys to conduct questionable if not outright illegal wiretaps.

At a forum held at MIT in 1994, professor Ronald Rivest argued that the fundamental question Clipper raises is: Should American citizens have the right to have communications and records that the government cannot access even when properly authorized? A case can be made that from a constitutional standpoint, no such absolute right exists. The Fourth Amendment specifically protects against unreasonable searches and seizures while allowing those conducted with a court order.

While abuse of the Clipper system cannot be ruled out, it is unlikely. Neither the public nor Congress has tolerated such activity in the past, and federal wiretap laws, government regulations and procedures, and congressional committees have been established to protect against their occurrence in the future. Wiretaps are conducted under tight controls and subject to considerable oversight. Clipper includes an additional layer of protection since anyone wishing to conduct a wiretap must also acquire a special decrypt processor and keys from the escrow agents.

The opposition to Clipper makes its widespread adoption by no means assured. But escrowed encryption offers the best hope for reaping the benefits of encryption while minimizing its potential harm. Rejection of key escrow would have profound implications for criminal justice. As computer networks continue to expand into every area of society and commerce, court-ordered wiretaps and seizures of records could become tools of the past, and the information superhighway a safe haven for criminal activity.

Objectionable Computer Content Should Be Labeled, Not Censored

by Esther Dyson

About the author: *Esther Dyson is the editor of* Release 1.0, *a computer newsletter, and is a managing partner of EDventure Ventures, a fund devoted to bringing on-line services to central Europe and Russia.*

Something in the American psyche loves new frontiers. We hanker after wide-open spaces; we like to explore; we like to make rules instead of follow them. But in this age of political correctness and other intrusions on our national cult of independence, it's hard to find a place where you can go and be yourself without worrying about the neighbors.

There is such a place: cyberspace. Lost in the furor over porn on the Net is the exhilarating sense of freedom that this new frontier once promised—and still does in some quarters. Formerly a playground for computer nerds and techies, cyberspace now embraces every conceivable constituency: school-children, flirtatious singles, Hungarian-Americans, accountants—along with pederasts and porn fans. Can they all get along? Or will our fear of kids surfing for cyberporn behind their bedroom doors provoke a crackdown?

Cyberspace as Real Estate

The first order of business is to grasp what cyberspace *is*. It might help to leave behind metaphors of highways and frontiers and to think instead of real estate. Real estate, remember, is an intellectual, legal, artificial environment constructed *on top of* land. Real estate recognizes the difference between park-land and shopping mall, between red-light zone and school district, between church, state and drugstore.

In the same way, you could think of cyberspace as a giant and unbounded world of virtual real estate. Some property is privately owned and rented out; other property is common land; some places are suitable for children, and others are best avoided by all but the kinkiest citizens. Unfortunately, it's those places that are now capturing the popular imagination: places that offer bomb-making instructions, pornography, advice on how to procure stolen credit cards. They make cyberspace sound like a nasty place. Good citizens jump to a conclusion: Better regulate it.

[A] recent manifestation of this impulse is the Exon-Coats Amendment, a well-meaning but misguided bill drafted by Senators Jim Exon, Democrat of Nebraska, and Daniel R. Coats, Republican of Indiana, to make cyberspace "safer" for children. Part of the telecommunications reform bill passed by the Senate and the House in 1995, the amendment would outlaw making "indecent communication" available to anyone under 18. Then there's the Amateur Action bulletin board case, in which the owners of a porn service in Milpitas, California, were convicted in a Tennessee court of violating "community standards" after a local postal inspector requested that the material be transmitted to him.

> *"Using censorship to counter indecency and other troubling 'speech' fundamentally misinterprets the nature of cyberspace."*

Regardless of how many laws or lawsuits are launched, regulation won't work.

Aside from being unconstitutional, using censorship to counter indecency and other troubling "speech" fundamentally misinterprets the nature of cyberspace. Cyberspace isn't a frontier where wicked people can grab unsuspecting children, nor is it a giant television system that can beam offensive messages at unwilling viewers. In this kind of real estate, users have to *choose* where they visit, what they see, what they do. It's optional, and it's much easier to bypass a place on the Net than it is to avoid walking past an unsavory block of stores on the way to your local 7-11.

Put plainly, cyberspace is a voluntary destination—in reality, many destinations. You don't just get "onto the net"; you have to go someplace in particular. That means that people can choose where to go and what to see. Yes, community standards should be enforced, but those standards should be set by cyberspace communities themselves, not by the courts or by politicians in Washington. What we need isn't Government control over all these electronic communities: We need self-rule.

What makes cyberspace so alluring is precisely the way in which it's *different* from shopping malls, television, highways and other terrestrial jurisdictions. But let's define the territory:

First, there are private E-mail conversations, akin to the conversations you have over the telephone or voice mail. These are private and consensual and require no regulation at all.

Second, there are information and entertainment services, where people can download anything from legal texts and lists of "great new restaurants" to game software or dirty pictures. These places are like bookstores, malls and movie houses—places where you go to buy something. The customer needs to request an item or sign up for a subscription; stuff (especially pornography) is not sent out to people who don't ask for it. Some of these services are free or included as part of a broader service like Compuserve or America Online; others charge and may bill their customers directly.

Third, there are "real" communities—groups of people who communicate among themselves. In real-estate terms, they're like bars or restaurants or bathhouses. Each active participant contributes to a general conversation, generally through posted messages. Other participants may simply listen or watch. Some are supervised by a moderator; others are more like bulletin boards—anyone is free to post anything. Many of these services started out unmoderated but are now imposing rules to keep out unwanted advertising, extraneous discussions or increasingly rude participants. Without a moderator, the decibel level often gets too high.

Ultimately, it's the rules that determine the success of such places. Some of the rules are determined by the supplier of content; some of the rules concern prices and membership fees. The rules may be simple: "Only high-quality content about oil-industry liability and pollution legislation: $120 an hour." Or: "This forum is unmoderated, and restricted to information about copyright issues. People who insist on posting advertising or unrelated material will be asked to desist (and may eventually be barred)." Or: "Only children 8 to 12, on school-related topics and only clean words. The moderator will decide what's acceptable."

Different Types of Communities

Cyberspace communities evolve just the way terrestrial communities do: people with like-minded interests band together. Every cyberspace community has its own character. Overall, the communities on Compuserve tend to be more techy or professional; those on America Online, affluent young singles; Prodigy, family oriented. Then there are independents like Echo, a hip, downtown New York service, or Women's Wire, targeted to women who want to avoid the male culture prevalent elsewhere on the Net. There's SurfWatch, a new program allowing access only to locations deemed suitable for children. On the Internet itself, there are lots of passionate noncommercial discussion groups on topics ranging from Hungarian politics (Hungary-Online) to copyright law.

> *"Whether [porn-oriented] services encourage the fantasies they depict is subject to debate."*

And yes, there are also porn-oriented services, where people share dirty pictures and communicate with one another about all kinds of practices, often anonymously. Whether these services encourage the fantasies they depict is subject to debate—the same debate that has raged about pornography in other media. But the point is that no one is forcing this stuff on anybody.

What's unique about cyberspace is that it liberates us from the tyranny of government, where everyone lives by the rule of the majority. In a democracy, minority groups and minority preferences tend to get squeezed out, whether they are minorities of race and culture or minorities of individual taste. Cyberspace allows communities of any size and kind to flourish; in cyberspace, communities are chosen by the users, not forced on them by accidents of geography. This freedom gives the rules that preside in cyberspace a

> *"If you don't like the rules of a cyberspace community, you can just sign off."*

moral authority that rules in terrestrial environments don't have. Most people are stuck in the country of their birth, but if you don't like the rules of a cyberspace community, you can just sign off. Love it or leave it. Likewise, if parents don't like the rules of a given cyberspace community, they can restrict their children's access to it.

What's likely to happen in cyberspace is the formation of new communities, free of the constraints that cause conflict on earth. Instead of a global village, which is a nice dream but impossible to manage, we'll have invented another world of self-contained communities that cater to their own members' inclinations without interfering with anyone else's. The possibility of a real market-style evolution of governance is at hand. In cyberspace, we'll be able to test and evolve rules governing what needs to be governed—intellectual property, content and access control, rules about privacy and free speech. Some communities will allow anyone in; others will restrict access to members who qualify on one basis or another. Those communities that prove self-sustaining will prosper (and perhaps grow and split into subsets with ever-more-particular interests and identities). Those that can't survive—either because people lose interest or get scared off—will simply wither away.

The Answer Is Labeling

In the near future, explorers in cyberspace will need to get better at defining and identifying their communities. They will need to put in place—and accept—their own local governments, just as the owners of expensive real estate often prefer to have their own security guards rather than call in the police. But they will rarely need help from any terrestrial government.

Of course, terrestrial governments may not agree. What to do, for instance, about pornography? The answer is labeling—not banning—questionable material. In order to avoid censorship and lower the political temperature, it makes sense for cyberspace participants themselves to agree on a scheme for questionable items, so that people or automatic filters can avoid them. In other words, posting pornography in "alt.sex.bestiality" would be O.K.; it's easy enough for software manufacturers to build an automatic filter that would prevent you—or your child—from ever seeing that item on a menu. (It's as if all the items were wrapped, with labels on the wrapper.) Someone who posted the same material under the title "Kid-Fun" could be sued for mislabeling.

Without a lot of fanfare, private enterprises and local groups are already producing a variety of labeling and ranking services, along with kid-oriented sites like Kidlink, EdWeb and Kids' Space. People differ in their tastes and values and can find services or reviewers on the Net that suit them in the same way they select books and magazines. Or they can wander freely if they prefer, making up their own itinerary.

> **"We can have individual choice—and individual responsibility."**

In the end, our society needs to grow up. Growing up means understanding that there are no perfect answers, no all-purpose solutions, no government-sanctioned safe havens. We haven't created a perfect society on earth and we won't have one in cyberspace either. But at least we can have individual choice—and individual responsibility.

Government Should Not Censor the Internet

by Nat Hentoff

About the author: *Nat Hentoff writes a civil liberties column for the* Village Voice *weekly newspaper in New York City and is the author of* Free Speech for Me—But Not for Thee: How the American Left and Right Relentlessly Censor Each Other.

For almost 50 years, Anthony Comstock—until he died in 1915—was the nation's relentless chief censor. He made it a crime to send information through the mail about contraception and abortion, along with anything "obscene." And, as Edward de Grazia notes in *Girls Lean Back Everywhere: The Law of Obscenity and the Assault on Genius*: "Comstock claimed to have convicted 'enough persons [of obscenity] to fill a passenger train of sixty-one coaches—sixty coaches containing sixty passengers each and the sixty-first coach not quite full.'" And he went after a publisher of [French novelist] Honoré de Balzac's *Droll Stories*, who wound up with a two-year prison term. Comstock so cleansed the nation of indecency that, among the many honors he received, he was appointed to President Woodrow Wilson's International Purity Congress.

I do not like to diminish the dead, but Comstock's accomplishments were chump change compared to the achievement of Senator James Exon (Democrat of Nebraska) who on June 14, 1995, persuaded the United States Senate to include his Communications Decency Act as part of the huge telecommunications bill.

Sweeping Censorship

The Exon Act is the most sweeping imposition of governmental censorship in American history because it is deliberately and directly aimed at a new technology that goes far beyond any previous ways of communication. It opens up the worlds within the worlds of cyberspace.

The Senate, by a stunning and disgraceful 84 to 16 vote, has established—

From "The Speech Police Invade Cyberspace" by Nat Hentoff, *Village Voice*, July 11, 1995. Reprinted with permission.

under the Exon Act, co-sponsored by Dan Coats (Republican of Indiana)—fines of up to $100,000 and two years in prison for people who "knowingly make, or make available . . . obscene, lewd, lascivious, filthy, or indecent material" across electronic networks. [The House of Representatives subsequently passed the act.]

Designed to protect minors from coming upon what Senator Exon has described as "a red-light district in cyberspace," the language of the amendment is so broad and so ignorant of the new technology that it can entrap almost anyone committing an illegal act. (What is "lewd," "lascivious," "filthy," or "indecent"?)

> *"The Exon Act is the most sweeping imposition of governmental censorship in American history."*

And how, moreover, on the Internet, can it be shown that you are deliberately directing an indecent communication "to any person under 18 years of age," as Exon puts it as a requirement for punishment?

As the Center for Democracy and Technology in Washington, D.C., emphasizes, "this restriction on indecency, which includes sexually-explicit material, amounts to a total ban on all 'indecent' information in public areas of the Internet *since all users of the Internet know that public areas are accessible to minors.*" (Emphasis added.)

In a crisply pertinent editorial, "Censoring Cyberspace," the *Washington Post* pointed out precisely how ignorant most of the senators are about how communications in cyberspace actually move:

> The [Exon] clause was written without hearings on the new technologies and without a full appreciation of how differently they work. . . . The law would heavily penalize, jail, or fine anyone who "knowingly transmits" or "knowingly makes available" indecent content to someone under 18.

> But on the Internet, the traditional distinction between a sender and receiver of information doesn't hold. To post anything anywhere, here or abroad, "makes it available" to millions of unidentified users who may get to it by a variety of technical routes and then make a copy for their own use. *Material can thus be "received" without anybody's sending* [it], and conversations that function like ordinary "speech" in the public square can also be considered "publications" that are copied by innumerable users. (Emphasis added.)

How, then, to police this complex web? Be assured that government agents will find a way.

Second-Class Speech

This is only the beginning of the dangerous foolishness that Senator Exon and 83 of his colleagues have perpetrated. They have turned expression in cyberspace into second-class speech. As the Center for Democracy and Technology puts it, "The indecency ban creates the paradoxical result that speech which would be fully protected in books, magazines, newspapers, or other print-based publications, would be subject to criminal sanction if made available over the Internet."

A salient example is House Speaker Newt Gingrich's current novel, *1945*, which contains exuberantly "indecent" passages.

The Exon amendment so sanitizes language and other forms of expression on the Internet that, as Senator Patrick Leahy (Democrat of Vermont) says: "I can call my brother on the phone and say anything—but if I say it on the Internet, it's illegal."

In *Newsweek* (April 3, 1995), Steven Levy quotes Leahy: "None of us want children to be delving into pornography, but let's not deal with it in a way that cripples one of the best communications successes in decades. I'm not going to close down a beautiful city park because periodically some idiot comes to the corner and shouts obscenities."

Leahy tried hard during the Senate debate on the Communications Decency Act to bring some sense to the discussion. "The Internet," he said,

> has become the tremendous success it is because it did not have Big Brother, the federal government, trying to micromanage what it does and trying to tell users what they could do. If the government had been in charge of figuring out how to expand the Internet or make it more available, I guarantee it would not be one-tenth the success it is today.

How the Senate Voted

. . . I had not seen a voting tally on the Exon Act in any paper, so I got it from the *Congressional Record*. You ought to know who tried to keep the highway free of cops, and you ought to know who wants to sabotage what was becoming the most liberating advance in *interactive* communication in all fields of knowledge.

To begin with, the 16 who voted against the Exon Act—heroes of the First Amendment: Joe Biden, Jeff Bingaman, John Chafee, Russell Feingold, John Glenn, James Jeffords, Ted Kennedy, Patrick Leahy, Carl Levin, Joseph Lieberman, Carol Moseley-Braun, Daniel Patrick Moynihan, Patty Murray, Charles Robb, Paul Simon, and Paul Wellstone.

Among the 84 know-nothings in the majority were such self-professed constitutionalists as Arlen Specter and Paul Sarbanes. Even though Bob Kerrey vigorously opposed the overall telecommunications bill—which greatly benefits the giants of the industry and screws consumers—he voted for the censorship part of the bill. A big disappointment.

The majority also included some careless liberals (Barbara Boxer, Christopher Dodd, Bill Bradley, and Tom Harkin), along with the usual Tories [conservatives] when it comes to

> *"The Internet . . . has become the tremendous success it is because it did not have Big Brother . . . trying to micromanage what it does."*

the Bill of Rights—Al D'Amato, Bob Dole, Dianne Feinstein, Orrin Hatch, Jesse Helms, Frank Lautenberg, Trent Lott, Alan Simpson, Strom Thurmond, et al.

I doubt if the 84 censors—of what would have been boundless knowledge—know or care, but in 1957 Justice Felix Frankfurter, speaking for the Supreme Court in *Butler v. Michigan*, struck down a law that prohibited the sale of "lewd" material that might damage young people.

Said Frankfurter: "The state may not reduce the adult population of Michigan to reading only what is fit for children."

That is now the low ceiling of expression in cyberspace. One ray of hope is that cyberspace is, up to a point, very hard to regulate. In "The Net: It's Hard to Clean Up" (*The New York Times*, June 18, 1995), Steve Lohr wrote: "But the sprawling, protean nature of computer network-technology means that any major regulatory effort to 'clean up the Net' would require draconian forms of censorship unfamiliar to Americans."

> *"Any major regulatory effort to 'clean up the Net' would require draconian forms of censorship unfamiliar to Americans."*

From the Massachusetts Bay Colony to Anthony Comstock to what happens now in schools and libraries in small towns you've never heard of, Americans have been all too familiar with draconian censorship. As will be proved again by the enforcement of Senator Exon's communications Decency Act.

Lohr continued:

> There are now 30,000 sites on the Internet's World Wide Web, where users can retrieve pictures, sounds, and text. Pity the poor FBI (or FCC [Federal Communications Commission]) agent trying to keep up with those. The Justice Department worries that the Senate's proposal is unenforceable. But the darkest fear of civil libertarians is that there will be mandated software on every computer, blocking access to large portions of the Internet—overseen by a censorship board.

The alternative to government control is, of course, user control. Why should Congress and the FCC have the right and power to tell you what you can communicate from a computer in your own home? The democratic way is being shown by the Surfwatch Software Company in Los Altos, California, which has developed a program (as have other companies) that allows parents to block access to Internet locations where sexually explicit material thrives.

In the *Wall Street Journal*, Jay Friedland of the Palo Alto firm says: "The goal is to allow people [not only parents] to have a choice over what they see on the Internet by allowing them to block or filter 'various [other] kinds of material.'"...

It's ironic but predictable that the Republican senators in particular—led by the mechanical Bob Dole—who voted to place sentries on the electronic highway, are the very same urgent voices for stripping the federal government of its powers and restoring them to the people. But now, thanks to them, Big Government will squat in every home with access to cyberspace.

Prosecutors Should Not Excessively Target Pornography

by Bruce Sterling

About the author: *A science fiction writer and the author of the nonfiction book* The Hacker Crackdown, *Bruce Sterling is a contributing writer for* Wired, *a monthly magazine covering telecommunications.*

I'm an author and I'm interested in free expression. That's only natural because that's my bailiwick. Free expression is a problem for writers, and it's always been a problem, and it's probably always gonna be a problem. We in the West have these ancient and honored traditions of free speech and freedom of the press, and in the United States we have this rather more up-to-date concept of "freedom of information." But even so, there is an enormous amount of "information" today that is highly problematic. Just because freedom of the press was in the Constitution didn't mean that people were able to stop thinking about what press freedom really means in real life, and fighting about it and suing each other about it. We Americans have lots of problems with our freedom of the press and our freedom of speech. Problems like libel and slander. Incitement to riot. Obscenity. Child pornography. Flag-burning. Cross-burning. Race-hate propaganda. Political correctness. Sexist language. Tipper Gore's Parents Music Resource Council. Movie ratings. Plagiarism. Photocopying rights. A journalist's so-called right to protect sources. Fair-use doctrine. Lawyer-client confidentiality. Paid political announcements. Banning ads for liquor and cigarettes. The fairness doctrine for broadcasters. School textbook censors. National security. Military secrets. Industrial trade secrets. Arts funding for so-called obscenity. Even religious blasphemy such as Salman Rushdie's famous novel *Satanic Verses*, which is hated so violently by the kind of people who like to blow up the World Trade Center. All these huge problems about what people can say to each other, under what circumstances. And that's without computers and computer networks.

From "Good Cop, Bad Hacker" by Bruce Sterling, *Wired*, May 1995. Reprinted with permission.

Every single one of those problems is applicable to cyberspace. Computers don't make any of these old free-expression problems go away; on the contrary, they intensify them, and they introduce a bunch of new problems. Problems like software piracy. Encryption. Wire fraud. Interstate transportation of stolen digital property. Free expression on privately owned networks. So-called "data-mining" to invade personal privacy. Employers spying on employee e-mail. Intellectual rights over electronic publications. Computer search-and-seizure practice. Legal liability for network crashes. Computer intrusion. And on and on and on. These are real problems. They're out there. They're out there now. In the future, they're only going to get worse. And there's going to be a bunch of new problems that nobody's even imagined.

I worry about these issues because people in positions like mine ought to worry about these issues. I can't say I've ever suffered much because of censorship, or through my government's objections to what I have to say. On the contrary, the current U.S. government likes me so much it makes me nervous. But I've written ten books, and I don't think I've ever written one that could have been legally published in its entirety fifty years ago. I'm forty years old; I can remember when people didn't use the word condom in public. Nowadays, if you don't know what a condom is and how to use it, there's a pretty good chance you're gonna die. Standards change a lot. Culture changes a lot. The laws supposedly governing this behavior are gray and riddled with contradictions and compromises. There are some people who don't want our culture to change, or they want to change it even faster in a direction that they've got their own

> *"There's not a lot to be gained by playing up the terrifying menace of porn on networks."*

ideas about. When police get involved in a cultural struggle, it's always highly politicized. The chances of it ending well are not good.

It's been quite a while since there was a really good, ripping computer-intrusion scandal in the news. Presumably, everyone was waiting for [fugitive computer hacker] Kevin Mitnick to get really restless. Nowadays, the hot-button issue is porn. Kidporn and other porn. I don't have much sympathy for kidporn people; I think the exploitation of children is a vile and grotesque criminal act, but I've seen some computer porn cases lately that look pretty problematic and peculiar to me. There's not a lot to be gained by playing up the terrifying menace of porn on networks. Porn is just too treacherous an issue to be of much use to anybody. It's not a firm and dependable place in which to take a stand on how we ought to run our networks.

Different Community Standards

For instance, there's this Amateur Action case. We've got this couple in California, and they're selling some pretty seriously vile material off their bulletin board. They get indicted in Tennessee, and face sentencing on eleven obscenity convictions, each carrying a maximum sentence of five years in prison and U.S. $250,000 in fines. What is that about? Do we really think that people in Memphis can enforce their pornographic community standards on people in California? I'd be impressed if a prosecutor got a jury in California to indict and convict some pornographer in Tennessee. I'd figure that that Tennessee pornographer had to be pretty heavy-duty. Doing that in the other direction is like shooting fish in a barrel. There's something cheap about it. This doesn't smell like an airtight criminal case to me. This smells like someone from Tennessee trying to enforce the local cultural standards via a long-distance phone line. That may not be the truth about the case, but that's what the case looks like. It's hard to make a porn case look good at any time. If it's a weak case, then the prosecutor looks like a bluenosed goody-goody wimp. If it's a strong case, then the whole mess is so disgusting that nobody even wants to think about it or even look hard at the evidence. Porn is a no-win situation when it comes to the basic social purpose of instilling law and order on networks.

> *"People in California are never gonna behave in a way that satisfies people in Tennessee."*

You could make a pretty good case in Tennessee that people in California are a bunch of flaky, perverted lunatics; in California, you can make a pretty good case that people from Tennessee are a bunch of hillbilly fundamentalist wackos. You start playing one community off another, and pretty soon you're out of the realm of criminal law, and into the realm of trying to control people's cultural behavior with a nightstick. There's not a lot to be gained by this fight. You may intimidate a few pornographers here and there, but you're also likely to seriously infuriate a bunch of bystanders. It's not a fight you can win—even if you win a case, or two cases, or ten cases. People in California are never gonna behave in a way that satisfies people in Tennessee. People in California have more money and more power and more influence than people living in Tennessee. People in California invented Hollywood and Silicon Valley, and people in Tennessee invented ways to put smut labels on rock-and-roll albums.

This is what Pat Buchanan and Newt Gingrich are talking about when they talk about cultural war in America. If I were a cop, I would be very careful of looking like a pawn in some cultural warfare by ambitious radical politicians. The country's infested with zealots now—to the left and right. A lot of these people are fanatics motivated by fear and anger, and they don't care two pins about public order or the people who maintain it and keep the peace in our society. They don't want a debate. They just want to crush their enemies by whatever means possible. If they can use cops to do it, then great! Cops are expendable.

A Porn Raid

There's another porn case that bugs me even more. There's this guy in Oklahoma City who had a big Fidonet bulletin board, and a storefront where he sold

CD-ROMs. Some of them, a few, were porn CD-ROMs. The Oklahoma City police catch this local hacker kid, and of course he squeals—they always do—and he says, Don't nail me, nail this other guy, he's a pornographer. So off the police go to raid this guy's place of business, and while they're at it, they carry some minicams and they broadcast their raid on that night's Oklahoma City evening news (this is in August of '93). It was a really high-tech and innovative thing to do, but it was also a really reckless cowboy thing to do, because it left no political fallback position. They were now utterly committed to crucifying this guy, because otherwise it was too much of a political embarrassment. They couldn't just shrug and say, Well, we've just busted this guy for selling a few lousy CD-ROMs that anybody in the country can mail order with impunity out of the back of a computer magazine. They had to assemble a jury, with a couple of fundamentalist ministers on it, and show the most rancid graphic image files to the twelve good people. And, sure enough, it was judged in a court to be pornographic. I don't think there was much doubt that it was pornography, and I don't doubt that any jury in Oklahoma City would have called it pornography by the local Oklahoma City community standards. This guy got convicted. Lost the trial. Lost his business. Went to jail. His wife sued for divorce. He's a convict. His life is in ruins.

> *"I don't think this guy was a pornographer by any genuine definition."*

I don't think this guy was a pornographer by any genuine definition. He had no previous convictions. Never been in trouble. Didn't have a bad character. Had an honorable war record in Vietnam. Paid his taxes. People who knew him personally spoke very highly of him. He wasn't some loony sleazebag. He was just a guy selling disks that other people (just like him) sell all over the country, without anyone blinking an eye. As far as I can figure, the Oklahoma City police and an Oklahoma prosecutor skinned this guy and nailed his hide to the side of a barn, just because they didn't want to look bad. A serious injustice was done here.

A Reckless Move

It was a terrible public relations move. There's a magazine out called *Boardwatch*—practically everybody who runs a bulletin board system in this country reads it. When the editor of this magazine heard about the outcome of this case, he basically went nonlinear. He wrote this scorching furious editorial berating the authorities. The Oklahoma City prosecutor sent his little message all right, and it went over the Oklahoma City evening news, and probably made him look pretty good, locally and personally. But this magazine sent a much bigger and much angrier message, which went all over the country to a perfect target computer-industry audience of BBS sysops [bulletin-board system operators]. This editor's message was that the Oklahoma City police are a bunch of crazed no-neck Gestapo who don't know nothing about nothing, and hate anybody who does. I think that the genuine cause of computer law and order was very much harmed by this case.

There are a couple of useful lessons to be learned here. The first, of course, is don't sell porn in Oklahoma City. And the second is, if your city's on an antiporn crusade and you're a cop, it's a good idea to drop by the local porn outlets and openly tell the merchants that porn is illegal. Tell them straight out that you know they have some porn, and they'd better knock it off. If they've got any sense, they'll take this word from the wise and stop breaking the local community standards forthwith. If they go

> *"Don't jump in headfirst with an agenda and a videocam."*

on doing it, well, presumably they're hardened porn merchants of some kind, and when they get into trouble with ambitious local prosecutors, they'll have no one to blame but themselves. Don't jump in headfirst with an agenda and a videocam. It's real easy to wade hip deep into a blaze of publicity, but it's real hard to wade back out without getting the sticky stuff all over you.

A Government Computer Encryption System Would Threaten Civil Liberties

by Shari Steele and Daniel J. Weitzner

About the authors: *Shari Steele is a Maryland attorney for the Electronic Frontier Foundation. Daniel J. Weitzner is deputy director of the Center for Democracy and Technology. Both organizations seek to protect the civil liberties of users of telecommunications media.*

On April 16, 1993, the Clinton Administration announced a national standard for encryption. Under the Administration's Clipper Chip proposal, voice telephone conversations would be encrypted by chips built into the telephone units used by the caller and the call recipient. Put simply, when a call is made, the two telephones involved communicate with one another and establish a unique key based on information contained on each of their chips. The telephones then use that key to encrypt and decrypt the conversation. In this way, anyone attempting to wiretap the telephone conversation would not be able to understand what was being said.

However, in order to provide a means for law enforcement officers to decrypt messages for court-authorized wiretaps, the Administration's proposal suggested that the keys be held in trust by a third party, who would only release keys when presented with valid warrants to perform wiretaps. To further ensure that the keys would not be too easily obtained, the Administration's proposal suggested that each key be split in half, with each half of each key held by a different escrow agent.

Government Control of Encryption

The Clipper Chip, which was originally developed by the National Security Agency (NSA), does offer some measure of privacy to individuals while providing law enforcement officers with the means to conduct wiretaps. However,

Shari Steele and Daniel J. Weitzner, "Chipping Away at Privacy," *BBS Magazine*, September 1993. Reprinted with permission of the publisher.

there are some serious problems with the government's proposal. First, the Administration has not established that the Clipper Chip offers maximum privacy protection. An encryption algorithm cannot be trusted unless it can be tested, yet the Administration proposes to keep the Chip algorithm classified. What will give people confidence in the safety of their keys? Furthermore, while the use of the key escrow system is one way to balance privacy and law enforcement needs, the details of this scheme must be explored publicly before it is adopted.

> *"We are entering an era in which most of society will rely on encryption to protect the privacy of their electronic communications."*

But before we even begin to address these concerns, we need to start with one very basic question: Is the Clipper Chip an attempt by the federal government to control the use of encryption? A government-mandated encryption standard raises profound constitutional questions.

So far, the Administration has not declared that use of the Clipper Chip will be mandatory, but several factors point in that direction:

The government has justified keeping the Clipper Chip encryption algorithm secret by claiming that it is the only way to ensure compliance with the proposed key escrow system.

Many parties have already questioned the need for a secret algorithm, especially given the existence of robust, public-domain encryption techniques. The most common explanation given for use of a secret algorithm is the need to prevent users from bypassing the key escrow system proposed along with the Clipper Chip. If the system is truly voluntary, then why go to such lengths to ensure compliance with the escrow procedure?

A voluntary system does not solve law enforcement's problems.

The major stated rationale for government intervention in the domestic encryption arena is to ensure that law enforcement officers have continued access to criminal communications. Yet, a voluntary scheme seems inadequate to meet this goal. Criminals who seek to avoid interception and decryption of their communications would simply use another system, free from escrow provisions. Unless a government-proposed encryption scheme is mandatory, it would fail to achieve its primary law enforcement purpose. In a voluntary regime, only the law-abiding would use the escrow system.

Any attempt to mandate a particular cryptographic standard for private communications, to require that encrypted messages use an escrow system, or to prohibit the use of specific encryption algorithms would raise fundamental constitutional questions. In order to appreciate the importance of the concerns raised, we must recognize that we are entering an era in which most of society will rely on encryption to protect the privacy of their electronic communications.

Constitutional Concerns

If the Administration does intend to mandate the use of a particular encryption technology, such as the Clipper Chip, and to make the use of all other encryption technologies illegal, there are serious constitutional concerns. A mandatory key escrow system violates the First, Fourth, and Fifth Amendments of the Constitution.

A mandatory key escrow system violates the Fourth Amendment prohibition against "unreasonable search and seizure."

Wiretapping and other electronic surveillance have always been recognized as exceptions to the fundamental Fourth Amendment prohibition against secret searches. Even with a valid search warrant, law enforcement agents must "knock and announce" their intent to search a location before proceeding. Failure to do so violates the Fourth Amendment. Increasing reliance on advanced telecommunications requires that we re-examine the scope and application of the exception granted to wiretaps.

Until now, the law of search and seizure has made a sharp distinction between, on the one hand, seizures of papers and other items in a person's physical possession and, on the other hand, wiretapping of electronic communications. Law enforcement officers must inform an owner, through the presentation of a valid warrant, before searching and/or seizing papers or personal effects. Only in the exceptional case of wiretapping may law enforcement officers invade a person's privacy without simultaneously informing that person.

Today, the distinction between storage of information and communication of information is not so clear. Instantaneous access to encryption keys, without notice to the communicating parties, may well constitute a secret search if law enforcement officers seize the "papers" (now in electronic form) of a virtual corporation or an individual.

A key escrow system forces a mass waiver of all users' Fifth Amendment rights against self-incrimination.

The Fifth Amendment protects individuals facing criminal charges from having to reveal information that might incriminate them at trial. So far, no court has determined whether or not the Fifth Amendment allows a defendant to refuse to disclose his or her cryptographic key. As society and technology have changed, courts and legislatures have gradually

> *"Prohibiting the use of a particular form of cryptography . . . is akin to prohibiting someone from speaking a language."*

adapted fundamental constitutional rights to new circumstances. Such decisions require careful, deliberate action. But the existence of a key escrow system would have the effect of waiving this right for every person who used the system in a single step.

Prohibition against use of certain cryptographic techniques is a content-based restriction which violates individuals' right to free speech guaranteed under the First Amendment.

Prohibiting the use of a particular form of cryptography for the express purpose of making communication intelligible to law enforcement officers is akin to prohibiting someone from speaking a language not understood by law enforcement officers. And, while courts have upheld "time, place and manner" restrictions, such as laws that limit the volume of speakers from interfering with surrounding activities and confine demonstrators to certain physical areas, no court has ever upheld an outright ban on the use of a particular language. Moreover, in order for a time, place and manner restriction to be a valid restraint on speech, a government must show that it is the "least restrictive means" of accomplishing the government's goal. It is precisely this question—the availability of alternatives that could solve law enforcement's actual problems—that we must be able to explore before we can promote a solution such as key escrow.

Further Discussion Is Needed

On May 14, 1993, the Digital Privacy and Security Working Group sent a list of over one hundred questions to President Bill Clinton, expressing the Group's concerns and asking that a public dialogue be initiated to discuss the issue further. The Digital Privacy and Security Working Group is a coalition of over fifty organizations—from computer software and hardware firms, to telecommunications companies and energy companies, to the American Civil Liberties Union and the Electronic Frontier Foundation—that was formed over a decade ago and is chaired by EFF's executive director, Jerry Berman. The Working Group identified several other aspects of the Administration's encryption proposal that warranted further discussion, including:

- the security of the key escrow system;
- the advisability of a government-developed and classified algorithm;
- The Clipper Chip's practicality and commercial acceptability;
- the effect of the proposal on American competitiveness and the balance of trade;
- possible implications for the development of digital communications; and,
- the effect on the right to privacy and other constitutional rights.

The Administration has agreed to slow down the process in order to enable a deliberate government policy on encryption to be developed before any one encryption technology is embraced.

Computer Technology Can Filter Out Objectionable Material

by Walter S. Baer

About the author: *Walter S. Baer is a specialist in communications and information policy at the RAND Corporation, a public policy research institution headquartered in Santa Monica, California.*

In June 1995, the U.S. Senate passed [Senator James Exon's Communications Decency Act] that would make electronic transmission of any materials deemed "obscene, lewd, lascivious, filthy or indecent" a federal crime, punishable by up to two years in prison and/or a $100,000 fine.

This definition would criminalize sending electronic excerpts from many newspapers, magazines and books that are readily found on newsstands or in convenience stores and public libraries. And if the Senate's action isn't tough enough, a high-level government task force is set to propose a new federal agency to police the nation's information superhighway.

But on a June 1995 cable television program, Speaker of the House Newt Gingrich said he thought the Senate bill was "very badly thought out and not very productive," meaning the debate over regulation is likely to be long.

Of course, there are legitimate concerns about what is available on the Internet and other computer networks. Many people worry about children being exposed to sexually explicit pictures or lured away from home by seductive messages on computer chat lines.

Others fear that the Internet provides too easy access to information about bomb-making and other illegal activities. Still others object more generally to sexually oriented material and neo-Nazi or other fringe-group polemics on Internet bulletin boards and on the rapidly growing World Wide Web.

Yet, there are better ways to deal with offensive materials than new laws or government agencies that would restrict the flow of desirable information and

Walter S. Baer, "Filtering Pornography from the Internet Files," *San Diego Union-Tribune*, June 23, 1995. Reprinted with permission.

likely infringe on the freedom of speech guarantees in the First Amendment. It would be far preferable to place control of information content with users rather than with the government. In particular, parents and educators should be able to determine the suitability of children's access to electronic information sources, just as they do for books and other conventional materials.

How might this work? Technically, it is quite feasible to build a "filter" into the computer software used to browse the Internet that blocks access to certain areas. Many businesses and government agencies today restrict access to some Internet bulletin boards from computers within their organizations. This does not prevent other users from accessing these sites, nor does it deny employees the ability to reach them using a personal account at home.

> *"Some commercial networks have introduced 'parental control' buttons to restrict access to certain chat lines and bulletin boards."*

Although the software used today in school and home computers does not include "filters" or similar features, the industry is beginning to respond to parents and other citizen complaints. At least one firm, SurfWatch Software—offers a service that blocks several hundred Internet sites which the company judges contain sexually explicit or racist materials.

Some commercial networks have introduced "parental control" buttons to restrict access to certain chat lines and bulletin boards. And just before the Senate vote, three software industry leaders, including Microsoft, announced their intent to develop standards that would enable users to "lock out" access to materials they deem inappropriate.

The industry response may be late in coming, but we should welcome it. What we need now is for parents, teachers and other consumers to demand software and services that make it easy for users to exercise control over content.

Positive Steps

Ironically, in [its 1995 telecommunications reform bill] that would give government a heavy hand over content on the Internet, the Senate strengthened parental controls over content on television. The bill requires that new television sets include a "choice chip" which permits parents to block violent or sexually-oriented programs they do not want shown in their homes.

This approach is by no means a panacea. It requires the television industry to come up with program ratings and transmit them as codes to trigger the "choice chip."

It will add several dollars to the cost of new TV sets, and it will only work for parents who take the time and trouble to use it. But the "choice chip" seems far superior to imposing government censorship or threatening criminal penalties on television programs that some consider offensive.

In fact, we are surrounded by information and entertainment that many people find offensive in all the media—in books, magazines, dial-in telephone service, radio, television and the new electronic information networks.

The First Amendment largely gives the creators of such materials the right to disseminate them and seek a willing audience. However, they have no rights to force their wares on recipients who don't want them for their children or for themselves.

The new technologies bring us a profusion of information—many would say an information overload. But technology can also make it easier for the users of information to say "no."

Government laws and regulations should encourage technical and other means to enable us to determine what kinds of information we let into our homes. Technological developments along the lines of the "choice chip" are positive steps in that direction. Rather than seeking to criminalize offensive information, we need to let users control what they and their children gain access to in the new world of cyberspace.

Bibliography

Books

Frederick B. Cohen   *Protection and Security on the Information Superhighway.* New York: Wiley, 1995.

Les Freed and Frank J. Derfler Jr.   *Building the Information Highway.* Emeryville, CA: Ziff-Davis, 1994

Bill Gates   *The Road Ahead.* New York: Viking, 1995.

George Gilder   *Life After Television.* Rev. ed. New York: Norton, 1994.

Danny Goodman   *Living at Light Speed.* New York: Random House, 1995.

William J. Mitchell   *City of Bits: Space, Place, and the Infobahn.* Cambridge, MA: MIT Press, 1995.

Nicholas Negroponte   *Being Digital.* New York: Knopf, 1995.

Howard Rheingold   *The Virtual Community.* Reading, MA: Addison-Wesley, 1993.

Michelle Slatalla and Joshua Quittner   *Masters of Deception—The Gang That Ruled Cyberspace.* New York: HarperCollins, 1995.

Mark Slouka   *War of the Worlds: Cyberspace and the Hi-Tech Assault on Reality.* New York: BasicBooks, 1995.

Bruce Sterling   *The Hacker Crackdown: Law and Disorder on the Electronic Frontier.* New York: Bantam, 1992.

Clifford Stoll   *Silicon Snake Oil: Second Thoughts on the Information Highway.* New York: Doubleday, 1995.

Steven L. Talbott   *The Future Does Not Compute: Transcending the Machines in Our Midst.* Sebastopol, CA: O'Reilly and Associates, 1995.

Periodicals

Michael Antonoff et al.   "The Complete Survival Guide to the Information Superhighway," *Popular Science,* May 1994.

Brent Baker   "Damn the Consumers—Full Speed Ahead," *Vital Speeches of the Day*, May 1, 1994.

Deborah Baldwin   "If This Is the Information Superhighway, Where Are the Rest Stops?" *Common Cause Magazine*, Spring 1994.

David S. Bennahum   "Getting Cyber Smart," *New York Times*, May 22, 1995.

The Information Highway

Business Week	"Planet Internet," April 3, 1995.
Julie Chao	"Internet Pioneers Abandon World They Created," *Wall Street Journal*, June 7, 1995.
Barry Diller	"Don't Repackage—Redefine!" *Wired*, February 1995. Available from 520 Third St., 4th Fl., San Francisco, CA 94107.
Ethics & Behavior	Forum on ethics and the Internet, vol. 5, no. 1, 1995.
James M. Fallows	"Not Yet Net," *Atlantic Monthly*, May 1995.
John J. Fialka	"U.S. to Propose Data-Highway Agency," *Wall Street Journal*, June 14, 1995.
James Gleick	"The Information Future: Out of Control," *New York Times Magazine*, May 1, 1994.
Laurie Hays	"PCs May Be Teaching Kids the Wrong Lessons," *Wall Street Journal*, April 24, 1995.
Albert G. Holzinger	"The Virtual Future," *Nation's Business*, May 1995.
Brandon Musler	"An Internet User's Lament," *Wall Street Journal*, April 10, 1995.
National Review	Special section on information, technology, and culture, August 15, 1994.
Newsweek	Special issue on the information revolution, February 27, 1995.
David Noble	"The Truth About the Information Highway," *Monthly Review,* June 1995.
Laura B. Randolph	"Blacks in the Fast Lane of the Information Superhighway," *Ebony*, January 1995.
Joshua Wolf Shenk	"The Robber Barons of the Information Highway," *Washington Monthly*, June 1995.
Daniel J. Silver	"Computers and Their Discontents," *Commentary*, July 1995.
Julian Stallabrass	"Empowering Technology: The Exploration of Cyberspace," *New Left Review*, May/June 1995.
Clifford Stoll	"The Internet? Bah!" *Newsweek*, February 27, 1995.
Television Quarterly	Special section on the information highway, Winter 1995.
Time	"Welcome to Cyberspace," special issue, Spring 1995.
UNESCO Courier	Special issue on communications and media, February 1995.
Utne Reader	"Cyberhood vs. Neighborhood," March/April 1995.
Jason Wehling	"Netwars," *Z Magazine*, July/August 1995.
World & I	Special section on the information highway, November 1994. Available from 3600 New York Ave. NE, Washington, DC 20002.

Organizations to Contact

The editors have compiled the following list of organizations concerned with the issues debated in this book. The descriptions are derived from materials provided by the organizations. All have publications or information available for interested readers. The list was compiled on the date of publication of the present volume; names, addresses, and phone numbers may change. Be aware that many organizations take several weeks or longer to respond to inquiries, so allow as much time as possible.

Center for Civic Networking (CCN)
PO Box 65272
Washington, DC 20037
(202) 362-3831
fax: (202) 986-2539
e-mail: ccn@civicnet.org

CCN is a nonprofit organization dedicated to applying information technology and infrastructure for the public good, particularly to improve access to information and the delivery of government services, to broaden citizen participation in government, and to stimulate economic and community development. It conducts policy research and analysis and consults with government and nonprofit organizations. The center publishes the weekly *CivicNet Gazette*.

Center for Democracy and Technology (CDT)
1001 G St. NW, Suite 700 E
Washington, DC 20001
(202) 637-9800
fax: (202) 637-0968
e-mail: info@cdt.org
Web site: http://www.cdt.org

The mission of CDT is to develop public policy solutions that advance constitutional civil liberties and democratic values in new computer and communications media. Pursuing its mission through policy research, public education, and coalition building, the center works to increase citizens' privacy and the public's control over the use of personal information held by government and other institutions. Its publications include issue briefs, policy papers, and *CDT Policy Posts*, an on-line, occasional publication that covers issues regarding the civil liberties of those using the information highway.

Center for Media Education (CME)
1511 K St. NW, Suite 518
Washington, DC 20005
(202) 628-2620
fax: (202) 628-2554
e-mail: cme@access.digex.net

CME is a nonprofit public interest group concerned with media and telecommunications issues, such as educational television for children, universal public access to the information highway, and the development and ownership of information services. Its projects include the Campaign for Kids TV, which seeks to improve children's education; the Future of Media, concerning the information highway; and the Telecommunications Policy Roundtable of monthly meetings of nonprofit organizations. CME publishes the monthly newsletter *InfoActive: Telecommunications Monthly for Nonprofits.*

Electronic Frontier Foundation (EFF)
PO Box 170190
San Francisco, CA 94117
(415) 668-7171
fax: (415) 668-7007
e-mail: eff@eff.org
Web site: http://www.eff.org

EFF is an organization of students and other individuals that aims to promote a better understanding of telecommunications issues. It fosters awareness of civil liberties issues arising from advancements in computer-based communications media and supports litigation to preserve, protect, and extend First Amendment rights in computing and telecommunications technologies. EFF's publications include *Building the Open Road*, *Crime and Puzzlement*, the quarterly newsletter *Networks & Policy*, the biweekly electronic newsletter *EFFector Online*, and on-line bulletins and publications, including *First Amendment in Cyberspace.*

Electronic Privacy Information Center (EPIC)
666 Pennsylvania Ave. SE, Suite 301
Washington, DC 20003
(202) 544-9240
fax: (202) 547-5482
e-mail: info@epic.org
Web site: http://www.epic.org

EPIC is an organization that advocates a public right to electronic privacy. It sponsors educational and research programs, compiles statistics, and conducts litigation. Its publications include the biweekly electronic newsletter *EPIC Alert* and on-line reports.

Institute for Global Communications (IGC)
18 De Boom St.
San Francisco, CA 94107
(415) 442-0220
fax: (415) 546-1794
e-mail: support@igc.apc.org

The institute provides computer networking services for international communications dedicated to environmental preservation, peace, and human rights. IGC networks include EcoNet, ConflictNet, LaborNet, and PeaceNet. It publishes the monthly newsletter *NetNews.*

Interactive Services Association (ISA)
8403 Colesville Rd., Suite 865
Silver Spring, MD 20910
(301) 495-4955
e-mail: isa@aol.com

ISA is a trade association representing more than three hundred companies in advertising, broadcasting, and other areas involving the delivery of telecommunications-based services. It has six councils, including Interactive Marketing and Interactive Television, covering the interactive media industry. The association publishes the brochure *Child Safety on the Information Superhighway*, the handbook *Gateway 2000*, the monthly newsletter *ISA Update*, the biweekly *Public Policy Update*, and *ISA Weekly Update* (delivered by fax or e-mail), and other reports.

National Public Telecomputing Network (NPTN)
30680 Bainbridge Rd.
Solon, OH 44139
(216) 498-4050
fax: (216) 498-4051
e-mail: info@nptn.org
Web site: http://www.nptn.org

NPTN is a nonprofit organization dedicated to the development of public-access community computer systems. It serves as the parent organization for the "Free-Net" community computer network systems worldwide and has information kits available to help organize and develop a community Free-Net. The network publishes the quarterly electronic *NPTN Newsletter.*

Office of the Vice President
Communications Office
Old Executive Office Bldg., Rm. 272
Washington, DC 20501
(202) 456-7035
fax: (202) 456-2685
Web site: http://www.whitehouse.gov

Under the leadership of U.S. vice president Al Gore and others, together with the Office of Science and Technology Policy and other federal offices, the White House in 1994 unveiled a program called "Welcome to the White House: An Interactive Citizens' Handbook," which is accessible on the World Wide Web, a feature on the Internet. The program provides a single point of access to all electronic government information available on the Internet. Accessible material includes detailed information about cabinet-level and independent agencies and commissions, a subject-searchable index of federal information, and "hotlinks" to related areas of interest.

Voters Telecommunications Watch (VTW)
233 Court St., Suite 2
Brooklyn, NY 11201
(718) 596-2851
e-mail: vtw@vtw.org

VTW is a coalition of civil liberties organizations that actively participates in the democratic and legislative processes to promote civil liberties for telecommunications users. It recommends legislation, monitors the positions and voting records of elected officials, and informs and alerts the public on relevant issues. VTW publishes *VTW-Announce*, a weekly on-line newsletter that chronicles federal legislation affecting telecommunications and civil liberties. Subscribe by sending e-mail to vtw-announce-request@vtw.org.

Index

Index

Index